The Failure of the Neo-Liberal Approach to Poverty

Brian Caterino

The Failure of the Neo-Liberal Approach to Poverty

The Rochester Monroe Anti-Poverty Initiative

palgrave
macmillan

Brian Caterino
Rochester, NY, USA

ISBN 978-3-031-10605-7 ISBN 978-3-031-10606-4 (eBook)
https://doi.org/10.1007/978-3-031-10606-4

This Palgrave Macmillan imprint is published by the registered company Springer Nature Switzerland AG.
The registered company address is: Gewerbestrasse 11, 6330 Cham, Switzerland

Acknowledgements

I would like to thank Phillip Hansen and Sanford Schram for their helpful comments on an earlier version of the manuscript. Howard Eagle and Isabelle Bartter also shared some their experiences with RMAPI as did several anonymous sources.

Contents

CHAPTER 1

Introduction

Some years ago, I consulted a lawyer who had just moved into what was once a large revolving restaurant called "The Changing Scene," on the 21st Floor of Rochester's First Federal Building. New York State's first revolving restaurant, at the time of its opening, the scenic view was said to do more for Rochester's image than any Chamber of Commerce promotion could ever achieve. It was now little more than a rundown relic of Rochester's more prosperous past or more precisely the last throes of its economic heyday. It never lived up to its full promise closing a scant a decade after its debut.[1]

The building had seen better days. The small vestibule that contained the dedicated elevator to the former restaurant was cold, dank and in need of a paint job. Still as we ascended the straining and creaking glass enclosed elevator on the outside of the building rising to about three hundred feet over the Rochester skyline, the panoramic view began to emerge.[2] Just below was the High Falls of the Genesee River where the water powered

[1] Allen Morell, "Whatever Happened to the Changing Scene," *Rochester Democrat and Chronicle* November 22, 2013. https://www.democratandchronicle.com/story/lifestyle/rocflavors/2013/11/22/whatever-happened-to-the-changing-scene-/3682233/

[2] The Major Historian of Rochester NY is Blake McKelvey, see *Rochester On the Genesee: The Growth of a City*, Second Edition (Syracuse: Syracuse University Press 1979) and Ruth Rosenberg-Naparstek, *Rochester: A Panoramic History* (American Historical Press 2001), and many others. More recently Warren Kling, America's *First Boomtown—Rochester NY: The Early Years and the Notables Who Shaped It* (Rochester: Rochester History Alive 2008).

B. Caterino, *The Failure of the Neo-Liberal Approach to Poverty*, https://doi.org/10.1007/978-3-031-10606-4_1

flour mills made Rochester a boom town in the early 1800s. Looking north and west you could see the shores of Lake Ontario, once fertile lands that were once abundant with fruit farms and nurseries (giving Rochester its second incarnation as the flower city) when my parents moved to the suburbs. Soon the farms were to disappear converted into housing tracts for Kodak workers fleeing the city. Now they were just tangles of suburban blight that contrasted with flotillas of yachts and pleasure boats on the lake in the summer. When I grew up everyone had boats in their yards. But when I returned years later, the boats slowly disappeared from working-class neighborhoods.

A couple of miles inland was Kodak's old office building, and the miles long sprawling Kodak Park complex. Once bustling with manufacturing, it was now largely empty land. With its tall coal fired smokestacks, no longer spewing a smoky particulate stream over the area, it now held toxic chemical wastes, buried in aging, rusting barrels just below ground on the abandoned land owned by the old photography giant. Once one of the largest polluters in the nation, both of the air and water; the one positive result of deindustrialization meant that the air is now much cleaner and breathable around Kodak Park.[3] To the east and south, you could see the wealthier suburbs of Rochester, several of which have average incomes among the highest in the nation. Here you could find world class golf courses beautiful homes and spacious parks. Farther south on a cloudless day you could see the picturesque foothills of the Finger Lakes region and Canandaigua where Rochester's wealthiest scions, like Wegman's CEO Danny Wegman, and Paychex founder Tom Golisano had their estates. The whole area was bisected by the Genesee River. In its heyday when downtown was still abuzz with activity, it was quite the scene. Nostalgic memory aside the contrast with the dreary visage it now presented could not be more obvious.

The well-appointed digs of the lawyer's office complete with several prized vintage motorcycles, was a counterpoint to the desolate tableau of the center city. It was a gloomy site that had turned a Chamber of Commerce dream into its worst nightmare. Downtown Rochester was now bereft of the large department stores that populated downtown it its heyday half a century earlier or of much commerce at all. Midtown Plaza the first urban indoor mall in the United States with its innovative town

[3] Lisa Foderaro, "Pollution by Kodak Brings Sense of Betrayal," *New York Times* March 8, 1989, documents this legacy.

square design was once considered a harbinger of a new urbanism in the early 1960s. Now it lay empty and abandoned, soon to be partially demolished, being a victim of white flight to the suburbs. The office buildings that were once the corporate headquarters of Xerox and Bausch and Lomb and Gannett newspapers were sparsely occupied, and corporate headquarters moved to other cities. Kodak was on the verge of bankruptcy. Except for several festivals in the summer, the area emptied out around 6 pm after offices and government buildings closed, and nighttime activity was nil. Looking south from the building there was a large, blighted swath—a remnant of rail and industrial activity. Just past the central core and the cultural district were large areas of substandard housing. The main activity downtown the day I visited consisted of some students at a downtown branch of the local community college, located in long since closed department store (Sibley's. once the largest department store between New York and Chicago) getting on and off buses and tepidly shuffling into classes without a hint of enthusiasm.

As a city in decline, Rochester, New York has had a serious poverty problem for decades, on par with other ravaged industrial cities like Detroit. Rochester has similar levels of poverty, especially childhood poverty, poor schools, and a disproportionately incarcerated minority population. While the crime rate had declined in recent years, like many urban areas, it still was quite high. The violent crime rate was nearly double the national average, and in the top 10 percent of the nation.[4] (During the COVID outbreak, crime, especially murder, rose. In 2021, Rochester recorded its highest number of homicides, eclipsing the previous number of 69 in 1991 by mid-November.[5]) Rochester's decline was visible not just in the downtown landscape but in the old working-class neighborhoods. With the exceptions of a few gentrified areas, much of the housing stock in the city was shabby at best. The area where my grandparents and other Italian immigrants settled, and where we all gathered for generous holiday dinners, was littered with run down housing and empty lots, where even

[4] For some data see City-Data.com "Crime rate in Rochester, New York (NY): murders, rapes, robberies, assaults, burglaries, thefts, auto thefts, arson, law enforcement employees, police officers, crime map" http://www.city-data.com/crime/crime-Rochester-New-York.html

[5] "The number of murders in 2020 was forty-eight. It skyrocketed to almost 80 in 2021. "Major crimes unit faces major caseload after Rochester homicide rates rise" *WHAM* Monday, December 6th 2021 https://13wham.com/news/local/major-crimes-unit-faces-major-caseload-after-rochester-homicide-rates-rise

more dilapidated houses had been demolished. Nothing was rebuilt in their place. The area is bleak, unwelcoming, and foreboding. It has now become a center of drug and gang violence. Every week the news reports a shooting there often drug related. Disputes, not just drug related, ones are settled by guns. The main routes to downtown we used to travel first by bus and later by cars for holiday shopping trips, were once filled with car dealerships, grocery and furniture stores restaurants and music stores, serving well paid Kodak workers, but are now depleted of commercial services. Instead, the street is a mixture of tattoo parlors, smoke shops convenience stores and the now ubiquitous CBD[6] stores. There's little activity or anything inviting you to stay. Instead, downtown Rochester is a place you must go through on the way to somewhere else or just bypass on the expressways. Despite the existence of pockets of prosperity too much of it reflects substandard living conditions.

Of course, if you grew up in the suburbs, and have come to see the city as a foreign territory, the Rochester area can be a place where you can live a satisfying life. It's small enough to be easily drivable, has well-paying jobs, has cultural amenities above its weight class, good educational institutions, nice parks, natural beauty, and affluence at a cost of living far less than major cities. That, however, is the crux of the problem. Its prosperity comes at the expense of the suffering of others.

Poverty Takes the Stage

For years, Rochester area leaders neglected and denied the seriousness of its poverty problem. With the denial of poverty came a second disavowal, the collective suppression of the history of discontent and uprising that stemmed from poverty and racism among minorities. The racial problems Rochester experienced in the past were barely a blip on the radar of most white Rochesterians. In the last decade however, this situation changed. Perhaps prompted by the attention drawn to race and poverty by the police shootings of often unarmed African Americans, resulting in the Black Lives Matter movement these issues finally came to the fore in Rochester. After racial incidents involving police in Ferguson and other places, local public interest groups, from 2013 onward issued reports calling for action on Rochester's own poverty problem.

[6] Cannabidiol, a derivative of cannabis found in oil and gummies sold in New York state.

A 2015 report by ACT Rochester, *Benchmarking Rochester's Poverty*[7] (an update of their 2013 Special Report on Poverty)[8] documented the disheartening state of poverty in Rochester. The report notes that Rochester was the fifth poorest city among the nation's 75 largest urban areas, and the second poorest among cities of comparable size. Only Detroit was worse. 32.9 percent of Rochester residents lived in poverty. Rochester also had the highest rate of extremely poor families, those with annual incomes under $11,000 a year. The childhood poverty rate was also one of the highest in the nation.

In lieu of these findings Rochester political leaders following an initiative by the Governor Andrew Cuomo, formed a coalition to fight poverty in the Rochester Area. Known by the acronym RMAPI, the Rochester Monroe Anti-Poverty Initiative began with much fanfare, and grand expectations. It had an ambitious program: to reduce poverty by 50 percent in 15 years. This goal was unrealistic given the resources and the situation. From the start, the program was mired in organizational and political problems and had trouble garnering public support. Many who had become skeptical of government programs, had little faith in RMAPI, and it did not do enough to address these concerns. More than five years into the project, little, if any, progress in reducing the poverty rate has been made. Even with slight fluctuations from year to year, the rate remained virtually unchanged. RMAPI officials have their own explanations for the lack of progress, they point to inflated expectations, a lack of public understanding of the project as well as organizational barriers, but I want to argue that the problem lies elsewhere. The major flaws in the poverty initiative stem from its attachment to an approach driven by neo-liberal welfare reform which it unsuccessfully tries to combine with an anti-racist approach concerned with problems of structural racism. The latter it approaches from the viewpoint of racial liberalism that emphasizes equal opportunity.

Nancy Fraser has argued that this combination of neo-liberal economic programs with some commitment to equality and justice can be called

[7] ACT Rochester. *Benchmarking Rochester's Poverty* https://www.urmc.rochester.edu/MediaLibraries/URMCMedia/pediatrics/training/plc/documentochester-s-Poverty-Report-Update-2015.pdf

[8] ACT Rochester. *Poverty and the Concentration of Poverty in the Nine-County Greater Rochester Area December 2013* https://www.actrochester.org/tinymce/source/2013%20Poverty%20Report.pdf

progressive neo-liberalism.[9] She views this grouping as the dominant "hegemonic bloc" in American politics. In her view, the fundamentalist version of neo-liberalism as envisioned founders like Hayek and Friedman was incapable of finding general acceptance. In contrast, the more progressive version could. Progressive neo-liberalism has two major social carriers, the liberal wing of new social movements, and "the most dynamic symbolic and financial sectors of the US economy," which include wall street, silicon valley, and Hollywood. This constellation has been described by others as the new coalitions of a democratic party which has abandoned the working class. Fraser in fact sees this as a class based social formation. It promises liberation for members of well-off educated classes from cultural prejudices they have experienced (e.g., gender, sexual preference or race) while leaving the less well-off more impoverished.

While I would take issue with Fraser's characterization of this bloc as "progressive" it is center left at best, she has formulated an ideal type which captures the contradictory elements of the new democratic coalition. To call it dominant however, is an overstatement. By all measures, a more right-wing version of neo-liberalism has been equally powerful in American politics leading to an essential stalemate. To be sure, this coalition did not share the libertarianism of fundamentalist neo-liberalism, but elements of ethnonationalism, racism, and increasing authoritarianism. Increasingly, the republican party had been dominated by more reactionary interests which not only sought to roll back gains in civil rights but also sought to limit democratic participation and create even greater autocratic control of elements of social life.

From its beginning in the Clinton era, third wave liberalism played footsie with these more reactionary elements. His Sister Souljah moment, 1994 crime bill and welfare reform, are more indicative of the blue dog democrats that were prominent under the influence of the Democratic Leadership Committee (DLC). His strategy of triangulation was meant to bring in swing voters, who did not identify with more progressive ideas. The emancipatory promise Fraser finds is lacking here. In moving the center of gravity in American politics to the right, the "progressive" bloc paved the way for the more brutal politics of the present.

In dealing with poverty, Clinton accepted the reality and even desirability of neo-liberal approaches and was unwilling to return to Keynesian

[9] Nancy Fraser, "From Progressive Ne0-Liberalism to Trump—and Beyond" *American Affairs* vol 1, no 4 (2017).

redistributive polices. His alternative was to promote wrap around services that provide the community support for the development of entrepreneurial subjects. However, his attempts to create community led to what Timothy Weaver called neo-liberalism by default.[10] The possibility of political mobilization on the part of the poor is subordinated to the creation of market conforming behavior.

The contradictions of the neo-liberal approach, especially its more "progressive" variant, are clear when the question of poverty is considered. First, it attempts to change the nature of the welfare state itself. It attacks the welfare programs of the Keynesian era as promoting dependency and as government solutions as ineffective. Seeking to restore the primacy of an unregulated or at least less regulated economy, it seeks not only to eliminate redistributive policies of government replacing them with means testing, but it also sought to privatize and financialize the remaining elements of the welfare state. It creates in its place a more precarious condition in which social risks are passed down to poor individuals: all under the guise of self-sufficiency.

Neo-liberalism with is emphasis on deregulation and privatization, was an inequality machine. It reversed the gains in the distribution of wealth during the Keynesian era and created the greatest gap between the rich and poor since the Gilded Age. The "progressive" neo-liberal outlook is, as Fraser rightly notes, a class based one. While it may be beneficial to the well-off, it degrades the life of the poor.

Instead of increasing respect and equality for the less well-off, neo-liberalism fostered disrespect and subordination for major elements of society especially the poor. They were labeled as deficient or even criminal in character, and incapable of functioning without guidance from social and economic elite. They have to become entrepreneurial subjects in order to survive. Under Neo-liberal welfare policies, subjects, especially the poor, are required to construct their subjectivity to conform to economic virtues of saving, accumulation, work discipline, and future oriented behavior. The emphasis on liberal rights wih the creation of entrepreneurial selves is incompatible.

RMAPI's programs attempts to extend the "progressive" neo-liberal outlook to the problem of poverty. They claim a commitment to both poverty reduction and to racial justice conceived as promoting equal opportunity. However, these are not fully compatible. Neo-liberal

[10] Timothy Weaver, *Blazing the Neoliberal Trail: Urban Political Development in the United States and the United Kingdom* (Philadelphia University of Pennsylvania Press, 2016).

"welfare" policies individualize the problem and shift the onus of responsibility from socio-economic structures to personal responsibility. Poverty is the result of personal character flaws. This leaves out questions of social power which can structure the potentials for acquisition of resources and of forms of public discussion. A restrictive definition of equal opportunity compatible with neo-liberal thought also excludes questions of social rights and social equity which are needed to address poverty.

The main organizational structure employed by RMAPI also lacks a conception of equity that is sufficient to address questions of poverty. **Collective impact** is a system theoretical model which seeks efficiency in providing services, not political change. Collective Impact theories diagnose social problems as system ones caused by the complexity of organization in advanced capitalist societies. System theories have an affinity with neo-liberal ideas because system approaches to social problems also deny the centrality of political power and domination.

Collective impact organizations are usually public private partnerships. There is in fact little public governance in its structure. It creates a privatized administrative apparatus that mixes legislation and administration and bypasses public accountability. Although it often pays lip service to the participation of the community it is an elite governed and CEO level organization which in fact downplays the perspectives of participants in social policy.

The two elements of the "progressive" program stand in an uneasy tension in the RMAPI program. Even where RMAPI did emphasize an issue that could have been considered progressive, the idea of structural racism and its interpretation was restricted. Structural racism suggests that social problems do not stem from individual deficiencies but they are embedded in social institutions and rules. Its source then is social power which creates oppression and domination. It is not clear how such problems of structural force can be addressed with individual solutions. Making individuals better competitors in a market system does not solve the problem that generates widespread poverty without large scale solutions. These imperatives lie in an uneasy, even contradictory relationship. Perhaps for this reason, RMAPIs attempts to address structural racism have been up to now quite limited. They primarily consist of voluntary pledges, not structural change.

A broader interpretation of structural racism, however, would entangle them in questions of social equity which they shied away from addressing. A crucial weakness which critics of such approaches including collective impact as well, is the lack an expansive vision of social equity and justice. RMAPIs commitment to structural racism never developed a critical diagnosis of neo-liberal arrangements. Looking to mitigate poverty, RMAPI made no effort at least in its first five years to eliminate its root causes.

Neo-liberals argue that poverty is the result of deficient reasoning and behavior on the part of the poor. Neo-liberals view the free market as a sphere of uncoerced voluntary action, a view that blinds them to the inequalities and power asymmetries inherent in market structures. For the neo-liberal government intervention and redistribution do not correct problems caused by markets, it distorts these markets. The existing distribution of wealth is simply a reflection of the operations of the market, and under free market conditions, the outcomes are fair. It does not link the existence of these unequal outcomes to political power or domination.[11] Thus, they have little to say about social justice. Even the center-left version of neo-liberalism cannot effectively address the question of equality for the worse off in society, not to speak of social rights.

Bibliography

Act Rochester. *Poverty and the Concentration of Poverty in the Nine-County Greater Rochester Area December 2013.* https://www.actrochester.org/tinymce/source/2013%20Poverty%20Report.pdf

Act Rochester. *Benchmarking Rochester's Poverty* 2015. https://www.urmc.rochester.edu/MediaLibraries/URMCMedia/pediatrics/training/plc/documentochester-s-Poverty-Report-Update-2015.pdf

City-Data.com. "Crime rate in Rochester, New York (NY): murders, rapes, robberies, assaults, burglaries, thefts, auto thefts, arson, law enforcement employees, police officers, crime map." http://www.city-data.com/crime/crime-Rochester-New-York.html

Foderaro, Lisa. "Pollution by Kodak Brings Sense of Betrayal." *New York Times* March 8, 1989.

Fraser, Nancy. "From Progressive Neo-Liberalism to Trump—and Beyond." *American Affairs* vol 1, no 4 2017.

Kling, Warren. *America's First Boomtown—Rochester NY: The Early Years and the Notables Who Shaped It.* Rochester: Rochester History Alive 2008.

[11] Among others the work of Thomas Piketty, *Capital in the Twenty-First Century* (Cambridge: Belknap Press 2014), has shown that unregulated free markets necessarily lead to significant inequalities and asymmetries of power. Robert Reich has also argued that unregulated free markets lead to oligarchy. Among his many books, see his most recent statement *The System: Who Rigged it, How we fix it* (New York: Vintage 2021).

McKelvey, Blake. *Rochester On the Genesee: The Growth of a City*, Second Edition. Syracuse: Syracuse University Press 1979.

Morell, Allen, "Whatever Happened to the Changing Scene." *Rochester Democrat and Chronicle* November 22, 2013.

Piketty, Thomas. *Capital in the Twenty-First Century*. Cambridge: Belknap Press 2014.

Reich, Robert. *The System: Who Rigged it, How we fix it*. New York: Vintage 2021.

Rosenberg-Naparstek, Ruth. *Rochester: A Panoramic History*. American Historical Press 2001.

Weaver, Timothy. *Blazing the Neoliberal Trail: Urban Political Development in the United States and the United Kingdom*. Philadelphia: University of Pennsylvania Press, 2016.

WHAM. "Major crimes unit faces major caseload after Rochester homicide rates rise." *WHAM* Monday, December 6th 2021. https://13wham.com/news/local/major-crimes-unit-faces-major-caseload-after-rochester-homicide-rates-rise

CHAPTER 2

Critical Theory, The Welfare State, and Neo-liberalism

The Welfare State in Neo-liberal Times

The modern welfare state is a response to the pathologies of industrial capitalism, both in the form of economic exploitation, and social fragmentation. With the rise of industrial society came a whole host of new social problems, well noted by the critics of the day: low wages, poor and unsafe working conditions, exploitative child labor; the persistent economic problems caused by the periodic fluctuations of capitalist economies such as unemployment resulting in a reserve army of unemployed; slums and crowded living conditions, poor nutrition, and starvation; social displacement and fragmenting of intergenerational families; breaking of the traditional bonds of support of preindustrial societies; delinquency, crime as well as a growing population of elderly and disabled or otherwise incapacitated. All these led to a growing divide and antagonism between, workers and capitalists. While industrial capitalism spawned an emerging middle class, being a member of the industrial working class often meant a life of poverty.

Nations like the US never had a pure laissez-faire philosophy. They were active in creating conditions for successful accumulation through the creation of transportation and communications infrastructures and often employed high tariffs to protect national industries. Infrastructure initiatives by local governments also included creating public utilities.

B. Caterino, *The Failure of the Neo-Liberal Approach to Poverty*,
https://doi.org/10.1007/978-3-031-10606-4_2

Government measures also extended beyond providing conditions for successful accumulation. Out of necessity, it came to address social problems created by the new industrial era.

Preindustrial forms of "welfare" were based both in family support and offered through parishes. Poorhouses existed to take care of the poor the elderly and those with no relations in urban areas. Attempts to expand poorhouses and institutions private and public were not successful. Debates around these institutions and on non-institutional "outdoor relief" tread familiar territory. Proponents often wanted to exclude those who were "able bodied" and the "undeserving poor" from receiving assistance; even poor women with children were sometimes classed among the unworthy poor. Because of the insufficiency of private reforms, the burden fell to the state to provision for these goods to society, although it was not the exclusive provider of social services. By the 1890's in the US, the beginning of what Michael Katz called a "semi-welfare state" could be discerned.[1] This version involved state regulation of the public and private institutions of child welfare. A professional non-profit sector was also spurred on by the crises of industrial capitalism. The rise of "experts" who often assumed authority over clients based on superior knowledge. Still, the protections we came to call the social safety net expanded to include health and safety protections on foods and medicines, humane work conditions unemployment insurance, abolition of childhood labor, social security, later aid to dependent families. In some countries universal health insurance was developed. Each of these represents, significant developments in the welfare state.

Both Hegel and Marx were cognizant of the poverty problem. Their differing conceptions of the role of the state however were the precursors of two major and conflicting approaches to analyzing the welfare state. For Marx, the state was an instrument of the ruling classes. Its laws and practices justified the private property system. Inequality was an inevitable result of its workings. Though Marx died before the welfare state was created, Marxists using his conception of the state held that the welfare state's main function was social control of the populace. It provided just enough help to keep individuals from starvation or other serious privation but kept in place the exploitative relations of capitalism. The welfare state

[1] Michael Katz, *The Undeserving Poor: Americas Enduring Confrontation with Poverty* 2nd edition (New York: Oxford, 2013).

is little more than a way of blunting the protest potential of class conflict which with the rise of unions and the conditions of the great depression was considerable. Union activism and strikes put pressure on both industrialists and political leaders to forward reforms which muted the power of capital and increased the unions. At least part of the welfare state is based on this idea of saving capitalism from its own flaws. Such reforms contain no inherent commitment to social justice or a better society. They just served the interests of the powerful.

Hegel in contrast, viewed the state as the expression of objective spirit. The state was totality of ethical life in which it played a positive role in promoting social welfare and integration. Against Marx's reading, Hegel did recognize that private property was not the basis of ethical life.[2] This normative approach claims that welfare state reforms are based on notions of human flourishing and social justice. This interpretation was forwarded first by nineteenth century liberal democrats and social democrats who expanded our notion of rights and freedoms. To exert the civil rights of citizenship guaranteed by democratic constitutions, those citizens need minimum social conditions. Humans are social beings who are both dependent on others and capable of autonomy. They need economic and social security, and access to education among other important condition, if they are to develop their human capacities. For example, John Stuart Mill and later T. H. Green held that the right of access to education became critical for the full development of citizens including the working classes in the emerging industrial society of their times. These developmental theories also influenced socialists of various stripes who also stressed the need for social rights appropriate to the new industrial society. They would include not just formal equality but notions of equal dignity and respect. Some contemporary Marxists incorporate Hegelian perspectives.

Both of these views can be seen in the work of the critical theory of the Frankfurt School. The major theorists of first generation of critical theory (the "inner circle") did not focus on these questions. The critical theorists, however, were concerned with the fact that the working class was not rebelling, despite their situation and saw the state as important in creating conformity.

[2] Shlomo Avineri, Hegel's Theory of the Modern State (Cambridge: Cambridge University Press, 1974).

The first generation of Frankfurt School theorists argued that the Keynesian welfare state was an instrument of social control. The interventionist character of late capitalism substitutes government and administrative steering of the economy for the workings of the free market. The stabilization of the economy from cycles of boom and bust muted the revolutionary nature of union and working-class activity. This control extended beyond steering the economy and resulted in the rise of a culture industry that placed emphasis on private life and bland entertainment. It supported a consumer-oriented society in which satisfaction of private needs replaced political and social consciousness.[3]

Because the first-generation theorists equated bourgeois law with formal reason and equality, they regarded attempts to claim that equality required social rights and redistribution as flawed non-formal law was illegitimate and potentially authoritarian. They were not sympathetic to social democracy. There was to be sure a measure of dissent within the so-called outer circle of the Frankfurt School, such as Franz Neumann and Otto Kirchheimer. They emphasized elements of social democratic states that Horkheimer and the inner circle neglected. Neumann for example, while he was quite critical of the Weimar republic did accept its emphasis on the expansion of social and political rights. He thought we had to adopt a developmental approach that started with Rousseau, Hegel and Marx. Something similar was used by British thought to justify the welfare state.[4] This line of though had an influence on the work of Claus Offe and Jurgen Habermas.

Horkheimer and Adorno had come to see the late modern world in the terms adopted by Weber and later Lukacs. Advanced capitalist societies employ science and technology for production and in these circumstances,

[3] On the Frankfurt School see Friedrich Pollock, "State Capitalism: Its Possibilities and Limitations" 71-94 and Max Horkheimer, "The Authoritarian State": 95-117 both in Andrew Arato and Eike Gephardt Editors *The Essential Frankfurt School Reader* New edition (London: Bloomsbury Academic 1982); Max Horkheimer and Theodor Adorno, *The Dialectic of Enlightenment Philosophical Fragments* (Stanford: Stanford University Press, 2002).

[4] On Neumann see William Scheuermann *Between the Norm and the Exception: The Frankfurt School and The Rule of Law* (Cambridge MA: MIT Press, 1996); David Kettler and Thomas Wheatland, *Learning from Franz L. Neumann: Law, Theory and the Brute Facts of Political Life* (Anthem Press, 2019); William Scheuerman ed., *The Rule of Law Under Siege: Selected Essays of Franz L. Neumann and Otto Kirchheimer* (Berkeley: University of California Press, 1996).

reason had become entirely instrumental. The state was managerial. It adopted a means end rationality in which normative concerns is eliminated or reduced to pure choice.

Habermas at first followed the one-dimensionality thesis, but later saw that normative elements of reason were not fully excised under late capitalism. This position can be seen in his analysis of the crises of the welfare state. While he certainly accepted that the welfare state could be an instrument of control, it also retained a normative component found in the notion of legitimation. When the state takes on the role of steering the economy, it creates a new set of requirements for successful governance. Managing the economy is no longer the role of a depoliticized market, in which class rule is ideologically concealed, but it creates demands for justification. The relations of production are repoliticized. The latter requires questions of whether a regime ought to be recognized. While this can sometimes mean little more than delivering the goods, it can also entail more elaborate notions of social and political justice involving redistributive schemes.

Karl Polanyi tried to capture the conflicting tendencies within capitalism with his notion of a double movement.[5] While capitalists sought a free-market economy with few or no controls in order to commodify social relations, this provoked a reaction or a counter movement that recognized collective goods such as social welfare and social rights. Like the later Frankfurt School, Polanyi argues that the welfare state is more than a mode of control but contains normative concerns. The rule of capital even when it is on the ascent is not total; it carries the possibility of opposition, if not revolution. In a similar vein, T.H. Marshall's formulation the notion of social citizenship identifies the rights and conditions necessary for the exercise of democratic citizenship, and that a vital public life required forms of social welfare.[6]

Gasta-Esping Andersen's analysis of the three worlds of welfare also contains elements of the positive interpretation of the welfare state. Welfare measures can act to counter the commodification and reification of social relations and decommodify social relations. While the welfare state can

[5] Karl Polanyi, *The Great Transformation The Political and Economic Origins of Our Time* 2nd ed. (Boston: Beacon Press, 2001); Fred Block and Margaret Somers, *The Power of Market Fundamentalism: Karl Polanyi's Critique (*Cambridge MA: Harvard, 2014). Nancy Fraser identifies a third dimension in Polanyi, Nancy Fraser, "A Triple Movement: Parsing the Politics of Crisis after Polanyi" *NLR* 81, (May/June, 2013): 119-32.

[6] T H. Marshall, *Citizenship and Social Class And Other Essays* (Cambridge: Cambridge University Press, 1950),

and does reinforce stratification, in its attempts to compensate for the side effects of the capitalist system it also removes workers and others from its direct control. The basic idea of decommodification is contained in the notion that: "The degree to which individual, or families, can uphold a socially acceptable standard of living independently of market participation."[7] In contrast, commodification is the condition under which workers lose control over their work in return for wages—the condition under which their dependence on the market is affirmed.[8] The decommodification of labor recognizes to some degree social rights. The fulfillment of basic needs at least is detached from the market. One is entitled to some basic provision as a citizen of an affluent society.

Decommodification was not achieved evenly in all industrial societies. Andersen identified three worlds of welfare, a liberal one, a conservative and a social democratic one.[9] Each of these worlds presumes a different relation of state and market. The social democratic welfare state has a more expansive notion of social rights. Welfare is more extensively removed from market participation. Liberal welfare states have a lesser level of decommodification. They often rely on means tests or other more limited forms of assistance which emphasize market participation; thus, they only detach needs from the market to a limited extent. Conservative welfare states use benefits to maintain existing status hierarchies. Still even the liberal state like all welfare states makes some provision for the risks associated with the capitalist market. The difference lies in the fact that the liberal welfare state restricted the scope of welfare to those who can't participate in the labor market, (the truly needy), or those who pass a means test, and avoids formulating a fuller notion of social rights. These ideals tended to retreat as the welfare state developed in places like Great Britain and the United States. The actual structure of the welfare state tended to privatize these needs, and to treat citizens as consumers rather than as equal participants. Welfare gained legitimacy primarily through middle class programs (social security). Instead of widespread participation, the welfare state cultivated mass loyalty in which citizen participation was most limited to voting, combined with civil privatism.[10]

[7] Gasta-Esping Andersen, *Three Worlds of Welfare Capitalism* (Princeton: Princeton University Press, 1990): 37

[8] Andersen, *Three Worlds*: 45

[9] Andersen, *Three Worlds*:

[10] For example, see Jurgen Habermas, *Legitimation Crisis* (Boston: Beacon Press, 1975)

The Rise of Social Rights and Questions of Recognition

The theories of the welfare state that developed in the latter half of the nineteenth century did not follow the line of formal reason that liberal thought employed, and which emphasized civil rights, but followed a developmental model that they inherited from Hegel, Marx, and German Romanticism and some elements of republican thought. For the developmental theorist humans are social beings who need certain conditions to develop their own capacities. This notion of development could be used to criticize existing formal notions which failed to fulfill its own ideals for democratic citizenship. For example, John Stuart Mill and later T. H. Green held that the right of access to education became critical for the full development of citizens including the working classes. The possibility of effective democratic participation required at least some degree of basic education. Equally, it is hard to live a good life if one is in poverty or is subject to the social and political effects of discrimination. Thus, an expanded notion of rights is needed which codify the conditions of social citizenship. These developmental ideals could also become part of a critique of an unregulated capitalist economy, which limited the possibilities for achieving social citizenship for most citizens.

Developmental theories also influenced socialists of various stripes who also stressed the need for social rights appropriate to the new industrial society. The notion of social citizenship encompasses these elements. They would include not just formal equality but notions of equal dignity and respect.

Third generation critical theorists have more directly taken up questions of poverty and inequality. David Ingram for example has addressed poverty in a global context in *World Crisis and Underdevelopment.* Recently those influenced by Axel Honneth, have introduced questions of mutual recognition drawn from Hegel, into discussions of poverty. The Hegelian notion of recognition as employed by Honneth includes essential elements of solidarity, trust, and mutual respect.

The formal recognition of others based on civil rights, is not a sufficient basis for mutual respect. Here poverty not just a matter of material deprivation, which still remains important but also invokes questions of dignity. The poor are treated with disrespect and degradation. They are only partially human. They are often stigmatized and excluded from political participation and social membership.

Social life is constituted by the intersubjective web of communicative relations through which we connect and bind our actions. However, the binding force of communicative action is not a matter of coordinating previously existing individual interests. The very constitution of individuals is a product of the intersubjectivity of social life. Humans are self-interpreting actors who reflexively understand their own situation against a background horizon of shared knowledge and shared understanding, This shared horizon is usually called the life world. Habermas for one, stresses the consensual nature of action; its basis is found in the reasonable agreement between participants. His emphasis is critical to understand the ways in which consent is manipulated, The ability to consent is crucial not only to freedom of choice but autonomy the ability to choose a path of life; notions of mutual recognition entail question of mutual respect needed to maintain relations of trust and solidarity in communities. Honneth's emphasis on the subjective features of mutual recognition identifies social pathologies like disrespect and exclusion that are the result of subordination and causes of psychic injury.

Honneth's work has raised the objection that he gives insufficient consideration to political economic issues.[11] In contrast, Habermas recognizes the issue of social power. Understanding the genesis of domination, exploitation, and inequality that are the sources of poverty requires a conception of social power.

While questions of recognition are important to the analysis of poverty, in isolation recognition does not explain how such pathological expectations are formed and shaped. Social power is distinct from communicative power which is the ability to formulate norms and practices through mutual understanding. Social power in Max Weber's definition is the ability an individual or a group has to achieve their own aims even in the existence of opposition. This type of strategic power differs from communicative power because it aims to achieve the goals of the individual or group, and not the consensual coordination of action. Strategic power is a way of inducing action in others through threats, or rewards, benefits, or losses. Economic and sometimes political status and power are sources of social power. Social power can affect the ways we make sense of the world.

[11] Axel Honneth and Nancy Fraser. *Redistribution or Recognition: A Political-Philosophical Exchange* (London: Verso, 2003).

Power: Theoretical Debates

The debate between pluralists and elitists in the sixties, had implications for understanding questions of power. Pluralists such as Robert Dahl concluded that power was evenly (or evenly enough) distributed throughout society so that no group or interest could dominate, while elitists argued that power was concentrated in a small group of social and political elite. Critics of pluralist theory contended that a simple one-dimensional notion of power failed to identify the more subtle dynamics of power and domination. Dahl followed Weber's notion of social power. It was exerted when A was able to control B's responses in the direction A desires. He failed to see however, the way that social power could be used to impact communicative power and manipulate consent.

Dahl is aware of a variety of forms ranging from rational convincing to influencing to deception, coercion, and force. Yet these still leave out key features of power. Critics pointed out that the pluralist model failed to grasp the way that power can operate in covert ways that occlude the way a dominant group can exert power. These concerned the ways the very structure of discussion or deliberation is shaped, including the way in which we raise problems, set agendas, articulate concerns, and interests, and decide what is relevant in political deliberations. An interest-based notion of democracy cannot theorize these issues.

The assumption of an unimpeded process of deliberation does not depict its workings under conditions of unequal power. The critique of the pluralist notion of power by Peter Bachrach and Morton Baratz can be understood as raising concerns about the communicative aspects of decision making and the notion of power needed to explain them. They formulated the notion of non-decision-making to interpret the situation in which social power excludes critical questions from political deliberations.[12] Bachrach and Bachrach identified ways of restricting discourse such that salient issues are not raised. Control of the agenda to selects what comes up for discussion, who gets to participate and what are considered valid reasons. In non-decision-making, certain concerns or reasons that are relevant never come up for discussion.

[12] Peter Bachrach and Morton S. Baratz, "Two Faces of Power," *The American Political Science Review* Vol. 56, No. 4 (Dec. 1962), pp. 947-952; Peter Bachrach and Morton S. Baratz, "Decisions and Nondecisions: An Analytical Framework," *The American Political Science Review* Vol. 57, No. 3 (Sep. 1963), pp. 632-642.

This line of analysis (what they call the second dimension of power) illustrates the constraint of communicative power. They had in mind situations in which because of the power of group A, the concerns of group B are not considered relevant to issues at hand. The concerns of B the less powerful group are suppressed. Because these objections or sources of dissent never come to the fore, the dominant groups can claim the policies or norms are the result of a fair process. Here power works unobtrusively because it is not an overt case of a claim being rejected. Only when we take a counterfactual attitude can we make these forms of power visible. Relations of domination are embedded in asymmetrical forms of public opinion making and more formal deliberative processes. Of course, this control is not absolute, but they identify ways that discussion and deliberation can be restricted to the benefit of some in a covert manner.[13]

Steven Lukes also criticized the one-dimensional notion of power found in pluralist thought. Like Bachrach and Baratz, he emphasizes a second notion of power which is exerted by keeping people out of the decision-making process or by setting the agenda so that certain issues do not come to the fore. However, he adds a third dimension related to the second. The third dimension concerns the shaping of expectations which is prior in a sense to participating in any decisions. Lukes noted "Is it not the most supreme and insidious exercise of power to prevent people, to whatever degree, from having grievances by shaping their perceptions, cognitions and preferences in such a way that they accept their role in the existing order of things, either because they can see or imagine no alternative to it, or because they see it as natural and unchangeable or because they value it as divinely ordained and beneficial?"[14] However, instead of structuring public discussion of issues, it reaches through socialization into the processes of personality and identity formation. It constrains the way that individuals make sense of the world.

John Gaventa employed Lukes' third dimension of power in order to show how the expectations of miners and community members could be shaped.[15] He stressed the manipulation of a political agenda by influential

[13] Matthew Crenshaw, *The Unpolitics of Air Pollution: A Study of Non-Decision Making in the Cities* (Baltimore: Johns Hopkins, 1971) was an attempt to illustrate the notion of non-decision making in the context of local deliberations over air pollution.

[14] Steven Lukes, *Power: A Radical View* second ed. (London: Palgrave Macmillan Springer. 2005): 28

[15] John Gaventa, *Power and Powerlessness: Quiescence & Rebellion in an Appalachian Valley* (Chicago: University of Illinois Press, 1982).

groups to make it appear that community power is at play when in fact it was generated by a few. The suppression of interests also can lead to what Gaventa calls quiescence or political inactivity. Although some miners showed resistance in the sense that they did not accept the prevailing definition of the situation, they also had low expectations about their ability and the efficacy of change. Gaventa's work is significant because it also emphasizes the way in which participants both take up dominant forms of meaning and show resistance to them.

Lukes and Gaventa especially compliment the recognition perspectives. Structurally embedded power causes social inequalities, but power also reaches into the personality structures that typify a society.

Discourse Theory

Discourse theories also identify the way in which forms of speaking and writing are impacted by power. In this sense, discourse theory is not primarily a linguistic theory but a political one. I do not discuss all versions of discourse theory here but focus on an influential version developed by followers of Foucault.

Discourse theory recognizes the leading role that language plays in social life. Social actors make sense of the world through language, and social reality is itself constituted through language. Discourse theories often focus on the rules and practices through which meaning is created and the context through which practical social action is carried out. Unlike theories of ideology which stress the way material interests distort or occlude reality, discourse theories want to see how practices are constructed so as to constitute a reality structured by dominant interests. In order to indicate the authoritative role these discourses play Foucault calls them **regimes of truth**.[16] He holds that power (as a strategic act of disclosure) constitute these rules and norms themselves. Power lays down the rules and norms of interaction including the standards of truth and validity prior to the communicative power of subjects.

[16] Michel Foucault, *Power/Knowledge: Selected Interviews and Other Writings, 1972-1977* (New York: Pantheon, 1980): 131. He used the term regime of Disciplinary power in *Discipline and Punish: The Birth of the Prison (*New York: Vintage, 1978). For a critical discussion that bears on my account, see Charles Taylor. "Foucault on Freedom and Truth" *Political Theory* 12, no. 2 (1984): 152–83. http://www.jstor.org/stable/191359.

Discourse theories can help us understand the way the social world in interpretatively structured and are suggestive about the ways they analyze the structure of authority in specific regions or regimes. However, discourse theories employ a one-sided notion of the formation of understanding. In Foucault's view, the forming power of disclosure is independent of the communicative power of participants. Here knowledge in Foucault's terms is an effect of power. It loses any independent power and it subordinates the interpretive power of actors to goal oriented actions. The kinds of power regimes Foucault have in mind shape discourses but cannot create them or eliminate communicative power. As self-interpreters, social actors have to accept interpretations, which strategic actors induce them to have. Thus, they also have an independent power to resist in theory any such interpretations. To be sure, Foucault recognizes a degree of opposition but makes it dependent and constrained by the regime of power. But the interpretive capacities of subjects can break the limits of strategic power. They can imagine and introduce new conceptions of validity or truth.[17] A theory that reduces communicative power to strategic ends cannot account for the nature of the social bond itself.

Critical Theory and Practice: Social Diagnosis

Critical Theories differ from traditional social scientific theories because they have a practical intent. The critical theorist does not see the social world as a set of objects to be observed by the theorist and manipulated to gain a desired result; they are participants in the same social world that they share with others. Critical theories aim to oppose domination and coercion and to provide insight that can lead to greater freedom: political, social, Cultural, and personal. They also differ from Rawlsian inspired theories which draw a distinction between ideal theories and real theories. The former stands for an ideal theoretical state which is the construct of the theorist, and the latter the actually existing conditions. In such cases, the difference between the two theories is never breached.

In contrast, critical theories begin from the socio-historical situations of subjects and through an analysis of the conflicts in society to draw out the

[17] I think this is a limit in Sanford Schram's otherwise informative discussion of discourse of poverty in *Welfare Discipline: Discourse, Governance and Globalization* (Philadelphia: Temple University Press, 2006).

possibilities for transformation. The latter is not a project carried out by the theorist, but by the participants themselves, through insight into their own situation and their understanding of the possibilities for change. Even when theorists have some specialized knowledge, their knowledge stands on the same terrain as the non-specialist member of a society. It is the agency of participants which must be activated in projects of social change and greater freedom.

The approach of critical theory has close affinities with interpretive approaches to social inquiry. These approaches begin from the idea that the social sciences are different from the natural sciences to the extent that the subject matter of the social science is the meaningful behavior of other subjects in the social world. Thus, the social scientist is involved in a double hermeneutic. Not only does she communicate with other scientists in a common pursuit, but the "objects" the social scientist studies are other subjects who engage in meaningful action in the social world. Thus, social science does not just seek knowledge of the laws of behavior of objects but to understand the action of others, that is their ways of making sense of the social world. Social science can never be value free; the very act of understanding others entails evaluation. Neither the social scientist nor the participant in ordinary social life can understand themselves or others without being able to evaluate the rightness of their actions or the truthfulness of what they may assert about the world. Practical forms of understanding require the ability to follow a rule. The interpreter has to be able to determine whether the other person is following a norm or rule correctly in order to understand them. There is a critical component to all forms of understanding. This critical component cuts both ways. The subjects that the social scientist studies, is equally capable of evaluating the research of social scientists. These subjects are agents capable of both reason and consent. Thus, the social scientist in order to bring about a change, must win the assent of the subjects to their research.

Critical Theorists accept the practical orientation of interpretive approaches to social science, they also hold that the practical project of such a theory requires the assent of and mobilization of citizens who want to limit or end inequality, oppression, or domination. However, it also requires a diagnosis of the sources of such coercion in forms of illegitimate social power. Thus, it seeks to understand the structural bases of social power and links them to the problems that members of society experience. In the case of this study that means understanding the pathologies of contemporary neo-liberal society, which is the way it creates greater inequality and poverty and the social arrangements it employs to maintain such inequality.

The Breakdown of the Welfare State

The Keynesian welfare state was a response to the crisis ridden nature of capitalist economies, culminating in the Great Depression. For Keynes, the capitalist market operating on its own was inherently flawed and needed correction. Keynesians sought to use the power of government to regulate the economy to manage and mitigate economic cycles. Stimulating consumption was one of the primary ways economic management and stability was achieved, along with the use of central banks to control inflation. Other means were used such as breaking up monopolies and unfair competition, correcting market failures, provisioning for public goods which were not satisfied by markets, and compensating for externalities, costs not calculated in market reasoning. These were also means to obtaining full employment. Keynesian polices were redistributive. They aimed to transfer money and resources, to stimulate consumption.

On the other hand, Keynesianism did not challenge the capitalist economy in toto. Keynesians sought to guarantee conditions for successful accumulation. In the post-World War II era, it provided substantial funds for research and development and mega project investments, as well as support of social infrastructure such as health and welfare transportation and energy sectors. These "social overheads" were necessary to attract capital investment but were absorbed by the public. [18] This activity carried a tax burden that the business community did not always accept. While Keynesian policies may have been acceptable to get out of the depression and during the period of high growth in the post war era, by the 1970s growth had slowed. The burden on the federal government the states and especially cities became excessive. Governments could not generate the revenues needed to cover the costs of welfare state policies. In addition, at the end of the Keynesian era, the balance between unemployment and inflation which macroeconomic policy had successfully managed could no longer be maintained. The combination of high unemployment and high inflation created serious problems.

[18] John Keane, "Introduction" to Claus Offe, *Contradictions of the Welfare State* (London: Routledge, 1984): 11-32.

At the end of the Keynesian era then the demands of accumulation and legitimation could not be reconciled. Instead, it faced an accumulation crisis. Business interests felt that the conditions of successful accumulation were no longer fulfilled especially due to inflation and slow growth, and the taxation level necessary to fund the welfare state also made it difficult to make sufficient profit. Thus, business went on a capital strike. They began to withdraw from investments needed to maintain growth.

Neo-liberalism touted itself as the economic solution to the twin problems of inflation and unemployment. As an economic ideology, neo-liberalism contended that excessive regulation and taxation were the sources of our economic dilemma. The solution lies in lower taxes, deregulation, and privatization of government services. These they claimed would restore the conditions of growth in a competitive market economy that Keynesians had distorted. They opposed the redistributionist policies of Keynesian economics and sought to cut back or eliminate the welfare state. The paring back of social "entitlements" was to be a solution to the fiscal crisis of the state too. With less spending on social programs, there would be less stress on the fiscal health of cities states and the nation. Thus, where the Keynesians thought the flawed capitalist economy was the problem neo-liberals saw flawed government intervention as the problem.

Neo-liberalism was not a simple revival of classical laissez-faire liberalism. It no longer relied on a spontaneously arising market and a minimal watchman state but it sees the market as something that is socially constructed. It requires a strong state to establish and maintain the conditions for a free market. This conception was derived from the earlier German Ordo Liberalism, which formulated the idea of a of a social market. The state has to both guarantee conditions of accumulation and market structure through legal structure and shape the behavior of individuals who participate in the market.[19] Neo-liberals think that humans, especially from the lesser classes, are deficient, must be shaped, and socialized. The ordo liberals and later the neo-liberals held that the experiences of the labor movement and socialist movements in the nineteenth and twentieth

[19] On Ordo Liberalism see Werner Bonefeld, "German Ordo-Liberalism and the politics of vitality" *Renewal* 20.4 (2013). Also Bonefeld, *Strong State Free Economy* (Lantham: Rowman and Littlefield, 2017); Michel Foucault also discussed Ordo Liberalism in Michel Foucault, *The Birth of Biopolitics: Lectures at the College de France (1978–9)* (New York: Palgrave Macmillan, 2010).

centuries illustrated workers were incapable on their own of entrepreneurial behavior. Deliberate political authority was needed to maintain free markets and shape market like behavior.[20]

These concerns were apparent in the founding documents of the Mont Pellerin Society in which a neo-liberal outlook was first organized. Socialism and social democracy were not just economic errors but existential threats. Socialism (which included some features of the welfare state) corrupted the body politic. It had to be eliminated if society was to be saved.[21]

Here I want to note a second manner in which the emerging neo-liberal model shaped society and culture. The marketization, deregulation, and privatization of the economy result in an increasing commodification of spheres of social life. To be sure, such processes of reification took place earlier, but neo-liberalism marks a new stage in the process. Jurgen Habermas has expressed this in his notion of colonization of the life world.[22] When the market expands beyond its legitimate uses and takes over spheres that are constituted by other forms of interaction like the family and education, it threatens the integrity of these spheres of interaction. In short, neo-liberal capitalism creates even greater social dislocation, alienation, and pathology in social life than its predecessors. Because they deny the need for these independent elements, and want social actors to be more like entrepreneurs, Neo-liberals are indifferent to the effect of these larger social problems.

Neo-Liberalism and the Welfare State

The welfare state in the United States has followed a liberal model. It has only partially decommodified welfare benefits. Many benefits have been tied to notions of deserving (and undeserving) poor combined with some

[20] Among many analyses of neo-liberalism see David Harvey, A Brief History of Neo-Liberalism (New York: Oxford, 2007); Thomas Biebriche, *The Political Theory of Neoliberalism* (Stanford: Stanford University Press, 2019; Wolfgang Streeck, *Buying Time: The Delayed Crisis of Democratic Capitalism 2nd Edition* (London: Verso, 2015).

[21] Daniel Steadman-Jones, Masters *of the Universe: Hayek, Friedman, and the Birth of Neoliberal Politics* (Princeton: Princeton University Press, 2014).

[22] Jurgen Habermas, *The Theory of Communicative Action Volume 2: Lifeworld and System: A Critique of Functionalist Reason* (Boston: Beacon Press, 1985)

notion of means testing.[23] However, neo-liberalism introduced a new iteration of this formulation that changed interpretations of poverty and threatened the existence of welfare. Not only must the poor be submitted to the logic of the commodity to get aid, but the subject of welfare discourse must also literally become a commodity-like person who conforms to the religion of entrepreneurialism. If you will, the poor are asked to become self-exploiters.

Thus, the neo-liberal approach to welfare differs significantly from its predecessors. From the New Deal until the end of the Keynesian era in the 1970s welfare was a safety net. The safety net could be seen in the first instance a set of programs that aim to protect those with low incomes from poverty and hardship. This would include those who are able to work and those who for several reasons can't work. In the first case, it attempts to get those able back on their feet and in a second, to provide disabled and others with a minimum standard of living. But the social safety net also included programs like Social Security, Medicare and unemployment which benefited the middle class. Low-income programs were transfer programs, (i.e., Redistributive) that do not require participation. The second group requires contributions by the individual and usually the employer. In each case, they seek to reduce the risks the individual faces in industrial societies.

Neo-liberals, while they are happy to reduce the risks to business via public funding and sharing of risk, think that social risks should be passed down to the individual. Though with little success so far, they have sought to privatize social security, Another failed example was Mitt Romney's proposal to privatize unemployment in 2012. Welfare programs create dependency and weakness rather than mitigating risks. In this way, they go beyond the discourse of means testing. They want to remove social guarantees and privatize welfare functions.

Neo-liberals reject the very notion behind welfare. Instead of decommodifying needs, they want to recommodify them and colonize the forms of subjectivity through which our lives are carried out. In addition to creating the conditions for a free-market economy and eliminating features of government and social life that distort markets of render them incomplete state then also creates conditions to produce subjects who conform to the demands of the economy. However, not all public authority is exercised

[23] See for example Michael Katz, *The Undeserving Poor: Americas Enduring Confrontation with Poverty* 2nd edition (New York: Oxford, 2013).

directly by the state. As part of the privatization of services, private groups like charities and non-profits come to provide the social services once provided by the state, but now under the terms of the state. Under these private public partnerships, the role of such groups changes. They are less advocates for disadvantaged groups, then agents of that public authority. The privatized welfare state is an agent of discipline.

The new social discipline requires however, a more punitive attitude toward the poor. Sociologist Loic Wacquant has written extensively about the development of a new "common sense" that has emerged in the last 30+ years, which criminalizes poverty, marginalizes the poor, and normalizes insecure low wage exploitive work at the bottom of the economic ladder. What he calls the government of social insecurity is based on the notion that the subaltern are "others" are not playing by the rules of the game, and hence not entitled to benefits.[24] Notably, in the Reagan era, welfare recipients (females) were labeled as welfare queens trying to game the system. Similarly, fears of a permanent underclass that was the source of increasing crime and disorder were prevalent when crime was decreasing. But these perceptions were used to justify punitive measures against the poor. Workfare and the carceral state became central to the project of disciplining and controlling the poor. Women especially single mothers and minority women were the most susceptible to this. For minority males, imprisonment was the main mode of social discipline. Despite a long-term decline in the crime rate, Black men in the US, are incarcerated at the highest rate in the world. Minorities are incarcerated more frequently, than the rest of the population, are incarcerated at a higher rate for similar crimes like drug possession and serve longer sentences.

Similarly, Sanford Schram, Joe Soss, and Richard Fording stressed the way in which neo-liberal policies are forms of disciplining the poor to create personally responsible market compliant actors. Like other social institutions, welfare functions have become marketized. "there has been a dramatic shift to relying on private providers, where clients are turned into consumers who get to make choices, and both are held accountable via

[24] Loic Wacquant, *Prisons of Poverty* (Minneapolis: University of Minnesota Press, 2009a). Also, Wacquant. *Punishing the Poor: The Neo-Liberal government of Social Insecurity* (Durham: Duke University Press, 2009b).

performance measurement systems that indicate whether market-based objectives have been met."[25]

Jaime Peck has characterized these developments as the creation of a "shadow" welfare state, comprised of "grant dependent institutions engaged in service roles in the community non-profit and faith-based sectors."[26] This grant dependence as Peck and others notes, effects primarily the poor, who receive either restricted or ideologically loaded services.

What Peck views as a secret welfare state turns out to be far from secret. For example, in welfare administration most job placement programs are now run by private firms or non-profits. One of the main organizational tools used by RMAPI, collective impact, is I think, quite clear in its attempt to consolidate such a private welfare state. Thus, not only are individuals disciplined to see themselves as responsible for their own fate, but the social service sector is also being transformed to be a tool of neoliberal "responsibilization." The idea of the entrepreneurial self is one of a rational calculator who has internalized market logic and accepts risk but is also compliant and adaptable to market forces. The individual must understand herself as applying an economic logic in all aspects of life to develop one's own social capital and think in terms of return on investment. Everyone is seen to be a self-sufficient actor creating value for the corporate bosses.[27]

This marks a major change in the idea of social work. Schram in fact thinks of it as the end of social work in its traditional form. It is no longer concerned with wider matters of social justice or critical understanding of the social world but becomes a set of psychological services that help clients adapt to the demands of the disciplinary state. It is a form of managing rather than serving needy populations.

[25] Joe Soss, Sanford Schram and Richard Fording, "Governing the Poor: The Rise of the Neoliberal Paternalist State." This is drawn from their book *Disciplining the Poor: Neoliberal Paternalism and the Persistent Power of Race* (Chicago University of Chicago Press 2011) also see Schram, "Neoliberalizing the Welfare State: Marketizing Social Policy/ Disciplining Clients" in Damien Cahill, Melinda Cooper, Martin Konings and David Primrose, *Sage Handbook of Neoliberalism* (Thousand Oaks CA: Sage Publishing, 2018): 308-322

[26] Jamie Peck, "Austerity urbanism: American cities under extreme economy" *City: Analysis of Urban Change, Theory, Action vol* 16, no 6 626-55: 644

[27] A different version of this point was made by Richard Sennett who emphasized the socialization of actors to accept the flexible fast capitalism in which they have to be able to adapt quickly to changing circumstances, See *The Culture of the New Capitalism* (New Haven: Yale, 2006). He draws on the work of Zygmunt Bauman, *Liquid Modernity* (London: Polity, 2000).

Neo-liberalism as critics like Peck noted has a deep-seated anti-democratic strain, which has intensified in the later stage of neo-liberalism. Here it is not just that the risks of social life are shifted from the structural level to the personal. More than this shift of focus toward the priority of economically rational behavior is a fundamental transformation of the idea of citizenship. The citizen is not a political one who acts together with others to create a collective democratic life, but an isolated economic actor, who is not concerned with the good of others. Rather than being a political problem to be solved through collective action, poverty is an individual one caused by the lack of skills or proper attitudes and behavioral expectations.

This feature of political culture was presaged in the theories of the first neo-liberals. They held that economic freedom precedes and trumps political freedom. Neo-liberal theorists like Milton Friedman, held that a capitalist dictatorship is preferable to a socialist democracy (as shown in his support of Chilean dictatorship under Pinochet). On this basis, neo-liberals justify an authoritarian paternalist attitude toward the mass of the populace. Authority is justified in enforcing economic discipline on those who lack it.

Wacquant takes this analysis one step further. Liberal paternalism employs a double standard. It is permissive regarding the transgressions of the well off and corporations, punitive and paternalistic toward the less well off. They are labeled as criminals or lazy miscreants subject to surveillance and sanctions. Of course, this parallels the general inequality of what has become a winner take all society. A few at the top are reaping great rewards while the quality of life and economic reward for the rest is stagnant or in decline.

Transforming the Non-profit Sector

As Soss, Schram, and Fording argued, neo-liberalism transforms the non-profit sector into a vehicle for social discipline and marketization. It changes the relationship of non-profits to both the state and to civil society. Non-profits have always been seen as a part of civil society, which is the network of voluntary association and institutions independent of government. Two elements of this sphere are important for my discussion. Civil society is a realm of solidarities and social bonds outside of the family, and it is the space of a public sphere in which social problems are identified, public opinion in formed and issues of interest to all or important segments of the public can be discussed.

In neo-liberalism however, these elements of civil society are under siege. Neo-liberal thought rejects the idea that there is a common good or a public good. These are collectivist (i.e., socialist) illusions. The only things that count are consumer preferences. This yields a constricted notion of democracy limited to the free choice among one's preferences. Neo-liberals have little interest in expanding or even maintaining a robust democratic debate. Thus, the "public" is reduced to a concatenation of preferences without any need or value in public discussion unless it concerns a compromise among the interest positions of actors. True public deliberation about the rightness soundness or even wisdom of an action is discouraged.

Similarly, questions of solidarity cannot be grasped from the individualistic standpoint of the strategic subject. The bonds that link us through compassion, care, and trust for those who are part of our community, even broader transnational ones, escape the boundaries of this theory. The latter are features of communicative forms of action. They require mutual understanding. To be sure neo-liberal welfare schemes presuppose a model of the intact family, they cannot explain the kind of normative bonds that family members but more importantly all members of a society can share however weakly.

The privatization of the welfare system has worked to weaken both elements. Non-profits have often become partners in neo-liberal governance rather than advocates of justice for the poor oppressed or underserved. Much non-profit service is mediated through government outsourcing and foundations that are increasingly run by financiers or information technology partners. Non-profits have been drawn into the project of creating entrepreneurial selves.

This was not always true. In the progressive era, and through the new deal to the Reagan era non-profits often were advocates for social rights, and championed anti-poverty, health care, childcare policies, and rights for the elderly and disabled. In one sense, they were advocates for decommodification. Certainly, this advocacy has been uneven, but overall non-profits employed notions of social citizenship -- the idea that individuals need a minimum of economic and social security as well as a basic education to fully participate in society. As Hassenfeld and Garrod note, under the conditions of the welfare state, "The nonprofit human-service sector operated in a policy environment that at least partially encouraged social equality and the expansion of social rights."[28] Here the non-profit sector served to develop and enhance civil society. It promoted solidarity with the poor and disadvantaged, and greater social and political equality for all.

Public Administration Scholars Angela Eikenberry and Jody Kluver have also analyzed the marketization of the public sector rasing many of the issues I have noted.[29] The end of the Keynesian approach to political-economic organization has led to its replacement by a neo-liberal model of political economy which stressed deregulation, privatization, and decentralization. One aspect of this is the changing relation of state and civil society and the public-private and governmental sectors. Now non-profits carry out "responsibilization": one must prove one is worth by willingness to work to get government aid. When non-profits carry out these imperatives, they become less a civil society building organization and they become colonized by economic political-administrative imperatives. They become partners is the commodification and financialization of the clients they serve. They enforce the discipline of the state in creating entrepreneurial selves. For example, if a private entity administers a job training program which individuals must certify they are engaged in to receive welfare benefits, then they no longer act as advocates for justice in civil society, or promote equity or solidarity, but enforce the norms of "responsible" agency that government programs require.

Thus, non-profits no longer serve to build solidarities between the poor or the poor and the larger community. To the contrary civil society has shrunk under neo-liberalism, as policies are increasingly shifted to corporate and government collaboration, the formation of public opinion even in the limited form of mass media become superfluous.

The outsourcing of social welfare functions to the private service providers was another mechanism for creating marketization. While government funding for not profit social services decreased. non-profits were able to grow in the 1980s and early 1990s due to a 52 percent growth in these commercial services. Also, government contracts have moved from grants to vouchers that use quasi-market competition to enforce norms of "accountability and performance measures for the delivery of social

[28] See Joan Roelofs, *Foundations and Public Policy: The Mask of Pluralism* (Albany: SUNY Press, 2003) :301

[29] Angela M. Eikenberry and Jodie Drapal Kluver, "The Marketization of the Nonprofit Sector: Civil Society at Risk?" *Public Administration Review* Vol. 64, No. 2 Mar.—Apr. (2004): 132-140.

services." Governments have also outsourced services to private enterprises, much of elder care services and many health care's services have been outsourced. An increase in market structures and market-like behavior in non-profits such as fees for services product sales and other commercial ventures have come to be the norm. Here non-profits function as instruments of entrepreneurial policy in order to maintain funding. Non-profits shift their aims to fit middle class needs rather than the poor, a strategy that is successful for sustaining funding but not for helping the poor.

One major element of this privatized welfare state is exemplified by the New Public Management. Employing neo-liberal ideas of privatization, this theory aimed to change the way that non-profit social services were administered: it seeks to use a contract approach to social services. The contract approach incorporates the language (risk-sharing, pay-for-performance, and bonuses) and methods of the market, shifting risk to providers who get paid only for completed assignments on a fixed-rate basis.[30]

They eliminate the ideas of reciprocal obligations and mutual aid that non-profits have employed. To the extent that citizens became consumers, they bear the full individual responsibility of obtaining the services. Non-profits can no longer provide services to all who need them.

The Dilemma of Neo-liberal Welfare Reform

The neo-liberal approach to welfare rejects the traditional notions of welfare and its values. Instead of seeking to decommodify forms of social life, it seeks to recommodify them. This feature separates the neo-liberal attempt to dismantle the welfare state, from a similar left-wing critique. Going back as far as the Frankfurt School's critique of advanced capitalists, some progressive thinkers have emphasized the destructive features of the welfare state. Through its connection to the administrative state, citizens are reduced to clients, charges of the state who must be treated as subject to therapeutic intervention.[31] Some critics extended this to the family. Christopher Lasch for example thought that the therapeutic nature of

[30]William P. Ryan, "The New Landscape for Non-Profits" *Harvard Business Review* 77, 1 (1999): 127-36.

[31]Max Horkheimer. "The End of Reason" *in The Essential Frankfurt School Reader:* 26-47; Max Horkheimer, *The Eclipse of Reason* (New York: Continuum, 1974).

state bureaucracies transferred authority over the family and personal life from the parents to the state itself. He thinks the emotional work previously done by the family was now done by the state, thus undermining the family.[32] Following Foucault, Jacques Donzelot took a similar view. He saw the in the development of the welfare state, a "policing of families" in which families are stripped of rights and rendered dependent on the state.[33]

Each of these critiques contends that state bureaucracies negate the autonomy of subjects. The problem with these approaches lies in their one-sided interpretation of the welfare state. No doubt, the welfare state can treat individuals as clients and sometimes promoted a therapeutic culture. Yet it also can serve to promote autonomy and solidarity. The safety net can play a role in preserving social bonds. Just as the economic interventions of the state in stabilizing the economy led to new claims about legitimacy that need to be addressed, the social welfare elements of state action also raise claims, if not always explicit ones about social rights. Such social rights counter the imperatives of the bureaucratic administrative state. They provide conditions of autonomy that an unfettered free market constrict. So, they may well lead to claims against forms of state intervention in personal life that are intrusive rather than empowering. The left critique usually issues from a non-statist vision of community that transcends the rule of the market. The neo-liberal one however, retains a strong state hand. Without forgetting the bureaucratic aspects of welfare in our societies, it can also serve a socially integrative function. To be sure, fully realizing this would require considerable reform. It could preserve and enhance social bonds of solidarity that critics like Lasch contend it destroys.

Neo-liberalism rather than promoting autonomy threatens to undermine the values that provide political support for the welfare state. As Peter Taylor-Gooby notes:

> Welfare state citizenship rests on the values of reciprocity inclusion and institutional trust. Endorsement of these values by a substantial and politically effective part if the population is essential to ensure that the welfare state continues in a recognizable form. The shift toward an individualization of

[32] Christopher Lasch, *Haven in a Heartless World: The Family Besieged* (New York: Basic Books, 1977).

[33] Jacques Donzelot, *The Policing of Families* (New York: Pantheon, 1979).

> responsibility toward welfare outcomes constrains reciprocity, contradicts inclusion, and undermines important aspects of trust[34]

Gooby describes the loss of socially integrative power in the neo-liberal version of the welfare state. In agreement with other critics a punitive conception of service provision means the welfare recipient is labeled as an "other," one who is deficient us, they cease to be partners in solidarity, but become threats that need to be controlled. Discipline is outsourced, to induce individuals to adopt the right entrepreneurial behavior. Even more than the supposed "nanny state" it criticizes, neo-liberalism controls and shapes subjectivity.

Neo-liberal welfare is singularly unable to deal with the emerging social problems that it creates. To the extent that neo-liberalism maintains its position as the dominant economic outlook, it will continue to generate crises in the economy and undermine mutual obligations. Questions of the mutual obligations between citizens remain problematic.

The social and economic conditions of the contemporary economy, also, pose current issues for the welfare state. The early welfare state was based on the quest for full employment with social insurance (unemployment and social security) and it saw social assistance as the supplement for those who were displaced. It rested on the assumptions of the single breadwinner, a stable nuclear family, and the issues that arose from its maintenance and pathology. Today the problems facing individuals and families stem from another set of problems that produce new vulnerabilities. These new social risks (NSR) emerge from the conditions of globalization, of deindustrialization, and contingent employment.

One set of NSRs stems from the dualized, precarious character of contemporary labor markets. Long-term unemployment and social exclusion; part-time or temporary work that brings insufficient security; caretaker interruptions that reduce pension entitlements; having one's skills become obsolete in mid-career; and being 'working poor' (i.e., full-time employed while earning poverty-level wages) are all examples. A second set—resulting from changes in family forms, gender relations, demography, and migration—includes being a single parent; being a divorced spouse; a child living in poverty; a dual-earner couple or lone working mother

[34] Peter Taylor-Gooby, *Reframing Social Citizenship* (New York: Oxford, 2009): 3.

experiencing difficulties obtaining childcare or balancing work and family life; the very elderly in need of intensive support; and immigrants.[35]

> This fragmentation influences our understanding of the unemployed.
>
> The category of 'the unemployed,' for example, no longer refers to a relatively homogeneous group of out-of-work male breadwinners. It now includes the underemployed; part-time or temporary workers; people who stay in school or retire early because they cannot find work; people who are deemed disabled but who are really unemployed; the long-term unemployed; and those who are temporarily out of work as they move between jobs."[36]

Unlike the Keynesian Welfare state which was designed to address the negative side effects of the market, the neo-liberal state lacks the capacity to address the precarity and vulnerabilities created by its own operation. The well-known hollowing out of the state, especially its administrative and regulative capacities, has resulted in a state that is unable to respond to the problems caused by its economic activity. The shortfalls to municipal revenues are one result, but as federal tax cuts, outsourcing and privatization have become the norm, both the financial and the administrative capacity to respond have been reduced. Ironically however, the decreased capacities, as Peck's analysis of Detroit discussed in the next chapter shows, lead to crises that justify extraordinary government authority through a state of emergency. Far from resolving the problems however, the state of emergency only increases the financialization of public services leading to more crises in the future. It makes urban governance less democratic.

Neo-liberalism does not recognize these new social risks as problems at all unless and until they impact the performance of the economy. It has a notion of dependency but not socially induced vulnerability. However, there is a dialectic if you will between autonomy and vulnerability. Because human beings depend on each other and the natural environment for survival and for development they are vulnerable. Our autonomy takes place in social contexts, and it depends on protection from excessive vulnerability. Mutual respect and mutual aid are connected. The neo-liberal welfare regime has no space for mutuality.

[35] David Garland, The *Welfare State A Very Short Introduction* (New York: Oxford University Press, 2016): 126-7.

[36] Garland, *The Welfare State:* 125

There are no longer large-scale anti-poverty programs at the federal level in the US. This has left the matter to states but even more often to municipalities. Yet municipalizes are the least autonomous and have the fewest resources for addressing the problems. And there are few attempts to address the long terms problems of poverty. Much of the slack has been taken up by private foundations and for-profit operations. These may have the virtue of flexibility and innovation, but they often have priorities that are unacknowledged and stand at a remove from democratic accountability. Whereas in the past, such programs might be seen as pilot programs that suggest forms of government action that could be publicly debated and considered, now these programs take on a more autonomous role. They come to act as quasi administrative agencies who influence and often dictate the direction of policy. On the municipal level, they are associated with privatization of public services and support of charter schools and gentrification. These new forces employ conceptions of "fairness" that are highly restricted.

The new conditions of the social welfare system in the US pose challenges. Forty years of neo-liberal economic policies has deepened the gap between the rich and the poor and created a situation in which many have significant debt and are close to the edge of poverty. Neo-liberalism has created increased precarity. Eighty percent of Americans do not have 400 dollars to deal with an emergency like a car breakdown, a home repair, or a medical emergency. Any of these could send American families into bankruptcy poverty or even homelessness. The economic regime of neo-liberalism has generated a set of new social risks (to use the current term of art) which it has not addressed.

Bibliography

Avineri, Shlomo. *Hegel's Theory of the Modern State.* (Cambridge: Cambridge University Press, 1974).

Bachrach, Peter and Morton S. Baratz. "Two Faces of Power." *The American Political Science Review* Vol. 56, No. 4 Dec. 1962: 947-952

Bachrach, Peter and Morton S. Baratz. "Decisions and Nondecisions: An Analytical Framework." *The American Political Science Review* Vol. 57, No. 3 Sep. 1963: 632-642.

Bauman, Zygmunt. *Liquid Modernity.* London: Polity, 2000.

Biebriche, Thomas. *The Political Theory of Neoliberalism.* Stanford: Stanford University Press, 2019.

Block, Fred and Margaret Somers. *The Power of Market Fundamentalism: Karl Polanyi's Critique*. Cambridge: Harvard, 2014.

Bonefeld, Werner. *Strong State Free Economy*. Lathan: Rowan and Littlefield, 2017.

Bonefeld, Werner. "German Ordo-Liberalism and the politics of vitality." *Renewal* 20.4. 2013.

Crenshaw, Matthew. *The Unpolitics of Air Pollution: A Study of Non-Decision Making in the Cities*. Baltimore: Johns Hopkins, 1971.

Donzelot, Jacques. *The Policing of Families*. (New York: Pantheon, 1979).

Eikenberry, Angela M., and Jodie Drapal Kluver. "The Marketization of the Nonprofit Sector: Civil Society at Risk?" *Public Administration Review* Vol. 64, No. 2 Mar.—Apr. 2004: 132-140.

Esping-Andersen, Gasta. *Three Worlds of Welfare Capitalism*. Princeton: Princeton University Press, 1990.

Foucault, Michel. *The Birth of Biopolitics: Lectures at the College de France (1978–9)*. New York: Palgrave Macmillan, 2010.

Foucault, Michel. *Power/Knowledge: Selected Interviews and Other Writings, 1972-1977*. New York: Pantheon, 1980.

Foucault, Michel. *Discipline and Punish: The Birth of the Prison*. New York: Vintage, 1978.

Fraser, Nancy. "A Triple Movement: Parsing the Politics of Crisis after Polanyi." *NLR* 81, May/June, 2013: 119-32.

Garland, David. The *Welfare State A Very Short Introduction*. (New York: Oxford University Press, 2016): 126-7.

Gaventa, John. *Power and Powerlessness: Quiescence & Rebellion in an Appalachian Valley*. Chicago: University of Illinois Press, 1982.

Habermas, Jurgen. *Legitimation Crisis*. Boston: Beacon Press 1975.

Habermas, Jurgen. *The Theory of Communicative Action, Volume 2: Lifeworld and System: A Critique of Functionalist Reason*. Boston: Beacon Press, 1985.

Harvey, David. *A Brief History of Neo-Liberalism*. Oxford: Oxford University Press, 2007.

Honneth, Axel, and Nancy Fraser. *Redistribution or Recognition: A Political-Philosophical Exchange*. (London: Verso, 2003).

Horkheimer Max, and Theodor Adorno. *The Dialectic of Enlightenment: Philosophical Fragments*. Stanford: Stanford University Press, 2002.

Horkheimer, Max. "The Authoritarian State." Andrew Arato and Eike Gephardt Eds., *The Essential Frankfurt School Reader* New edition (London: Bloomsbury Academic, 1982): 95-117.

Horkheimer, Max. *The Eclipse of Reason*. (New York: Continuum, 1974).

Horkheimer. Max. "The End of Reason" in The Essential Frankfurt School Reader: 26-47;

Katz, Michael. *The Undeserving Poor: Americas Enduring Confrontation with Poverty* 2nd edition, New York: Oxford, 2013.

Keane, John. "Introduction" to Claus Offe. *Contradictions of the Welfare State* (London: Routledge, 1984): 11-32.

Kettler, David and Thomas Wheatland. n.d. *Learning from Franz L. Neumann*. Anthem Press.

Lasch, Christopher. *Haven in a Heartless World: The Family Besieged.* (New York: Basic Books, 1977).

Lukes, Steven. *Power: A Radical View* second ed, London: Palgrave Macmillan Springer, 2005

Marshall, T.H., *Citizenship and Social Class: And Other Essays*. Cambridge; Cambridge University Press, 1950.

Peck. Jaime "Austerity urbanism: American cities under extreme economy." City: Analysis of Urban Change, Theory, Action vol 16, no 6: 626-55.

Polanyi, Karl. *The Great Transformation: The Political and Economic Origins of Our Time* 2nd ed. Boston: Beacon Press 2001.

Pollock, Friedrich. "State Capitalism: Its Possibilities and Limitations." Andrew Arato and Eike Gephardt Eds., *The Essential Frankfurt School Reader* New edition (London: Bloomsbury Academic, 1982): 71-94.

Roelofs, Joan. *Foundations and Public Policy: The Mask of Pluralism.* Albany: SUNY Press 2003 :301.

Ryan, William P. "The New Landscape for Non-Profits" *Harvard Business Review* 77, 1 (1999): 127-36.

Scheurmann, William, *Between the Norm and the Exception: The Frankfurt School and The Rule of Law.* Cambridge MA: MIT Press, 1996a.

Scheurmann, William. *The Rule of Law Under Siege Selected Essays of Franz L. Neumann and Otto Kirchheimer.* Berkeley: University of California Press, 1996b.

Schram, Stanford. "Neoliberalizing the Welfare State: Marketizing Social Policy/ Disciplining Clients." in Damien Cahill, Melinda Cooper, Martin Konings and David Primrose, *Sage Handbook of Neoliberalism* Thousand Oaks CA: Sage Publishing, 2018: 308-322

Schram, Sanford. *Welfare Discipline: Discourse, Governance and Globalization.* Philadelphia: Temple University Press, 2006.

Sennett, Richard. *The Culture of the New Capitalism.* New Haven: Yale, 2006.

Soss, Joe, Sanford Schram and Richard Fording. *Disciplining the Poor: Neoliberal Paternalism and the Persistent Power of Race.* Chicago: University of Chicago Press, 2011

Steadman-Jones, Daniel. *Masters of the Universe: Hayek, Friedman, and the Birth of Neoliberal Politics*—Updated. Princeton: Princeton University Press, 2014.

Streeck, Wolfgang. *Buying Time: The Delayed Crisis of Democratic Capitalism 2nd Edition*. London: Verso, 2014.

Taylor, Charles. "Foucault on Freedom and Truth." *Political Theory* 12, no. 2 1984. 152–83. http://www.jstor.org/stable/191359.

Taylor-Gooby, Peter. *Reframing Social Citizenship*. New York: Oxford, 2009.

Wacquant, Loic. *Prisons of Poverty*. Minneapolis: University of Minnesota Press, 2009a.

Wacquant, Loic. *Punishing the Poor: The Neo-Liberal government of Social Insecurity*. Durham: Duke University Press, 2009b.

CHAPTER 3

Deindustrialization, the Welfare State and Urban Decay

The Deindustrial Condition

Deindustrialization was one of the main factors in the decline of cities especially those in the Northeast and Midwest during the 1970s and 1980s. Its effects on restructuring the American economy are still seen today. When manufacturers fled to the suburbs, the sunbelt and to foreign countries, they not only emptied cities and rural areas of good paying industrial jobs, but the network of small business and commercial services that grew up to serve industries. With a loss of income in taxes and investment, cities faced looming fiscal crises. Without any satisfactory replacements for industrial jobs, deindustrialization led to disinvestment in urban areas. When neither industries nor government provided investment in the depressed areas, they suffered intensified decline. They lacked the fiscal resources to adapt to changing conditions. Where there were new jobs, they paid far less than the jobs lost. Deindustrialization created a new form of inequality in American society.

Throughout much of the twentieth century, the United States was the world's leading industrial power. In the years after World War II, the US benefitted from the devastation of Europe and Japan. It used its advantage to create the post war industrial and financial order based on international institutions which favored the US. During its period of dominance, the strength of US manufacturing created a large and stable middle class, many of whom owned their own homes, and provided the basis of

B. Caterino, *The Failure of the Neo-Liberal Approach to Poverty*,
https://doi.org/10.1007/978-3-031-10606-4_3

widespread prosperity. Unions played a significant role, even if they were not as strong as those in Europe. Of course, the cold war played a role too. A working class pacified by good wages and benefits was a guarantee against the rise of socialist or even social democratic impulses. During the postwar years, social inequality declined significantly. Whereas the top 10 percent made 45 percent of all income in the first decades of the twentieth century in the postwar years from 1950-80 that percentage declined to close to 30 percent.

The post war years contrast starkly to the situation from 1980 onward. Even though the US was still the second leading manufacturer in the world (China is now number 1) manufacturing's percentage of total economic output has declined to 12 percent. At its height, it was closer to 20 percent. Estimates of the total loss of manufacturing jobs are at least 7.5 million.[1] While the manufacturing output in toto has not declined, new industrial production is both capital intensive and requires higher education and fewer employees. Many traditional manufacturing sectors have declined or disappeared altogether and where they have been retained, wages have decreased. They no longer represent a path to the middle class. The loss of these traditional higher paying manufacturing jobs especially in the Northeast and Midwest, were a major factor in the growing inequality and poverty. Since 1980 income inequality (and concomitantly inequality of wealth) except for some short periods of retreat under Obama, has increased significantly. Now it approaches or exceeds the levels found in the turn of the century. Today, according to a 2018 UN Report, the US has the most inequitable income distribution of any industrialized nation.[2] Even though US workers are among the most productive in the world, wages have not kept up with these productivity increases. [3]

There were, certainly, some indications of problems even during the post war years. Manufacturers began to move plants to the suburbs, affecting workers who lacked adequate transportation and associated jobs

[1] Kerwin Kofi Charles, Erik Hurst, and Mariel Schwart, "The Transformation of Manufacturing and the Decline in U.S. Employment" *NBER* working paper 24468. https://www.nber.org/system/files/working_papers/w24468/w24468.pdf

[2] Susan McFarland, "U.N. report: With 40M in poverty, U.S. most unequal developed nation" *UPIJUNE* 22, 2018. U.N. report: With 40M in poverty, U.S. most unequal developed nation—UPI.com

[3] Robert Reich, *Aftershock: The next economy and America's Future* (New York: Vintage, 2010), and Thomas Piketty, *Capital in the Twenty-First Century* (Cambridge: Belknap Press 2014).

connected to supply chains. A more substantial challenge to industrial centers in the Northeast and Midwest came from the recovering economies of Japan and Europe, especially Japan which manufactured similar goods at lower prices. Manufacturing also migrated internally to the South and the Sunbelt. These areas had nonunion workers, lower wages, and more lax regulations than other parts of the country and lower operating costs. However, these decisions were not just economic but political. Moving jobs reduced the extent of and power of unions. The increased power of capital led to legal and regulatory changes which weakened workers, consumers, and citizens. Though organizations like NAM (National Association of Managers), manufacturers were beginning to assert greater power over political policy. This was a signal of the fundamental rewriting of the social contract that was established in the Keynesian era. The new social power of business resulted in greater political power to enact more measures favoring capital over labor.

Even Sunbelt areas were not entirely immune to new economic forces. They also found themselves losing manufacturing jobs to offshoring by multinational corporations, making American workers compete against low wage foreign workers. Later free trade agreements like North American Free Trade Agreement (NAFTA) and tax breaks for large corporations made it easier to outsource production then to retain domestic factories, as did technological developments which reduced the importance of physical distance and enabled the globalization of production. Globalization altered the spatial relations of humanity and transformed the nature of the world economy. Communication and transportation technologies allowed for coordination impossible in early forms of production. Not only is production located offshore, technical support for a product for example, may be in India or some other country. Faster communications allowed control over distant production centers and control of flows and supply chains at least in theory. Global capitalism promises a fast-flexible system of production can respond quickly to changes in market demand.

Economists sometimes look at deindustrialization in a positive light. It is the inevitable result of the evolution of the global economy. On this view of deindustrialization, American industries and American workers must submit to the discipline of the market. The increasing interdependence of the global economy facilitates new international competition that cannot be resisted. Deindustrialization is a force of creative destruction which will clear the ground for capital to invest in new businesses. In many communities, of course, this did not happen. It is a mistake to look at deindustrialization and globalization as neutral or quasi natural processes unaffected by social power. Large corporate interests did much to shape its direction. The technological changes associated with these spatial exchanges and global interconnection are not inherently liberating and do not necessarily improve human welfare. Its role depends on the social and political organization of technology and economic activity. Neo-liberal globalization was not the only possible form a global economy could take. It could have been based on principles of equity and justice. The low wages paid to workers in poorer countries can be seem a form of exploitation not simply market forces.

To be sure, the absolute number of manufacturing jobs in the US continued to rise until 2004, but the relative percentage of jobs declined. Certain industries were destroyed and areas like Flint Michigan, Detroit, Youngstown, Ohio, and Rochester have yet to recover. The American economy has undergone a fundamental restructuring from a manufacturing economy to a service one. Services now constitute about two-thirds of the economic product, and financial banking and real estate services make up by themselves about 20 percent.[4] Among the fast-growing services were education, health care, and social services. At the same time, wages have remained stagnant for almost 30 years, and many of the benefits associated with industrial work such as health care and pensions were lost. While workers were forced to compete against low wage foreign workers, the wages of managers and CEOs of large corporations increased. The new jobs and the new situations that a more flexible capitalism created, combined with lower wages and benefits are more unstable and insecure.[5]

Disinvestment, the withdrawal of capital investment in an area, goes well beyond plant closures. It includes the reduction or loss of services and goods available. Writing in the early 1980s Barry Bluestone and Bennett Harrison noted that deindustrialization is also a "widespread disinvestment in nations basic productive capacity,"[6] that responded in part to

[4] "The economic benefits of improving social inclusion: A report commissioned by SBS" *Deloitte Access Economics* August, 2019. https://www2.deloitte.com/content/dam/Deloitte/my/Documents/risk/my-rsk-sdg10-economic-benefits-of-improving-social-inclusion.pdf

[5] Guy Standing, *The Precariat: The New Dangerous Class* (London: Bloomsbury, 2016). originally 2011

[6] Barry Bluestone and Bennett Harrison, *The Deindustrialization of America* (New York: Basic Books, 1982).

shifts in the global economy and business practices. Not only were plants closed but also communities were abandoned. It is one thing to close plants in an unprofitable business but another to use profits to boost salaries of CEO's or to pay shareholders and refuse to invest profits in redevelopment of these areas. Deindustrialization was a restructuring of the social contract. It was not a force of creative destruction, just destruction.

Equally important was disinvestment by local, state, and federal agencies. These entities also withheld and withdrew funds from cities or segments of cities and decided which areas would get business loans, housing revitalization and community development grants, and private capital investment. Cities were abandoned not just by industries but also by federal government policies which cut most funding to urban renewal programs. Unsurprisingly poor and minority neighborhoods often suffered the most from this kind of disinvestment.[7]

Poverty and Deindustrialization

In addition to the many displacements both cultural and personal, deindustrialization leads to impoverishment. The poverty generated by deindustrialization's transformation to a more service-based economy is different in character from poverty in earlier eras. Increasingly, poverty creates working poor; individuals were employed but did not make sufficient income to avoid poverty. The new jobs that workers found, if they found them, only replaced about two-thirds of their previous wages. According to one study, only 35 percent of laid off full-time workers in the 1990s found jobs with equal or better pay. This was significantly lower than the success of laid off or unemployed workers in previous decades. It was indicative of a downward mobility that resulted in the shrinking of the middle class and growing inequality. This decline continues into the present. A 2019 study by the Brookings institute found that by its criteria 44 percent of the work force can be considered low wage workers, with a national average of just over $10 an hour with a median income a little more than $17,000 a year. Only about 4 of 7 of these workers can work full time year-round, making their situation more contingent. These findings support the common perception that many Americans live close to

[7] John Sankofa, "Disinvestment in Baltimore's Black Neighborhoods Is Foreboding but Reversible" *Urban Wire* September 29, 2020. https://www.urban.org/urban-wire/disinvestment-baltimores-black-neighborhoods-foreboding-reversible

the edge of poverty.[8] In the long term, this creates further problems both economic and social. Much work is now contingent, that is temporary or short lasting. Even when the immediate effects of unemployment fade, the replacement jobs are at lower wages. Even with jobs, the new poor must draw on social services to make ends meet.

In a study of Lake County Indiana, the Gary Indiana area, hit hard by deindustrialization, Brady and Wallace found that Aid to Families with Dependent Children (AFDC) rose after plant closures.[9] Similarly, in Flint, the local United Way reported a 25 percent increase in calls for assistance during the months after GM closed its plant there. This figure was not changed by any rise in service sector jobs. They did not pay enough to make a difference. After closures, the poverty rate rose to 20 percent. In areas like Gary, these effects have not waned but increased. Today it has a poverty rate of over 30 percent. Flint has an incredible 41 percent rate.

While deindustrialization impacted the white working class, it affected a high percentage of the African American population too. Older workers, along with women and African Americans had the greatest impact and were and the least able to make up the loss. The loss of a pension or at least a significant part of it that would have been accumulated meant that a higher number of older workers lost money needed for a comfortable retirement. Wilson notably argued that deindustrialization was a major factor in the rise in the deepening inequality between African Americans and white workingmen.[10]

Wilson's conclusion was challenged by others who claimed that African Americans never had many manufacturing jobs because of existing discrimination, but other research supports Wilson's view. In the last half century, African American men faced a 13.3 percent decline in wages, and a 5.6 percentage point decline in employment rates. About a third of that was attributed to manufacturing decline. When it came to industrial wages there was a 12 percent increase in the racial wage gap for men, a 3.4 percentage point increase in the racial gap in male employment. African

[8] Martha Ross and Nicole Bateman, "Meet the Low Wage Workforce" *Brookings Institute Metropolitical Policy Program* November, 2019. https://www.brookings.edu/wp-content/uploads/2019/11/201911_Brookings-Metro_low-wage-workforce_Ross-Bateman.pdf

[9] David Brady, and Michael Wallace, "Deindustrialization and Poverty: Manufacturing Decline and AFDC Recipiency in Lake County, Indiana 1964–93" *Sociological Forum* 16, 2001: 321–358. https://doi.org/10.1023/A:1011008919557.

[10] William Julius Williams, *The Truly Disadvantaged: The Inner City, the Underclass and Social Policy* (Chicago: University of Chicago Press, 1987).

American men in particular face longer periods of unemployment, and more difficulty in finding re-employment. Other effects include a 9 percent increase in childhood poverty among African American children, and 8 percent in African American women.[11]

Of course, the effects of deindustrialization were exacerbated where de facto segregation was in place. The concentration of populations in certain inner-city areas, without the possibility of mobility led to intensified poverty in these African American areas.

A New Social Contract

The transformations of the American economy required a recasting of the basic social contract between workers and employers.[12] It is not simply an economic but a political economic transformation. The social contract involved a tacit set of social and political norms that specify if only informally, conditions of decent employment. Economies are embedded in political processes both national and global and employers and national governments have obligations to provide fair wages and working conditions. They contain some idea of a decent life of fundamental fairness. Under the conditions of neo-liberal globalism however, national governments often find their autonomy to act limited by transnational corporations.

Large corporations have also been able to change the basic economic terms of wages. Economic theory often argues that increases in productivity should mean increasing wages, but while productivity of US workers increased significantly, their wages have remained stagnant. The average salaries of CEOs in contrast have grown to 278 times the average wage earner (up one thousand percent since 1978).[13] The explanation lies not in strictly economic factors but is due to the power that corporations have to exploit workers.

[11] Eric Gould, "The impact of manufacturing employment decline on black and white Americans" *VoxEU* December 19, 2018. Manufacturing decline has hurt black Americans more | VOX, CEPR Policy Portal (voxeu.org)

[12] Here I use the term social contract not in the philosophical sense as a hypothetical agreement among members of a society to form a government, but to the formal and informal norms that govern the relations between employers and employees.

[13] Jeff Cox, "CEOs see pay grow 1,000% in the last 40 years, now make 278 times the average worker" *CNBC* Aug 16, 2019. https://www.cnbc.com/2019/08/16/ceos-see-pay-grow-1000percent-and-now-make-278-times-the-average-worker.html

The transformation of the social contract has entailed a waning obligation on the part of private enterprise, and the government, to the stability and prosperity of the American middle and working classes. In addition to the stagnant wages, many benefits such as health insurance, pensions, bonuses, education credits, and others have been reduced or eliminated. Service sector jobs rarely have pensions or benefits. In the 1970s and 1980s, economic alternatives were available but not seriously considered. They represent roads not taken in the quest for a humane economy.[14]

Lowered Expectations and Deaths of Despair

Bluestone and Bennett also identified some of the cultural and individual dimensions of the new social contract. Deindustrialization and disinvestment created a growing contradiction not just between workers and owners, but capitalism and community. They traced the increase in factory closing and the effects on social community through the creation of industrial ghost towns. Many cities lost up to 90 percent of their industrial jobs. While the plant closings of the eighties were seeming followed by the recovery of the nineties for many it was a jobless recovery in which economic growth was not followed by a decrease in unemployment. When displaced workers did find jobs, they were often more insecure contract or contingent work or low wage service jobs.

The effects of deindustrialization then went beyond job loss; it often represented a loss of identity for workers and communities. That is, it also affected the ways they understand themselves and their place in relation to the world. Any major change in circumstances is likely to result in changing interpretations, and a different conception of what is possible or likely. These changing expectations take on greater importance in neo-liberalism.

Deindustrialization resulted in lowered expectations and life chances. Several studies of workers in the spirit of Bluestone's work found, like Gaventa, that workers felt a sense of betrayal and helplessness in the face of these job losses. In one study of a closing of a North Carolina factory in the nineties workers felt that big business had lost its moral compass and violated the tacit agreement between workers, management, and

[14] Samuel Bowles, David M. Gordon, and Thomas E. Weisskopf, *Beyond the Waste Land: A Democratic Alternative to Economic Decline* (New York Anchor, 1983).

ownership.[15] They thought that corporate leaders overemphasized the effect of global competition and the market and undervalued the social capital of the workers and the values of community. Corporations neglected the harm done not just to individual workers but the community in which the industry was located, valuing the bottom line at the expense of that human capital. Still, worker's response was contradictory; they did not necessarily rebel-- though they resisted. On the one hand, they had feelings of helplessness in the face of these global forces, on the other, a sense of betrayal by big industry.

The workers at an International Harvester plant were blunter.[16] They pointed to mismanagement and poor decisions on the part of leadership for plant shutdowns. Management had sold off parts of the company that were still profitable and continued to be profitable in the hands of new owners. However, they also located another factor: the hatred of unions. Both the Harvester workers and the North Caroling workers were not wrong in their judgments. More than just a set of economic forces and economic theory, the emerging neo-liberal political economic order was also a type of moral order.

Deindustrialization and disinvestment have effects on the social fabric as well. It disrupts and destabilizes existing patters of social and familial relations and can lead to hopelessness and mental illness and crime. Often increasing poverty associated with deindustrialization was more highly concentrated in inner cities. In the absence of social and economic mitigation, poverty creates long-term hostilities to governments and often to social out-groups like immigrants or minorities on whom blame is displaced. While it was not the only cause, the social problems caused by deindustrialization were a factor in the rise of the populist right.

Deindustrialization has also been linked to lowered life expectancy, and poor health outcomes, especially in the Midwest. These persist even if service jobs take up the employment slack. Average life expectancy, in these regions especially for men has declined. In 2015 Ann Case and Angus Deaton published an article (followed by a book in 2020) detailing

[15] Steve May and Laura Morrison, "Making Sense of Restructuring: Narratives of Accommodation among Downsized Workers" in Jefferson Crowe and Joseph Heathcott eds. *Beyond the Ruins: The Meanings of Deindustrialization* (Ithaca: Cornell University Press, 2003): 259-283.

[16] Joy L Hart and Tracy E. K. Meyer, "Worker Memory and Narrative: Personal Stories of Deindustrialization in Louisville Kentucky" in Crowe and Heathcott *Beyond the Ruins*: 294-304.

the epidemic of deaths of despair among the working classes especially in middle America.[17] These are described as types of mortality resulting from suicide, drug overdose, and alcohol-related liver disease. While they disputed a direct link between deaths of despair and rising rates of inequality, they did propose a strong link between deindustrialization, higher rates of unemployment or underemployment and lack of education. Insecure and unstable jobs led working class men mostly white men to feel more stress and have fewer coping mechanisms. The link between opiate use and overdoses in deindustrialized areas in the South and Midwest has also been noted.[18]

Case and Deaton do not want to reject capitalism; they say they believe in a market system. However, they do think that the current forms of capitalism (its dominant neo-liberal variant) need to be reformed. Others express the need for a more radical change. David Stuckler and Lawrence King identify an existential crisis of capitalism that comes from loss of middle-class status and long-term decline. Whether one chooses the path of reform or of more radical challenges, both feel the center cannot hold.

Deindustrialization Hits Rochester

Rochester was shielded from the first wave of deindustrialization due to the influence of Kodak and to a lesser extent Xerox. In the early eighties, Kodak employment in Rochester peaked at about 62,000 workers. However, through the later eighties into the nineties, facing stiff competition from Fuji and later, from new digital technologies, Kodak employment declined precipitously to the point where today its employs only a few thousand in the Rochester area, less than 5 percent of its number at its peak. Like the criticisms made by the Harvester workers, Kodak had bad management who made poor decisions. As is well known, a Kodak employee made the first digital camera in 1975, but the company declined

[17] Anne Case and Angus Deaton, *Deaths of Despair and the Future of Capitalism* (Princeton: Princeton University Press, 2020).

[18] Atheendar S. Venkataramani, Elizabeth F. Bair, Rourke L. O'Brien, Alexander C. Tsai, "Association Between Automotive Assembly Plant Closures and Opioid Overdose Mortality in the United States: A Difference-in-Differences Analysis" *JAMA Intern Med.* 2020 180(2):254-262. doi:10.1001/jamainternmed.2019.5686

to develop it until it was too late.[19] They also sold off profitable subsidiaries like Kodak Chemicals while keeping unprofitable ones. Along with cuts by Xerox and other employers, Rochester's economic situation was in serious decline. By 1990, Rochester's poverty rate had increased to about 23.5 percent.

However, there is another factor in deindustrialization that must be considered: racism.[20] While racial discrimination does not explain all aspects of deindustrialization, it is a central feature in the continuing decline of many rust belt cities. The worse performing cities were those with high percentages of people of color and such communities also had higher rates of home demolitions and empty lots. According to the report *Industrial Flight and the Decline of Black Communities* prepared for the Alliance of American Manufacturing while all workers suffered from deindustrialization African American workers suffered proportionately worse. They had fewer resources to weather the storm, and often the areas where they lived were more damaged by deindustrialization. Smaller or medium sized cities, especially lost income and property tax revenues needed for vital public services like police and fire protection, clean water, and education. Due to restrictive housing practices and the inability to get mortgages, many are trapped in communities with substandard services.[21]

However, these economic trends were given a more political direction, The Conservative critiques of urban disorder created a narrative of decline which was due to bad governance. Thus, it tried to shift blame for these problems from deindustrialization, to municipalities, usually those with African American mayors or the ascendance of African American leadership.

[19] For a brief journalistic account of this see Nathan McAlone, "This man invented the digital camera in 1975—and his bosses at Kodak never let it see the light of day" *Business Insider* August 17, 2015. https://www.businessinsider.com/this-man-invented-the-digital-camera-in-1975-and-his-bosses-at-/kodak-never-let-it-see-the-light-of-day-2015-8

[20] Jason Hackworth, *Manufacturing Decline: How Racism and the Conservative Movement Crush the American Rust Belt* (New York Columbia University Press, 2019). Keeanga-Yamahtta Taylor, *Race for Profit: How Banks and the Real Estate Industry Undermined Black Homeownership* (Chapel Hill University of North Carolina Press, 2019).

[21] Gerald D. Taylor, "Unmade in America: Industrial Flight and the Decline of Black Communities" *Alliance of American Manufacturers* October, 2016. By https://s3-us-west-2.amazonaws.com/aamweb/uploads/research-pdf/UnmadeInAmerica.pdf

Urban Policy and Decline in the Postwar Era

While the beginnings of the suburban trek away from the cities began in the 1920s with rise of the mass-produced automobile, the role of the suburb was at first limited. Suburbs were at best a quarter of metro populations. It was only in the 1950s that suburban population began to overtake central cities in total population. Cities had continued to grow albeit at a slower rate, during this period. For example, both Buffalo and Rochester reached their highest population around 1950 and have, like other Northeastern and Midwestern cities, declined in population ever since. Population growth shifted to the suburbs and to cities in the west and southwest. By the 1970s, many central cities in the northeast and Midwest represented a third or less of the greater metro area population.

On David Harvey's reading the postwar expansion of the suburbs represented a "spatial fix," to the economic problems of capitalism in the wake of the great depression. Harvey uses a neo-Marxist analysis that is an analogue to Marx's notion of a technological fix in which increasing technology by replacing living workers with dead labor provides an ever-new stimulus for production. The suburban fix was based in the creation of a growth machine, a coalition of developers, automotive and oil interests, and consumer goods, along with Federal government policy to drive economic growth and expansion.[22] Cheap loans especially for veterans, guaranteed by the Federal Housing Agencies, along with government funded infrastructure and highway construction, supported, and reinforced the suburban trends.

This model of development can be seen as Keynesian. It sought to stimulate demand and consumption as the engine for economic growth. In large measure, it was successful and even mildly redistributive. In combination with high taxation and US economic dominance, the middle class grew at an unprecedented rate and income and wealth inequality declined. However, as with most forms of capitalist economic growth, it proved uneven and as much as it can be called a spatial fix, in the US at least it was largely a "racial fix." It drew on cultural dimensions that cannot be completely explained in Harvey's otherwise insightful analyses.

[22] Harvey Molotch and John Logan, *Urban Fortunes: The Political Economy of Place* (Berkeley: University of California Press, 1987); Molotch, "The City as a Growth Machine: Toward a Political Economy of Place" *American Journal of Sociology* 82: 2 1976: 309 322

While the 1950s still were prosperous times for cities, shifting populations meant a declining share of revenue and decreasing attention to poorer parts of the cities. Slums were symptoms of decay and decline in some city areas, but the central business areas needed work too. Cities needed the help of governments to assist in fixing its problems attract business and retain residents who were fleeing to the suburbs. Federal Urban Renewal programs were developed with the aim of stemming the tide of decline before it got serious. These often had however, unintended consequences. While no doubt well intentioned, they were poorly thought out. To the extent that they did not consider the spatial fix of suburbanization, they did not address the larger causes of urban decline. To the extent that such policies often supported infrastructure improvements like the construction of new highways, they contributed more to the problem than the solution. Urban renewal programs demolished slums and substandard housing and allowed cities to reconfigure these areas. They often replaced slums with housing projects displacing residents and severing existing community ties. Moreover, programs that began as attempts to replace substandard housing often morphed in programs aimed at stemming the loss of middle-class populations and keeping business and commercial operations in downtown areas. These too were not successful. The increasing number of interstate highways also meant that other neighborhoods were destroyed, most often on poorer parts of cities. Combined with the demolition of slum areas, the interstate highway system disproportionately displaced African Americans and caused anger and resentment. The rise of the highway system and population shifts to less densely populated suburbs meant that outside a few of the largest cities mass transit also declined.

White Flight and Poverty

One of the defining features of urban life in America is the phenomenon of white flight, the migration of white populations from urban areas to suburban ones. More recently, this has extended to the movement from suburbs to exurban and rural areas, and even the flight to the southwest and west. As a result, urban populations have in some cities shrunk and become more predominantly minority. It would be an exaggeration to say that the only motive driving suburbanization was racism; many sought a better life for their families and new ways of living.[23] They were no doubt motivated by images of a consumer society and generous financial terms held the promise of home ownership for all (white people at least). Certainly however, political financial and corporate leaders knew what they were doing. African Americans did not benefit from this financing and were unable to get loams for houses to move to the suburbs and exclusionary covenants and policies were enacted. In this respect, we can say that the postwar spatial fix was truly a racial fix. The suburban dream was primarily a white one, and African Americans and other minorities have been excluded from it, through covenants, Redlining, and other measures.

The early migrations of African American to the northern cities though small were met with significant resistance. The second wave of migration from the south to the cities (and to some southern urban centers like Atlanta) was much larger, around six million, and while not met with physical resistance was met with white flight. For every African American who moved into cities more than two white people moved out. However, white flight had another unintended consequence. Previously limited to ghetto areas, African Americans lived in geographically limited areas which had developed their own services. When more African Americans left these areas for other parts of the city, these communities were weakened but other new community bonds failed to form.

While flight was not a southern phenomenon, busing and other attempts at integration in the north led to flight. Many cities in the Northeast and Midwest saw declines in population as whites with resources moved to the suburbs, Detroit's population declined from 1.8 million to about 950,000 Cleveland from a post war high of over 900,000 to about 380,000 Upstate New York cities like Buffalo and Rochester have also suffered significant declines. When these groups left the cities, they took considerable resources with them.

White Flight was another element in the fiscal crises of cities. Their fiscal situation became more tenuous as the tax base shrunk. Those who were left were burdened with fiscal and resource deficits. Not only did they take taxable and spendable income from the city, but they also took services. Banking, grocery stores, other shopping, and personal services

[23] See for example Herbert Gans, *Levitowners: Ways of Life and Politics in a New Suburban Community* (New York: Columbia University Press. 1967)

followed to the more lucrative terrain of the suburbs. The support for schools and business centers disappeared.

Without the resources and infrastructure to flourish, these neglected urban areas suffered a variety of problems which reinforced their depleted condition. The poor were often located in areas where pollution and environmental degradation was prevalent leading to respiratory and other health problems. Lack of access to healthier food, and exorbitant prices at the few stores that remain meant that nutrition suffered, and along with the stresses of subaltern status has led to increased prevalence of diabetes circulatory problems and heart diseases. As a result, the average life span of an inner-city urban dweller in a poor area can be 5-15 years less than the general population.[24]

White populations came to perceive urban areas as centers of crime, drug abuse, deviance, and social disorganization. These areas were also associated with lower property values and family problems. The flight of the white affluent groups to the suburbs increased social stratification and racial segregation.

The Great Society

Michael Harrington's book *The Other America*, published in 1962 brought the problem of poverty (urban and rural) in America to popular awareness. Harrington's work stood in stark contrast to the widely held view of America as an Affluent Society where problems of poverty had been conquered. He argued that the US was not a truly middle-class society.[25] Up to a third of all American's lived at or below what he considered to be a decent level: $3000 a year (in 1962). The book had a major impact on political climate and spurred President Kennedy, and after his death, President Lyndon Johnson to action. Johnson declared a War on Poverty

[24] Michael Maciag, "Life Expectancy Varies Greatly Within Cities" *Governing* February 03, 2016. https://www.governing.com/archive/gov-life-expectancy-neighborhood.html; Lindsey Cook, "Why Black Americans Die Younger" *US News and World Report*, Jan. 5, 2015. https://www.usnews.com/news/blogs/data-mine/2015/01/05/black-americans-have-fewer-years-to-live-heres-why

[25] Michael Harrington, *The Other America: Poverty in America* with a new introduction (New York: Scribner, 1997). Maurice Isserman, *The Other American: The Life of Michael Harrington* (New York: Public Affairs, 2001). Maurice Isserman, "50 Years Later: Poverty and The Other America" *Dissent* Winter 2012. https://www.dissentmagazine.org/article/50-years-later-poverty-and-the-other-america.

as part of his Great Society Program. Among the initiatives in this program were Community Action Programs and model cities programs. In addition to poverty in areas like Appalachia, both programs responded to the civil rights movement, urban poverty, and growing unrest in cities.

Community Action programs were created by the 1964 Economic Opportunity Act. They represented a novel approach aimed not just to fight poverty but empower communities. On its own terms it was meant to provide “services, assistance, and other activities of sufficient scope and size to give promise of progress toward elimination of poverty or a cause or causes of poverty through developing employment opportunities, improving human performance, motivation, and productivity, or bettering the conditions under which people live, learn, and work.” Community Action Agencies were governmental and nonprofit agencies which at first were made up of members of the community served.

Community Action Programs were significant because unlike previous ideas, which often stressed the role of social science experts in designing and implementing social reform, the impetus was given to the members of the community to create social change. In line with the social reform movements of the time, Community Action agencies sought to incorporate elements of participatory democracy into its principles. It sought “maximum feasible participation” of local citizens. They were to be involved in determining the way that federal monies were to be used to combat poverty.

Some Johnson administration officials clearly meant Community Action Agency (CAAs) to be disruptive. Community participation was more than just a theoretical desideratum. They wanted to bypass traditional power structures found in state and local governments which gave jobs and funding to white and sometimes ethnically based groups. Some cities were run by Republicans who did not owe their success to Black voters and other Democratically run cities were controlled by ethnic machine politics. The only way, that the power structures of urban areas could be changed, they reasoned, was through a direct relationship with the federal government. Community action programs did in fact lead to contestation as empowered CAA leaders confronted local politicians. However, these policies generated a great deal of resentment from existing urban political leaders and opposition from elites and they did not get the backing they needed.[26]

[26] Frances Fox Piven and Richard Cloward, *Regulating the Poor: The Functions of Public Welfare* 2nd edition (New York: Vintage, 1993).

Not only did such programs find resistance from entrenched political leaders who had interests in maintaining the status quo, but not all members of the federal bureaucracy accepted them. There were those who still maintained the position that experts were needed to design programs and that these should be carried out in a neutral manner.

The model cities program was established in 1966, as an alternative to existing urban renewal programs. It sought a more comprehensive approach through coordinating services, emphasizing new projects along with rehabilitation and social services including neighborhood facilities. These programs also included citizen involvement initiatives.

Additional anti-poverty initiatives included programs like Medicare and Medicaid, expanded early educational programs like head start and school lunch programs, and expanded training programs. Anti-poverty programs helped establish community health centers, expanded social security, and created programs like Home Energy Assistance Program (HEAP). Other achievements included GINNY MAE the Government National Mortgage Association (GNMA) which promoted affordable housing through guaranteed mortgages and lower interest rates.

While there was a good deal of criticism of the programs—Community Action Program (CAP) was criticized for mismanagement and corruption—taken as a whole, Great Society programs did in fact lead to a significant reduction in poverty. The rate of poverty declined at least 8 percent to just around 11 percent, the lowest it would be in several decades. Though there were failures, a good deal of the problems with these poverty programs stemmed from their overly narrow political support and changes in the federal landscape that terminated these programs.

There was a major tension on the war on poverty. While some moved in the direction of true community involvement, the second group retained an approach more in common with the approach of Keynesians. They sought a more race neutral vision of poverty mitigation based on the Keynesian policies of economic growth full employment and increasing human capital. They did not want to attract the more politically risky problems of ending discrimination. They saw the problem as one of creating greater opportunity, not necessarily social equality. Everyone should have an equal opportunity to compete.[27] Attacking cultural barriers was

[27] Michael Katz, *In the Shadow of the Poorhouse: A Social History of Welfare in America*, Tenth Anniversary Edition (New York: Basic Books, 1996).

not necessarily antithetical to this project. They freed the individual to compete more fully.

Harrington, who had been brought in as a consultant, wanted a strong job creation program, but the focus became a term he adapted from Oscar Lewis, the culture of poverty. Harrington (and most likely Lewis) did not intend it to mean that the poor were poor because of cultural norms. Harrington linked the culture of poverty approach to unequal economic power and sought radical reform, but the conservative reading became the dominant interpretation. The culture of poverty view also was reflected in the Moynihan Report prepared by then Assistant Secretary of Labor, Daniel Patrick Moynihan which also influenced Johnson's War on Poverty. His view at first was not unequivocally conservative. He endorsed some social democratic programs including later an early version of a guaranteed income, yet he also argued that the reason that African Americans had not progressed like other ethnic groups was due to a culture in which males were often absent and matriarchy was the rule.

Moynihan's work illustrated the tension between participatory initiatives and expert cultures. Though his first report initiated the war on poverty, he was like other members of the administration severely critical of citizen participation.[28] The idea of cultural deprivation lent itself to the idea that expert guided intervention was needed because of the deficits in the culture of the poor.

In addition to tension in the nature of the war on poverty, the second problem was a lack of funding. By 1965, the rising costs of the Vietnam war meant that funds for a war on poverty were no longer abundant. Johnson decided to do it on the cheap. Programs failed because of lack of support. Implementation of community development and model cities programs required much greater funding then was available.

The third problem involved local politics. The participatory democratic reforms proposed by anti-poverty programs were more explosive and radical then the other proposals. Local activists funded by the federal government posed direct challenges to politicians. They met opposition by local politicians and power elites who did not accept the citizen participation.

[28] Daniel Patrick Moynihan, *Maximum Feasible Misunderstanding: Community Action in the War on Poverty* (New York: Free Press, 1970), On Moynihan, see Daniel Geary, *Beyond Civil Rights: The Moynihan Report and its Legacy* (Philadelphia: University of Pennsylvania Press, 2013).

The tensions within the Great Society poverty programs then lead to their demise. Marris and Rein in an early study of community action programs argue that federal officials were unable to deal with the internal conflicts their policies generated.[29] While some expected conflict as I noted above, others thought that they could generate a consensus that never materialized. By 1967, amendments were passed to the original act which limited or eliminated citizen participation and shifted power away from the poor. CAA boards had to be approved by state and local officials. Nonetheless, many activists who got a start in the community programs moved into positions of power in later years and tried to carry on reforms.

Neo-liberal Urbanism

Urban policy at the national level was fundamentally transformed in the neo-liberal era. Its beginning could be traced to Nixon, who declared the "Urban Crisis is over and done with" though he still retained many aspects of Keynesian thought. These changes truly began with Carter who despite some rhetorical support failed to help urban areas with problems of housing, poverty, or fiscal crises. Carter had already moved away from Keynesian solutions and embraced the new economic thinking. However, the Reagan administration brought about more fundamental changes in government policy toward cities: it reduced federal involvement in urban affairs and transferred most responsibility to the states (federalism) as well as transferring many urban welfare services to private providers. The creation of unfunded mandates and declining Housing and Urban Development (Department of) (HUD) initiatives continued through the Reagan era. Federal grants to cities declined by close to 40 percent during the Reagan years. There were further deep cuts under Bush. These policies entailed a change in the focus of service. Where Keynesian urban policy focused on places that is, states and municipalities, Reagan's neo-liberal policies shifted the focus to individuals. Thus, urban policy did not address the changes that occurred as traditional manufacturing jobs in the north and instead promoted white flight to the suburbs and to the sunbelt. Between 1975 and 1985 minority population of northeastern cities increased from 33 percent

[29] Peter Marris and Martin Rein, *Dilemmas of Social Reform: Poverty and Community Action in the United States* 2nd Edition (New York: Routledge, 2017).

to 42 percent.[30] This novel approach to urban policy also generated new social policies aimed at addressing poverty.

The emerging neo-liberal discourse on poverty rehabilitated a version of the underclass thesis in the 1980s. The underclass was not a new notion, going back at least to the 19th century. In the earlier version, however, the underclass was understood structurally by its place in the socio-economic order. For Marx, it was the group that was structurally below the working class, comprised of those often not fully engaged in the labor system of capitalism. It consists of the poor and unemployed or partially employed and often concentrated in urban settings. In the Reagan era however, this group was no longer a structural economic or institutional one but a behavioral and cultural one. The underclass was now characterized by its deficient individual behavior; its members lacked a moral compass and impulse control. These characteristics led to crime, single mothers on welfare, out of wedlock babies, violence, and devkant anti-social behavior by the poor.

The new underclass theory was as much a product of popular journalism as academic study and employed well-worn stereotypes in a new context. Mickey Kaus for example argued that the underclass was a "Black lower class" for whom "the work ethic has evaporated, and the entrepreneurial drive is channeled into gangs and drug-pushing." The underclass represented a culture of poverty that was invoked alongside a single motherhood, single parent welfare culture. Similarly, Ken Auletta saw the underclass as combining poverty and deviance. However, the underclass, in his view, was not exclusively poor. "The underclass usually operates outside the generally accepted boundaries of society. They are often set apart by their 'deviant' or antisocial behavior, by their bad habits, not just their poverty."[31] The underclass is the basis of a self-defeating culture that needs correction by bourgeois values.

[30] David Stoesz, "The Fall of the Industrial City: The Reagan Legacy for Urban Policy," *The Journal of Sociology & Social Welfare:* Vol. 19: 1, 1992. https://scholarworks.wmich.edu/jssw/vol19/iss1/9

[31] Cited in Adolph Reed, "The Underclass as Myth and Symbol: The Poverty of Discourse on Poverty" in Adolph Reed Jr,, *Stirrings in the Jug: Black Politics in the Post-Segregation Era* (Minneapolis: University of Minnesota Press, 1999): 179-96. For examples, see Nicholas Lemann, "The Origins of the Underclass", *The Atlantic* June, 1986. https://www.theatlantic.com/past/docs/politics/poverty/origin2.htm. Ken Auletta, The *Underclass*, (New York: Random House, 1982). Also see Herbert Gans, *The War Against the Poor: The Underclass and Antipoverty Policy* (New York: Basic Books, 1995).

In the academic work of Lawrence Mead, which was used to justify Clinton era welfare reform, the underclass is poor because it has behavioral deficits: "the urban underclass is made up of street hustlers, welfare families, drug addicts, and former mental patients."[32] While not statistically large, the underclass was implicated in a tangle of pathologies. It was a source of a significant percentage of the major social problems of American culture. Mead opposed William Julius Willson who saw the source of the underclass as a combination of social isolation, deindustrialization, off-shore outsourcing, and white flight.[33] Willsons' view is more in line with the earlier usage of "underclass" which locates it in socio-economic circumstances. In contrast, Mead saw the new underclass as a creation of a permissive welfare state which encouraged anti-social behavior. This permissive state and its welfare dependency are the immediate cause of all manner of social pathology such as illegitimate births, joblessness, and crime.

Due to the character deficiencies of the underclass, Mead argued that a coercive policy is justified to correct them. The poor must be compelled to work to change their behavior. This is the root of the idea of workfare; individuals can only receive social benefits when they work. This change from permissive to authoritative welfare entails the use of command power to induce behavioral change. Mead did not go as far as Charles Murray who wanted to abolish welfare altogether. He felt that willingness to work should qualify individuals and families for assistance.

The Clinton administration found these ideas, many of which came from centrist DLC affiliated thinkers, congenial to the political strategy of triangulation. Along with Tony Blair's Labor party in England, he was influenced by the Third Way outlook, which attempted to combine some commitment to social welfare with free market politics. He thought (as a "progressive" neo-liberal) he could address the problems of neo-liberalism by combining neo-liberal economic growth with a fundamental fairness, reconcile labor and capital, and rights and responsibilities.

Clinton believed the changes in the global economy ruled out a return to redistributive policies. The era of big government was over and electoral success relied on rejecting the democratic liberalism of the past. He

[32] Lawrence Mead, *Beyond Entitlement: The Social Obligations of Citizenship* (New York: The Free Press, 1986).

[33] William Julius Wilson, *The Truly Disadvantaged: The Inner City, the Underclass, and Public Policy* 2nd edition (Chicago: University of Chicago Press, 2012) originally 1987.

appealed to the middle class and those above them by guaranteeing that he would not reverse tax cuts and accept globalization, keeping labor demands on hold and keeping inflation low. He appealed to the working class by claiming that through investing in people he could help them compete and would use the increased revenue from economic growth to provide better public service. Here, Clinton also employed a communitarian rhetoric which emphasized repairing the social fabric. Clinton had no plans to challenge neo-liberalism. Clinton's approach to the economic problems of neo-liberalism then followed the supply side model, investing in education and skills, but not on the demand side as had the Keynesian model.

Third way approaches to poverty however, reflected the contradictions of this approach. In practice, Clinton followed a conservative view of the causes of poverty. He held that poverty was due to individual inclination, not structural problems with the new economy. The unwilling must be forced into participating in the economy. This meant in practice that welfare recipients were forced into a low wage economy if they were to survive at all. Promised spending on public works did not come about due to the neo-liberal emphasis on limiting spending and reduced revenue sharing. Any conflicts between the market and social welfare were resolved in favor of the market.

One of the most notable neo-liberal ideas for revitalizing urban areas was implemented in Thatcher's England. and championed in the US by Jack Kemp, was the creation of enterprise zones. In these zones, usually located in depressed areas, private companies could operate with limited taxation and regulation, and receive infrastructure improvements, in order to revitalize run-down urban neighborhoods otherwise not attracting new investment. This also a supply side approach, it sought to increase investment without necessarily stimulating demand. In the US unlike Britain, these programs were implemented at the state level. These were however not as generally as successful as advocates hoped. Like most supply side programs, they often benefitted the better off and not the poor they were meant to help.

The Clinton administration added onto the enterprise zones the notion of empowerment zones. They were meant to add a community development element consistent with communitarian ideas which promoted self-sufficiency and independence. In that respect, it stressed community involvement and participation. It was however still primarily an economic approach, based on incentives for investment. In all these policy initiatives,

Clinton practiced neo-liberalism by default. The force of the deregulation of and privatization of public services in a wide variety of area, including not just welfare but banking and communications overwhelmed any purported community forces. It negated any attempts to reconcile his economic program with a concern for the social fabric including the poor.

Timothy Weaver notes, “most important the overall economic and labor market framework of the Clinton administration which was more fundamentally aligned with neo-liberalism—deficit reduction, welfare reform and free trade- meant the urban poor and the working classes, most of whom were not touched by empowerment zones spending, were worse off at the end of the 1990s then at the beginning.”[34]

Cities as Entrepreneurs

After Richard Nixon proclaimed the end of urban renewal in 1969, funding to the cities for reform projects was significantly cut. As the fiscal crises of the states and cities increased, the change in political economic philosophy brought about by the end of Keynesianism and the rise of neo-liberalism, federal commitment to social programs waned. By the time, the Reagan era many of the programs created in previous administrations were dismantled. Responsibility devolved primarily to the cities themselves.

There were some who argued this had a positive aspect. Past urban programs tied the recipients of federal funds to specific federal programs. With the devolution of power to the cities, it was argued cities had the power to create programs designed to meet their specific circumstances. This interpretation was incorrect. The assumption that cities could act autonomously under neo-liberal conditions was superficial. Lacking federal and state support, they were subject to capture and control by other more powerful economic forces. Domestically, large corporate and commercial and real estate interests dominated urban interests, globally, a new political economy developed in which transnational corporations and financial interests had the extensive power to shape policies and steer agendas. Cities were constrained, they became dependent on private financial interests and international capital which set the rules of the game for financially troubled cities.

[34] Timothy Weaver, *Blazing the Neoliberal Trail: Urban Political Development in the United States and the United Kingdom* (University of Pennsylvania Press 2016).

Deindustrialization was an early indication of a sea change in the US economy. Its rise presaged the end of the Keynesian era, and the establishment of a new set of dominant economic assumptions. These took a specific form for urban areas. In the terms of David Harvey, it entailed a transition from managerialism to entrepreneurialism.[35]

Cities responded to these new conditions by becoming directly involved in economic projects that hoped to create jobs or bring revenue to cities. Lacking investment by the government or by manufacturing interests, cities were themselves acting as entrepreneurs to generate economic growth. Cities used their powers to attract external sources of funding, direct investment, or sources of employment. These projects often used mechanisms of private public partnerships. In order to attract these partnerships, cities took on most of the risk, immunizing those private interests from at least some of the losses. They socialized the risks of development projects while privatizing the profits. Most of these partnerships, Harvey argues, were speculative; they did not have a rational plan or a guarantee of success. Thus, many of them were risky. [36]

Cities responded to the loss of industrial jobs with several strategies which were not mutually exclusive but could be developed in tandem. They are linked by their shared aim of expanding the value of service sector revenues and not on improvement of their shrinking industrial base. Two of the main strategies did not seek to rehabilitate the industrial sector, but to bypass it.

The first strategy sought to turn cities into entertainment destinations. Baltimore's Inner Harbor redevelopment called "festival marketplace" is often held out as the model of successful redevelopment and revitalization using this strategy. Baltimore's inner harbor was able to attract more visitors than Disney World upon its opening in 1980.[37] The tourism strategy relied on large infusions of government money for redevelopment as well as use of eminent domain. The revitalization however, of a specific place within a metropolitan area does not necessarily mean the whole area benefits from redevelopment. This was true in the case of Baltimore. The success of the Inner Harbor revitalization did not lead to a general rise in

[35] David Harvey, "From Managerialism to Entrepreneurialism: The Transformation in Urban Governance in Late Capitalism" *Geografiska Annaler: Series B, Human Geography* Volume 71, 1989: 7ff.

[36] Harvey, "From Managerialism to Entrepreneurialism" 7ff.

[37] Allan Wallach, *The Divided City: Poverty and Prosperity in Urban America* (Washington: Island Press, 2018).

the prosperity of Baltimoreans. While some have prospered in Baltimore which has some affluent neighborhoods, and strong downtown employment, inequality has increased and crime and racial conflict over police violence has continued to rise. In 2013, the wealth gap in Baltimore was among the country's largest. "The typical Baltimore resident in the bottom fifth of earners made $13,588 in 2013, whereas those in top 5 percent made an average of $166,924 that year."[38] In 2013, the national average for the ratio of 95th percentile income to 20th percentile income was 9.1. Baltimore's 95/20 ratio was 12.3.

However, even seen on its own terms, these attempts were by no means universally fruitful in creating successful tourist areas. Many cities notably Toledo's Portside were less successful in creating festival marketplaces, but invested large sums of public money, tax abatements and other inducements on sports complexes. A related strategy included cities that have tried to leverage their cultural resources to bring tourism. To an extent these incentives combined with an era of cheap money did create a template of sorts in cities with new construction, but it proved illusory.[39] Museums, architecture, and culturally district entertainment traditions, have not proved to be as successful in attracting visitors as they had in the past.

Another way of developing entertainment venue, municipally funded stadiums for major league sports, has proved controversial and of dubious economic value. While it may provide a certain amount of civic pride, the downside is the loss of revenues for infrastructure and schools because of tax abatements. A good example is the City of Oakland which has one of the worst school districts in the nation and decaying transportation infrastructure. The city was asked to provide tax breaks and municipal funding for the Oakland Athletics to build a new stadium. However, once construction was completed (which was funded by tax breaks and often non-union labor) the temporary employment gains from construction were lost. Fewer people were employed by the stadium than a large department store. Often proponents inflate the economic benefits of stadiums and in the case of Oakland, the main benefit was from office space built near the

[38] Economic Inequality in Baltimore, MD https://wp.nyu.edu/economicinequality/2017/03/29/economic-inequality-in-baltimore-md/, The quote is from Rios, Edwin D. "7 Charts Explaining Baltimore's Economic and Racial Struggles." *Mother Jones.* Alan Berube, and Brad McDearman, "Good Fortune, Dire Poverty, and Inequality in Baltimore: An American Story" *Brookings Institution.* August 2. 2016.

[39] Wallach, *The Divided City.*

stadium.[40] Franchise owners in contrast have found the value of their franchises grow exponentially. Ironically, these complexes, funded by taxpayer money, have raised the prices of many major league sports beyond the reach of most ordinary citizens; instead they rely on attracting the well-heeled and corporate interests to exclusive box seating. As the amenities required for appealing to these high-end customers increase, the price tags for new stadiums has skyrocketed. Just recently, the owners of the Buffalo Bills proposed a $1.4 billon new stadium in economically depressed Western New York. This was almost double the cost of the previous high of 750 million for the stadium for the now Las Vegas Raiders. It would be the largest stadium subsidy in US History.[41]

The entertainment and culture strategy employed a different economic model than those employed during the Keynesian era. The latter depends on generating income through wages that in turn leads to consumption of goods produced by manufacturing. The entertainment-based model seeks to attract those who already have disposable income to spend, bypassing the production of goods altogether. It is parasitic and dependent upon pre-existing wealth. While this entertainment model does produce some jobs, these are lower paying service sector jobs often with limited benefits. They do not do much to decrease inequality and often increase it. Projects have a declining return for investment. There is a limit to the disposable income of families in an era of declining incomes.

A second strategy has been colloquially called the eds and meds approach.[42] It emphasizes the role that educational and medical facilities have come to serve as engines of economic development in postindustrial cities. This approach is also a response to the increasing necessity of post-secondary education to enter the job market. The number of Americans

[40] Rick Paulas, "Sports Stadiums Are a Bad Deal for Cities: But cities can fight back" *The Atlantic* November 21, 2018. https://www.theatlantic.com/technology/archive/2018/11/sports-stadiums-can-be-bad-cities/576334/ Gregg Easterbrook, "How Taxpayers Keep the NFL Rich" *The Atlantic* December 8, 2015 https://www.theatlantic.com/entertainment/archive/2015/12/how-taxpayers-keep-the-nfl-rich/418971/; Michael A. Leeds, Peter von Allmen, Victor A. Matheson, *The Economics of Sports* 6th Edition (New York: Routledge, 2018): chapters 6 and 7.

[41] "Buffalo Bills propose new $1.4 billion NFL stadium by 2027" *CNBC*, August 31, 2021. https://www.cnbc.com/2021/08/31/buffalo-bills-propose-new-1point4-billion-nfl-stadium-by-2027.html; Mark Scheer, "A record subsidy for Bills stadium?" *Investigative Post* November 16, 2021. https://www.investigativepost.org/2021/11/16/a-record-subsidy-for-bills-stadium/

[42] Wallach, *The Divided City:* 60-73.

attending colleges rose from about 9 percent in the mid-sixties to 32 percent in recent decades. Public University spending increased fourfold since the sixties. The modern research university has become what Clark Kerr predicted: a multiversity. It is a vast research complex of multibillion dollar institutions which not only educate students but also serve corporations, government, and policy institutes, as well as create business spinoffs. These institutions, which are public or receive substantial amounts of public money, serve as taxpayer funded research and development services for corporate interests. This corporate connection distinguishes it from earlier federally subsidized research and development. Many corporations which had their own research facilities have outsourced their research to universities or have funded research in applied sciences and medicine at universities in exchange for sometimes exclusive control of products developed. The modern university seems more like a large corporation, than a public service institution.[43]

Medical centers have pursued a similar model and have become global health service enterprises. In most cases, large hospitals have ties to research universities. Because of the size and scope of these enterprises, the ed med complex has become a leading if the not the leading employer in many cities, supplanting industry.

It might seem that the ed med complex would generate many high paying jobs, but this is not always the case. Hospitals, universities, and medical research facilities employ an extensive support staff that are not high paid or even highly educated. Even university instruction has not been immune to this process and has also been among the causalities. While some researchers who bring large grants to universities are highly compensated, and a few academostars in the humanities who can attract students and graduate students are well paid, most of the instruction in colleges and universities is done by lower paid adjunct instructors who, depending on their situation, do not receive benefits. Tenured professors are now in the minority. According to a 2020 report by the American Federation of Teachers, one-quarter of adjuncts are on food stamps and up to 40 percent have difficulty making ends meet. One third of the three thousand

[43] On the marketization and conversion of the university, Sheila Slaughter and Gary Rhoades, *Academic Capitalism and the New Economy: Markets, State, and Higher Education* (Baltimore: Johns Hopkins University Press, 2009); James E Côté, and Anton L. Allahar, *Lowering Higher Education: The Rise of Corporate Universities and the Fall of Liberal Education*. (Toronto: University of Toronto Press, 2011); Gaye Tuchman, *Wannabe U: Inside the Corporate University* (Chicago: University of Chicago Press, 2009).

adjunct surveyed made less than $25,000 a year, putting them close to or below the poverty level depending on the size of their families. In the process, the role of instruction has been significantly downgraded.[44] While instruction is becoming de-professionalized, administration staff and their salaries have increased, purportedly to manage the many new business-related functions, resulting in what is sometimes called administrative bloat. Similarly, many hospital workers are low paid. Hospital Janitors average only about $31,000 a year and orderlies make a similar amount. Food staff and phlebotomists around $35,000[45] Nursing home workers earned a mean salary of about $38,000.

A third strategy has been the attempt to attract employers using Industrial Development agencies. Here local authorities use a variety of incentives, such as tax breaks and reduction of sales taxes along with use of publicly owned land and other incentives to induce industries to relocate to an area. Sometimes this is a zero-sum game: A gain for one area means a loss for another; when no new industries or jobs are created but simply transferred, there is no total economic gain. Other times, businesses leave when tax breaks are exhausted and go to some other locality that provides tax breaks again. Here residents bear the burden of reduced revenue from school and property taxes, resulting in underperforming schools, declining infrastructure with little economic gain. Cities like Detroit, Flint Michigan, Akron, Youngstown, Buffalo, and Rochester have not been successful in adapting to the global economy or in attracting new industries. They have often undergone severe fiscal difficulties and in some cases have been subject to oversight by state commissions.

In some cases, cities have succeeded in finding new employment through industries or services that are less dependent on traditional manufacturing. New York City, which always had a financial sector, has become

[44] Colleen Flaherty, "Barely Getting By New report on adjuncts says many make less than $3,500 per course and live in poverty" *Inside Higher Ed* April 20, 2020. https://www.insidehighered.com/news/2020/04/20/new-report-says-many-adjuncts-make-less-3500-course-and-25000-year For the full report see *An Army of Temps: AFT 2020 Adjunct Faculty Quality of Work/Life Report.* https://www.aft.org/sites/default/files/adjuncts_quality-worklife2020.pdf

[45] Ivan De Luce, Emma Curt, and Madison Hoff, "Here's how much 30 types of hospital workers are paid" *Business Insider* May 10, 2021. https://www.businessinsider.com/how-much-everyone-makes-in-a-hospital-2019-5?amp; "The Average Salary of Nursing Home Office Staff Work" *Chron* August 13, 2020, https://work.chron.com/average-salary-nursing-home-office-staff-1651.html

a global financial leader. Other areas like Pittsburg and San Francisco have also succeeded in creating a financial service sector. A second area of job growth has been high-tech jobs, especially again in Northern California, in the North Carolina research triangle and in the hub around the Boston area—though even these areas have been impacted by outsourcing. While these areas have seemed successes, the high-tech strategy has not always reduced inequality. Even in these seemingly more successful areas, the poverty rate can be over 20 percent. Not all the jobs created in these cities have been good paying nor has greater economic prosperity led to a reduction in inequality.

While in the face of deindustrialization some cities have staged comebacks, more often, the result has been more segmented cities. A fourth mode of entrepreneurialism is through Gentrification: the resettlement of blighted and disinvested areas, by more affluent owners. By raising property values, and supporting business and services, gentrification promises to bring much needed revenues to cities. However, the nature of Gentrification has changed over time and has come to be dominated by corporate development rather than individual owners.

The first wave of gentrification, which extended to the early eighties, was primarily driven by individuals who bought homes in run-down and disinvested areas and rehabilitated them for individual use. To be sure, corporate development interests did enter the market, but only when individuals had already entered these areas. These new residents sought the advantages of city living such as arts and culture and proximity to work, but they displaced less affluent residents and renters, and demanded more costly services and amenities.

Ironically, the economic recession of the 1990s ushered in the second wave of gentrification. Real estate prices dropped significantly, and many overextended speculators and developers faced bankruptcy. Most inner-city developers survived however, through mergers and reorganizations which resulted in larger firms with more capital and resources. These larger firms were well positioned to take advantage of the changes in the conditions of inner-city development.

By the 1990s, many of the easily gentrified areas in major cities had been settled, and prices had risen to the extent that single investors could not afford down payments or mortgages. Only larger commercial and corporate groups had the resources to develop these areas. While governments had sometimes supported gentrification in Keynesian times, their efforts had been constrained by redistributive projects. As larger development projects took hold, cities became more assertive in supporting development projects. Opposition to such projects had been effectively neutralized and with the waning commitment to public housing during Reagan, when vouchers replaced public housing projects, there was little to stop developers. Even the Clinton administration's HOPE IV programs rolled back its commitment to replacing housing that had been demolished. Developers became involved at earlier stages of projects and with expansion of gentrification, more projects.

Gentrification has divided cities into area which are more affluent and those with greater poverty. Today's urban centers are no longer home to a middle-class population but consist of the poor along with some new immigrants and significant numbers of millennials who desire the cultural and entertainment amenities of the big city and shun suburban life. It is no longer a place to raise children and buy a family home. The share of middle-class income families in cities dropped from about 40 percent in 1970 to about 25 percent in 2014. Where two-thirds of all households were married families and 90 percent were two parents, today this is the exception not the rule. Only 19 percent of households are married, many families are single parents and others are unmarried parents.

Gentrification also drew on another entrepreneurial strategy rooted in real estate investment. It became part of a new spatial fix which involved attempting to bring back to life inner cities and outer ring suburbs or exurbs at the expense of the original inner ring suburbs which in many cases are in decline.

Sociologist Loic Wacquant has identified this phenomenon of increasing segregation as a larger process he calls double ghettoization.[46] After the civil rights movements of the sixties social and economic reaction created new ghettos that collapsed onto themselves. The neo-liberal economy was the source of decline of local economies which along with the retrenchment of the welfare state created a hyperghetto in which groups are relegated to a substandard environment based both in race and in class. Hyperghettos create a new form of marginalization. Unlike older African American ghettos in which there was a parallel middle class, the new ones suffer both from the declining African American middle class and from

[46] Loic Wacquant, *Urban Outcasts: A Comparative Sociology of Advanced Marginality* (Malden MA: Polity, 2008). Michelle Alexander, *The New Jim Crow: Mass Incarceration in an Age of Colorblindness* (New York: New Press, 2012).

their own flight. If anything, the new enclaves are more marginalized than before or during the civil rights movement.

From Entrepreneurialism to Financialization: Cities after 2008

While financialization was always an element of neo-liberal urban governance, it took on a more prominent role once other forms of growth stalled out. Jaime Peck has identified a new stage of urban governance that is the successor to the ones that Harvey identified. This new stage might be called austerity urbanism or extreme austerity. It is the outcome of the often-unsuccessful project of entrepreneurial urbanism, which resulted in years of slow revenue growth, risky new financial instruments, and processes. Entrepreneurial urbanism led to deepening debt, reduced financial ratings and defaults. Only some cities benefitted. In its place, austerity urbanism arose, an authoritarian technocratic form of governance, which eliminates what little democratic autonomy cities had.

Many of the strategies that cities attempted were with a few exceptions, unsuccessful. At the same time, cities were forced to borrow to pay for services, to finance development projects for entertainment, and to defray tax breaks for Industrial Development projects. Cities more than doubled their debt in the neo-liberal era. Compounding this problem, the neo-liberal era had lower growth than the post war era, and by the end of the twentieth century, cities exhausted some of the easiest ways to generate revenue. A third factor was the fundamental weakness neo-liberalism was showing in a series of financial bubbles and bust which required federal bailouts.

The result was an intensified process of financialization in the later stages of neo-liberalism especially in urban areas. Cities went deeper into debt, employed riskier financial strategies, and employed punitive adjustment measures, including selling off utilities, breaking or rolling back union contracts, and pensions and staff cutbacks. Though they have been around for more than a century, ratings came to play an expanded and crucial role.

Financial rating institutions also played a significant role. In the Keynesian era, for example, financial rating institutions played a small role. The loss of federal funding, however, meant that cities had to seek private funding and take on debt in order to pay normal expenditures no longer covered by federal funds like welfare and housing. More lending was now done through nontraditional sources like union pension funds to skirt limits on speculation grade investments. Credit worthiness became an essential element in obtaining funds. This, however, made cities far more dependent on financial institutions. Lacking any true autonomy cities had to develop plans that pleased lenders and often corporate interests. Projects that might serve public interests or address problems like poverty were often not possible.

One of the financialized instruments cities used were Special Districts, that is, independent limited purpose areas financially and sometimes administratively independent of local governments. Due to their status, they could bypass some of the state and locally imposed limits on debt. Fire districts for example are often used in to raise revenue, levy taxes, and get around tax and debt limits. Tax Investment Bonds which are based on future or anticipated tax revenues from development were also employed.

Though not identical, Peck's analysis has some affinities with critical political economist Wolfgang Streeck's analysis of the stages of neo-liberal fiscal crisis leading to austerity, and the increasing democratic deficit generated in the process.[47] Moving from the first deflationary monetary policies of the Federal Reserve in the 1970s through the accumulation of debt by cities followed by the privatization of debt, Streeck sees a series of attempts that are ultimately unable to stave off the fiscal crisis of the states and municipalities. The debt accumulation phase ran aground in the crash of 2007. Here he sees a transition from the debt state to the austerity/ consolidation state. Although central banks and fiscal policies like quantitative easing have stabilized the federal economy, states and municipalities have been forced into austerity measures that are enforced through anti-democratic means. Such austerity also has an economic function, as it tends to dampen demand which might lead to inflation. Here democratic legitimation is entirely bypassed and judged inadequate because of a state of emergency that is fiscal insolvency.

Detroit is the paradigm case of fiscal insolvency in the late neo-liberal era. While urban areas differ significantly in their financial situation, Detroit exhibits features other stressed areas share, and may be subject to a similar fate if neo-liberal conditions continue. Detroit has suffered from excessive debt, slow and sometimes negative growth, declining population, and a shrinking tax base for many years. It had borrowed heavily to

[47] Wolfgang Streeck, *Buying Time: The Delayed Crisis of Democratic Capitalism* (London: Verso, 2014). Brian Caterino and Phillip Hansen, *Critical Theory, Democracy and the Challenge of Neo-Liberalism* (Toronto: University of Toronto Press, 2019): 118-20.

cover cash flow problems. Revenues declined by 20 percent since 2008 and while expenses and staffing had already been cut, long-term commitments to pensions healthcare and debt servicing increased significantly. Declining revenues also followed from the results of the 2007-08 crash/recession, and many houses financed through derivatives were foreclosed. Property values sank further reducing revenue. State aid had also been reduced. By 2013, Detroit had become almost insolvent on a cash flow basis, with a deficit of $162 million.

In July of 2013, the city of Detroit declared bankruptcy, and the state of Michigan took over fiscal management of the city. It appointed an "emergency manager" Keyvn Orr, to oversee the city's finances. State law granted Orr exceptional powers that went beyond mere financial matters normally addressed by bankruptcy, and gave him the ability to vacate pension agreements, break union contracts sell off city assets among other powers. The emergency manager was allowed to function as a virtual dictator and override any democratically achieved agreements and processes.

Of course, financial analysts and the press presented Detroit's bankruptcy as its own fault, the result of poor management, political corruption, and union contracts. Even liberals who might have taken a more compassionate view seemed to the think that emergency management was a necessary precursor to righting the ship and get Detroit back on its feet. For example, President Obama who certainly helped corporate America get back on its feet after the 2007 crashed was notably inactive in helping Detroit and did not challenge dictatorial powers. There was little or no analysis of the structural features that caused the bankruptcy in the first place.

One of the most significant aspects of this forced restructuring was the extent to which it involved intensifying the financialization of Detroit. While bankruptcy may not be the future of all cities the financialization process it ushered in are models those other cities will adopt.

In Jaime Peck's analysis, four features of financialization are most important. First is the use of intermediation. The term intermediation refers in this case to the connection of lenders and borrowers. Financially troubled cities like Detroit, lacking internal revenues or sufficient federal or state aid, became more dependent on private funding through the bond market—not only for projects but also for day to day operations. The role of intermediary institutions like bond rating agencies came to be central. For their part, cities like Detroit sought riskier financing schemes involving leveraging future revenues from taxes and revenue sharing. However, making these loans though the bond market meant pleasing rating agencies by implementing business friendly policies like lower tax rates, or other incentives to developers.

Just as intermediation promoted the financialization, the instruments of financialization promote a greater control and exploitation of new opportunities for private companies to benefit from urban resources and enhance the financialization of urban government. These new financial instruments "includes RANs, TANs, and fiscal stabilization bonds, as well as revenue bonds, general obligation bonds, certificates of participation (COPs), swaps, bond insurance (wraps), private financing through P3s, TIFs, tax liens, and social impact bonds. Instruments like these, serve, in effect, as carriers for financial rationalities and imperatives they inaugurate and deepen financialized relationships between local and extra local actors and agencies; and they open up new horizons of financial opportunity and exposure."[48]

The third step in the process involves and institutionalization of the processes of devolution which have been in effect since the beginning of neo-liberalism. This is a contraction of revenue sharing funds. In Michigan, this was called the great revenue sharing hoax, and Michigan in fact withheld over $700 million in funds. Cities like Detroit are supposed to provide their own sources of revenue and be autonomous. This autonomy puts cities more at the mercy of financial interests and affects the poor populations disproportionately.

The final element, intensification, is similar to the idea of the shock doctrine discussed much earlier by Naomi Klein.[49] Both the earlier uses of the shock doctrine and the later fiscal crisis of Detroit in 2013 invoke notions of fiscal emergencies to allow radical restructuring without political deliberation and debate, but the in the latter case the result is more than punitive. The financialization of urban regimes is considerably enhanced and the dictatorial powers of financial manages is even more perverse. As Peck notes these processes were deliberately planned. The Michigan American Civil Liberties Union (ACLU) was able to obtain documents going back as far as 2011 where such measures were being prepared. "Crucially in Detroit's case, these legally enforced and technocratically managed emergency measures have been the subject of

[48] Jaime Peck and Heather Whiteside, "Financializing Detroit" *Economic Geography* Volume 92, 2016—Issue 3: 255.

[49] Naomi Klein, *The Shock Doctrine: The Rise of Disaster Capitalism* (New York: Picador, 2001).

meticulous and extensive planning. The raiding of public assets, the impairment of municipal employee and retiree benefits, and the imposition of radical restructuring on local-government systems and services were not isolated mishaps, but strategically envisioned measures."[50]

Peck's detailed analysis of the connection of intensified financialization, austerity, and the loss of democratic control suggests another feature of neo-liberal governance. Neo-liberalism does not reduce the scope of government; it requires a strong state to conduct its aims. Foucault and some critical theorists have emphasized this point. [51]

Bibliography

"The Average Salary of Nursing Home Office Staff Work." *Chron* August 13, 2020. https://work.chron.com/average-salary-nursing-home-office-staff-1651.html

"The economic benefits of improving social inclusion: A report commissioned by SBS." *Deloitte Access Economics* August 2019. https://www2.deloitte.com/content/dam/Deloitte/my/Documents/risk/-rsk-sdg10-economic-benefits-of-improving-social-inclusion.pdf

AFT. *An Army of Temps: Adjunct Faculty Quality of Work/Life Report. AFT 2020.* https://www.aft.org/sites/default/files/adjuncts_qualityworklife2020.pdf

Alexander, Michelle. *The New Jim Crow: Mass Incarceration in an Age of Colorblindness*. New York: New Press, 2012.

Auletta, Ken, The *Underclass*. New York: Random House, 1982.

Berube, Alan, and Brad McDearman. "Good Fortune, Dire Poverty, and Inequality in Baltimore: An American Story." *Brookings Institution*. August 2. 2016.

Bluestone, Barry and Bennett Harrison. *The Deindustrialization of America*. New York: Basic Books, 1982.

Bonefeld, Werner. *The Strong State and the Free Economy*. Rowman and Littlefield: Lanham MD, 2017.

Bowles, Samuel, David M. Gordon, Thomas E. Weisskopf. *Beyond the Waste Land: A Democratic Alternative to Economic Decline*. New York Anchor, 1983.

Brady, David and Michael Wallace. "Deindustrialization and Poverty: Manufacturing Decline and AFDC Recipiency in Lake County, Indiana

[50] Peck and Whiteside, "Financializing Detroit": 259.

[51] Werner Bonefeld, *The Strong State and the Free Economy* (Rowman and Littlefield: Lanham MD, 2017). Michel Foucault, *The Birth of Biopolitics: Lectures at the College de France 1978-1979* (New York: Picador, 2010). Foucault's exact view of Neo-liberalism has been subject to controversy. See Daniel Zamora and Michael C. Behrent eds., *Foucault and Neo-Liberalism* (Cambridge: Polity, 2014).

1964–93." *Sociological Forum* 16, 2001: 321–358. https://doi.org/10.1023/A:1011008919557.

Case, Annie and Angus Deaton, *Deaths of Despair and the Future of Capitalism.* Princeton University Press, 2020.

Caterino, Brian and Phillip Hansen. *Critical Theory, Democracy and the Challenge of Neo-Liberalism.* Toronto: University of Toronto Press, 2019.

CNBC. "Buffalo Bills propose new $1.4 billion NFL stadium by 2027." *CNBC*, August 31, 2021. https://www.cnbc.com/2021/08/31/buffalo-bills-propose-new-1point4-billion-nfl-stadium-by-2027.html

Cook, Lindsey. "Why Black Americans Die Younger." *US News and World Report*, Jan. 5, 2015, https://www.usnews.com/news/blogs/data-mine/2015/01/05/black-americans-have-fewer-years-to-live-heres-why

Côté, James E., and Anton L. Allahar. *Lowering Higher Education: The Rise of Corporate Universities and the Fall of Liberal Education.* Toronto: University of Toronto Press, 2011.

Cox, Jeff, "CEOs see pay grow 1,000% in the last 40 years, now make 278 times the average worker." https://www.cnbc.com/2017/07/20/ceos-make-271-times-the-pay-of-most-workers.html

CNBC Aug 16, 2019. https://www.cnbc.com/2019/08/16/ceos-see-pay-grow-1000percent-and-now-make-278-times-the-average-worker.html

De Luce, Ivan, Emma Court, and Madison Hoff. "Here's how much 30 types of hospital workers are paid." *Business Insider* May 10, 2021. https://www.businessinsider.com/how-much-everyone-makes-in-a-hospital-2019-5?amp.

Easterbrook, Gregg. "How Taxpayers Keep the NFL Rich." *The Atlantic* December 8, 2015. https://www.theatlantic.com/entertainment/archive/2015/12/how-taxpayers-keep-the-nfl-rich/418971/

"Economic Inequality in Baltimore, MD", https://wp.nyu.edu/economic-inequality/2017/03/29/economic-inequality-in-baltimore-md/.

Flaherty, Colleen. "Barely Getting By New report on adjuncts says many make less than $3,500 per course and live in poverty." *Inside Higher Ed* April 20, 2020. https://www.insidehighered.com/news/2020/04/20/new-report-says-many-adjuncts-make-less-3500-course-and-25000-year

Foucault, Michel. *The Birth of Biopolitics: Lectures at the College de France 1978-1979.* New York: Picador, 2010.

Gans, Herbert. *Levitowners: Ways of Life and Politics in a New Suburban Community.* New York: Columbia University Press. 1967.

Geary, Daniel. *Beyond Civil Rights: The Moynihan Report and its Legacy.* Philadelphia: University of Pennsylvania Press, 2013.

Gould, Eric. "The impact of manufacturing employment decline on black and white Americans." *VoxEU* December 19, 2018. Manufacturing decline has hurt black Americans more | VOX, CEPR Policy Portal (voxeu.org)

Hackworth, Jason. *Manufacturing Decline: How Racism and the Conservative Movement Crush the American Rust Belt.* New York Columbia University Press, 2019).

Harrington, Michael. *The Other America: Poverty in America* with a new introduction. New York Scribner, 1997.

Hart Joy L., and Tracy E. K. Meyer. "Worker Memory and Narrative: Personal Stories of Deindustrialization in Louisville Kentucky." in Jefferson Crowe and Joseph Heathcott eds. *Beyond the Ruins: The Meanings of Deindustrialization*. Ithaca: Cornell University Press, 2003: 294-304.

Harvey, David. "From Managerialism to Entrepreneurialism: The Transformation in Urban Governance in Late Capitalism." *Geografiska Annaler: Series B, Human Geography* Volume 71, 1989.

Isserman, Maurice. *The Other American: The Life of Michael Harrington*. New York: Public Affairs, 2001.

Isserman, Maurice. "50 Years Later: Poverty and The Other America." *Dissent* Winter 2012. https://www.dissentmagazine.org/article/50-years-later0 poverty-and-the-other-america.

Katz, Michael. *In the Shadow of the Poorhouse: A Social History of Welfare in America*, Tenth Anniversary Edition. New York, Basic Books, 1996.

Klein, Naomi. *The Shock Doctrine: The Rise of Disaster Capitalism*. New York: Picador, 2001.

Charles, Kofi Kerwin, Erik Hurst, and Mariel Schwart, "The Transformation of Manufacturing and the Decline in U.S. Employment." *NBER* working paper 24468. https://www.nber.org/system/files/working_papers/w24468/w24468.pdf

Leeds, A. Michael, Peter von Allmen, Victor A. Matheson. *The Economics of Sports* 6th Edition. New York: Routledge, 2018.

Lemann, Nicolas. "The Origins of the Underclass." *The Atlantic* June, 1986. https://www.theatlantic.com/past/docs/politics/poverty/origin2.htm

Maciag, Michael. "Life Expectancy Varies Greatly Within Cities" *Governing*. February 03, 2016. https://www.governing.com/archive/gov-life-expectancy-neighborhood.html

Marris, Peter, and Martin Rein. *Dilemmas of Social Reform: Poverty and Community Action in the United States* 2nd Edition. New York: Routledge, 2017.

May. Steve, and Laura Morrison. "Making Sense of Restructuring: Narratives of Accommodation among Downsized Workers." in Jefferson Crowe and Joseph Heathcott eds. *Beyond the Ruins: The Meanings of Deindustrialization*. Ithaca: Cornell University Press, 2003: 259-283.

McAlone, Nathan. "This man invented the digital camera in 1975—and his bosses at Kodak never let it see the light of day." *Business Insider* August 17, 2015. https://www.businessinsider.com/this-man-invented-the-digital-camera-in-1975-and-his-bosses-at-/kodak-never-let-it-see-the-light-of-day-2015-8

McFarland, Susan. "U.N. report: With 40M in poverty, U.S. most unequal developed nation." *UPIJUNE* 22, 2018.

Mead, Lawrence. *Beyond Entitlement: The Social Obligations of Citizenship.* New York: The Free Press, 1986.

Molotch, Harvey, and John Logan. *Urban Fortunes: The Political Economy of Place.* Berkeley: University of California Press, 1987.

Molotch, Harvey. "The City as a Growth Machine: Toward a Political Economy of Place." *American Journal of Sociology* 82: 2 1976: 309-322.

Moynihan, Daniel Patrick. *Maximum Feasible Misunderstanding: Community Action in the War on Poverty.* New York: Free Press, 1970.

Paulas, Rick. "Sports Stadiums Are a Bad Deal for Cities: But cities can fight back." *The Atlantic* November 21, 2018. https://www.theatlantic.com/technology/archive/2018/11/sports-stadiums-can-be-bad-cities/576334/

Peck, Jaime, and Heather Whiteside. "Financializing Detroit." *Economic Geography* Volume 92, 2016—Issue 3.

Piketty, Thomas. *Capital in the Twenty-First Century.* Cambridge: Belknap Press 2014.

Piven, Frances Fox and Richard Cloward. *Regulating the Poor: The Functions of Public Welfare* 2nd edition. New York: Vintage, 1993.

Reed Jr, Adolph. "The Underclass as Myth and Symbol: The Poverty of Discourse on Poverty." in Adolph Reed Jr, *Stirrings in the Jug: Black Politics in the Post-Segregation Era.* Minneapolis: University of Minnesota Press, 1999: 179-96.

Reich, Robert. *Aftershock: The next economy and America's Future.* New York: Vintage, 2010.

Ross, Martha and Nicole Bateman. "Meet the Low Wage Workforce." *Brookings Institute Metropolitical Policy Program* November, 2019. https://www.brookings.edu/wp-content/uploads/2019/11/201911_Brookings-Metro_low-wage-workforce_Ross-Bateman.pdf

Russo, John and Sherry Lee Linkon. "The Social Costs Of Deindustrialization." *Center for Working Class Studies,* Youngstown State University. https://ysu.edu/center-working-class-studies/social-costs-deindustrialization

Sankofa, John. "Disinvestment in Baltimore's Black Neighborhoods Is Foreboding but Reversible." *Urban Wire* September 29, 2020. https://www.urban.org/urban-wire/disinvestment-baltimores-black-neighborhoods-foreboding-reversible

Scheer, Mark. "A record subsidy for Bills stadium?" *Investigative Post* November 16, 2021, https://www.investigativepost.org/2021/11/16/a-record-subsidy-for-bills-stadium/

Slaughter, Sheila, and Gary Rhoades. *Academic Capitalism and the New Economy: Markets, State, and Higher Education.* Baltimore: Johns Hopkins University Press, 2009.

Standing, Guy. *The Precariat: The New Dangerous Class.* London: Bloomsbury, 2016.

Streeck, Wolfgang. *Buying Time: The Delayed Crisis of Democratic Capitalism.* London: Verso, 2014.

Taylor, Gerald D. "Unmade in America Industrial Flight and the Decline of Black Communities" *Alliance of American Manufacturers* October, 2016.

Taylor, Keeanga-Yamahtta. *Race for Profit: How Banks and the Real Estate Industry Undermined Black Homeownership.* Chapel Hill University of North Carolina Press, 2019. https://s3-us-west-2.amazonaws.com/aamweb/uploads/research-pdf/UnmadeInAmerica.pdf

Tuchman, Gaye. *Wannabe U: Inside the Corporate University.* Chicago: University of Chicago Press, 2009.

U.N. report: With 40M in poverty, U.S. most unequal developed nation—UPI.com

Venkataramani Atheendar S., Elizabeth F. Bair, Rourke L. O'Brien, Alexander C. Tsai. "Association Between Automotive Assembly Plant Closures and Opioid Overdose Mortality in the United States A Difference-in-Differences Analysis." *JAMA Intern Med.* 2020 180(2):254-262.

Wacquant, Loic. *Urban Outcasts: A Comparative Sociology of Advanced Marginality.* Malden MA: Polity, 2008.

Wallach, Alan. *The Divided City: Poverty and Prosperity in Urban America.* Washington: Island Press, 2018.

Weaver, Timothy. *Blazing the Neoliberal Trail: Urban Political Development in the United States and the United Kingdom.* Philadelphia, University of Pennsylvania Press, 2016.

Wilson, William Julius. *The Truly Disadvantaged: The Inner City, the Underclass and Social Policy.* Chicago: University of Chicago Press, 1987.

Zamora, Daniel, and Michael C. Behrent eds. *Foucault and Neo-Liberalism.* Cambridge: Polity, 2014.

CHAPTER 4

From a City of Quality to a City of Poverty

Race in Rochester: A Pattern of Discrimination and Neglect

Rochesterians are fond of citing Frederic Douglas and Susan B Anthony, who both spent considerable time in the city, as proof of its liberal progressive and tolerant heritage, and its enlightened attitudes on race. The reality of Rochester in the 20th century, however, was quite different. It shows a pattern of discrimination and neglect.

Rochester was not affected by the first great migration of African Americans to the North in the early part of the twentieth century, which had an impact on cities like Chicago, Detroit, New York, Philadelphia, and Baltimore. In Rochester until the 1950s, African Americans represented only about 1-2 percent of the population of 325,000. Perhaps this was because there were no industrial jobs available in Rochester as there were in other cities. In the 1930s, racial discrimination in Rochester was obvious. The assessment by the Roosevelt era federal Homeowners Loan Corporation (HOLC) is an illustration. HOLC was given the task of grading neighborhoods across the country to determine which would be

B. Caterino, *The Failure of the Neo-Liberal Approach to Poverty*,
https://doi.org/10.1007/978-3-031-10606-4_4

eligible for government insured home mortgage refinancing.[1] In Rochester the two areas in which African Americans were concentrated were given the lowest rating of hazardous and marked on maps in red (hence the term redlining). Such areas were ineligible for federal loans. Of one area, it said directly "Negroes have come into the area and today it is the poorest section of the entire city." They went on to note that pride in ownership was lacking and hence federal investment would be fruitless. These assessments created a vicious circle. The inability to buy houses made it difficult for African American families to build equity, since in most middle-class families the house is the largest asset. Paying rent without building equity made it hard to get out of limited circumstances. In the suburbs, restrictive covenants excluded African Americans from buying houses in these areas too.[2]

A second report in the late thirties from a state commission on the condition of the "colored urban population" also found dismal conditions.[3] Out of 35,000 employees at private industrial firms in Rochester, they found only 70 African Americans. Kodak, which at that time had about 16,000 employees, had only one black employee, a porter, and a handful of construction workers. Kodak did not hire African Americans and apparently neither did other companies. The members of the commission wondered how "Negroes in these and other communities in the up-State region managed to make a living and avoid starvation."[4]

[1] Justin Murphy, "1930s Rochester redlining maps show discrimination," *Rochester Democrat and Chronicle* October 26, 2016. https://www.democratandchronicle.com/story/news/2016/10/20/rochester-ny-redlining-map/92456536/; For the original data see *Mapping Inequality: Redlining in New Deal America*. https://dsl.richmond.edu/panorama/redlining/#loc=14/43.147/-77.621&city=rochester-ny

[2] The Landmark Society of Rochester has gathered a number of snippets of important documents. See Shane Wiegand, "History of Segregation and Racial Policy in Greater Rochester." *Landmark Society Web Site*. https://www.landmarksociety.org/wp-content/uploads/2019/05/ShaneWiegand_Redlining-Segregation_web.pdf

[3] *Second Report of the New York State Temporary Commission on the Condition of the Colored Urban Population to the Legislature of the State of New York* February, 1939. 1939 NYS Commission on Colored Urban Population.pdf—Google Drive

[4] *Second Report*

The Legacy of George Eastman

Any account of the issues of race in Rochester must come to terms with the legacy of Kodak's founder, George Eastman.[5] Kodak dominated Rochester's economic and cultural life throughout much of the twentieth century, and when Kodak spoke, the rest of the community followed its lead. Some have characterized George Eastman's view of race as "complicated." Eastman, they argue, gave generously to black institutions, especially the Tuskegee and Hampton Institute, and at his funeral, his hearse contained a wreath thanking him for all he had done for the "colored race." Yet in his home city, Eastman assiduously avoided any attempts at integration to better the conditions of local African Americans. He kept African Americans from Kodak jobs. He used Kodak's financial power, through its banking services, to assure suburbs would not be integrated.

Eastman's legacy is not complicated. He supported precisely the African American institutions that did not present a threat to a segregated social order especially that of Rochester. The Tuskegee institute founded by Booker T. Washington was a favorite of white industrialists who were comfortable adopting a paternalistic attitude toward race. They saw Washington as a self-made man much like themselves, who rarely challenged the existing social arrangements. Washington unlike other leaders such as W.E.B. DuBois or A. Phillip Randolph did not criticize the exploitation by the business classes and did not ask for too much in the way of social change.

Eastman did not favor integration. If he did secretly favor it as some like to think, none of his public actions ever indicated this. In his public statements, he opposed fraternization of the races and was concerned about any activity in which whites would have to encounter African Americans in a professional or cultural setting. The University of Rochester Medical School remained segregated because, according to officials, white women would not go to an African American doctor or have them deliver their babies. Eastman discouraged the medical and dental school from admitting African American applicants and encouraged the University of

[5] The information in this section is largely drawn from Justin Murphy's research on George Eastman. See Justin Murphy, "George Eastman's Complicated Legacy of Race Relations and Philanthropy," *Rochester Democrat and Chronicle,* June 7, 2021, although the evaluation of his "complications" is my own. https://www.democratandchronicle.com/in-depth/news/2021/06/07/george-eastman-kodak-rochester-ny-legacy-black-race-relations-philanthropy/4755198001//

Rochester to remain a white only institution. The University only relented, long after Eastman's death, when the federal government threatened to cut off aid. While Eastman did allow African Americans to attend the Eastman theater concert hall, they were only allowed to sit in the balcony, the spatial equivalent of the back of the bus. Nor did Eastman meet frequently, if at all, with local civil rights leaders of the time. He did not agree with their more assertive approaches to race issues. He consistently refused to consider issues they wanted to raise with him.

Eastman like many business leaders of his time believed in Eugenics, a pseudo-scientific theory that sought to improve the genetic quality of humans through "selective" breeding. Eastman funded the American Eugenics Society and believed that Eugenics could breed out misfits and criminals. Modern Eugenics arose as a feature of Social Darwinist theories. Besides the dubious scientific basis of the theory and its genetic determinism, it was primarily a political cudgel used to pass racist laws. Eugenics supporters passed miscegenation laws, banning interracial marriages, and forced sterilization of "defectives." It was an element in the more restrictive immigration measures of the 1920s. Eastman did not believe the vast majority of African Americans had the intelligence and discipline to work at Kodak. Eastman had similar views about the growing Italian American populations in Rochester. They too were not employed in significant numbers for many years. Eastman preferred Germans whom he thought had the intelligence and skill to perform manufacturing tasks. In addition, he was known to frequently use anti-Semitic tropes.

A Second Wave

The second wave of migration from the south occurred after World War II. Rochester's African Americans population increased from 7845 to about 32,000 by 1964. The new arrivals were not welcomed with open arms. The inability to get suitable housing and work was a major source of tension. As a result, the unemployment rate for African Americans was more than six times that of whites.[6] However, the extent of racial discrimination ran deeper. Reverend Franklin Florence who came to Rochester from Florida in 1959 to become a pastor at the Reynolds Street Church of Christ, and who later became a central figure in Freedom, Independence,

[6] *July 64,* Director, Carvin Eison. Producer, Chris Christopher (ImageWordSound, 2006). The Film details the uprising https://vimeo.com/349946856 ;

God, Honor, Today (FIGHT) a major civil rights group in Rochester, recalls that the situation he faced here was not much different from the one he experienced in the South. He observed, "It was like living in Mississippi or Alabama, no difference." [7] Similarly, organizer Saul Alinsky characterized Kodak as a plantation transplanted from the south. African Americans were often referred to as bean pickers, a reference to the migrant labor some had done in area farms before moving to the city. Others who came as university students were surprised by the discrimination they faced and found real difficulty getting housing. Walter Cooper, who also became a major figure in local civil rights, was denied housing 69 times when he came to Rochester in the 1950s as a chemistry graduate student. Police brutality was common. City Police officers, Florence stated, would go into black neighborhoods and "harass and intimidate" people using dogs. They even interrupted church services. Housing was still a serious problem. African Americans often had to live in rundown houses owned by absentee landlords who charged excessive rents. Fresh healthy food was hard to obtain, and schools were largely segregated. In short, Rochester was a powder keg.

Rochesterians had a smug, almost complacent, attitude toward these problems. If you were white and middle class, (especially Northern European) things were pretty good in Rochester. Wages were decent and business was prosperous. The unemployment rate in the white community was around 2 percent and jobs were begging. For most in the Rochester area including of course the burgeoning suburbs, these simply were not their problems. They saw no need to change.[8] If you grew up in the suburbs, you were likely unaware of the extent of the problems. There were no more than a handful of African American families in my suburb. The 1964 uprising was a shock to them.

The match was lit on July 24, 1964, when police came to break up a block party in the area. They arrested a 20-year-old for public intoxication and for harassment of a woman at the party. When he resisted, the police responded with force. Some in the crowd, already sensitized to police misconduct felt the police response was too strong. They started throwing rocks and bottles. The police then called in additional backup—and the

[7] Tim Louis Macaluso, "Franklin Florence on Rochester and Racism: Little has changed," *CITY Newspaper* September 28, 2018.

[8] See the comments of Journalist Jack Germond, who began his career in Rochester, City Historian Ruth Rosenberg-Naparsteck and Reverend Dr. Arthur Whitaker in *July 64*.

additional police came with K-9 dogs. Despite the official policy prohibiting the use of dogs for such purposes, two were used by the police for crowd control. That was a mistake. The use of the dogs was the trigger of the uprising. It no doubt invoked the memory of police dogs being used on protesters in the south. One week earlier the Harlem Riot had taken place, further raising tensions.

From the initial flash point, the resistance expanded first to about four hundred then up to two thousand people by the early morning hours, including some looting on the main commercial street in the area. Police lost control of the situation. The next day Governor Rockefeller declared a state of emergency and called in the national guard, but the disturbances carried on for several nights and did not end until July 26.

Confirming the notion that Rochester was out of touch with the realities, municipal leaders reacted with outrage that their city would be seen as a racial tinderbox. In their minds, this was simply impossible. City spokesman Arthur Deutsch, sent an angry telegram to Newsweek magazine in response to its "Rage in Rochester" headline, said: "This city has made more progress in helping minority groups than any other."[9] Frank Lamb then mayor of Rochester said in a 1964 PBS interview said, "People were stunned as to how could this happen in Rochester, you know, an affluent eastern city that had a reputation of being very benevolent and generous."[10] The police also were surprised by the action. Given the city's history of mistreatment of African Americans as outlined above, these statements strain credulity. However, it is consistent with the self-image that many Rochester leaders maintained.

A City of Quality?

Rochester's smug self-image was nowhere more in display than in the promotional film, *Rochester, City of Quality* produced in 1963 a year before the uprising. The city was portrayed as peaceful modern and prosperous.[11] Rochester was an exceptional city, with none of the problems of other

[9] James Goodman, "1964 riots revisited: 3 days that shook Rochester," *Rochester Democrat and Chronicle* July 20, 2014. https://www.democratandchronicle.com/story/news/2014/07/19/roberta-abbott-buckle-rochester-riots/12855941/

[10] Ty Clauss, "Rochester Race Riots: Unemployment and Unrest," *Reporter* (RIT) https://reporter.rit.edu/features/rochester-race-riots-unemployment-and-unrest

[11] *Rochester City of Quality*. Director Charles Christenberry Jr. (Rochester Gas and Electric, 1963) Accessed at https://www.youtube.com/watch?v=2yLKkxq0dH0

cities. While it is possible today to see this film as an amusing, nostalgic piece of kitsch for a Rochester that no longer exists, I want to take it seriously as an expression of the insular view of Rochester leaders.

City of Quality shows a self-satisfied community with no hint of racial troubles. It lauds Rochester's natural beauty, transportation hubs, and its progressive outlook as exemplified in its manufacturing base. Rochester is a leader in clean industrial technology, distinct from "dirtier" industries—perhaps meaning steel, auto, tire and parts manufacturing found in other Great Lake cities especially Buffalo—and the dirtier (working class) people who live in these towns. Rochester has the right kind of people. Here manufacturing was based in "quality" products that attracted "quality" people to live and work. Rochesterians are "clean and stable" people like its secure manufacturing base. Its well educated work force was adept at anticipating and adjusting to technological change. It required a forward-looking work force that was well disciplined (unlike unruly union workers).

I can imagine Donald Fagen's (ironically meant) IGY, with its invocation of a spotless high-tech utopian future, playing in the background of this film. This beautiful world was at least in the film, homogenous. Rochester is filled with conscientious people and has sensible government. Most of all Rochester is ***orderly***. But watching the film one is struck in retrospect with the incredible whiteness of its Being, There a few if any African Americans or even swarthy Italian Americans who made up a significant part of Rochester's population. Not many identifiably working-class people either. They are not the quality people the film wants business leaders to see. The men and women look like they stepped out of a 1950s sitcom and the male children all have Leave it to Beaver buzz cuts. Like Ward Cleaver, the men all looked like they were going to or coming from management level jobs. This was the imagined Rochester that soon would be confronted first by racial troubles which confronted its progressive image.

The Aftermath

Rochester leaders had been warned of the troubles ahead. A New York State Commission report on discrimination from that period noted that Rochester was "sitting on a pressure cooker" and Florence and several others had warned the city just a week before that the situation was critical. Far from showing the benevolence of Rochesterians, the uprising revealed the deep undercurrent of racial prejudices just below Rochester's complacent surface. Leaders did not want to believe the realities of Rochester racism.

In the aftermath of the uprising, several organizations notably FIGHT, and the Urban League arose to represent the African American Community. Members of FIGHT did not take a strict integrationist approach. Influenced by Black Power movements of the time FIGHT leaders felt that white liberals were often an impediment to progress. Florence was also an associate of Malcolm X who was a proponent of Black Nationalism rather than integration. Leaders like Florence did not seek positions on corporate boards but took to the streets seeking independence and community power for Rochester's African American population. FIGHT held that African Americans should speak for themselves. This stance meant that they could sometimes be unruly. They disrupted school board meetings, protested the use of police dogs and other police tactics, and confronted slum landlords. As Florence noted, if people would not listen, they had to be made uncomfortable to pay attention. Conflict was required. FIGHT gained some notoriety when it brought in organizer Saul Alinsky to work with community leaders to open employment opportunities at Eastman Kodak. None of Rochester's big three employers (Kodak. Xerox, and Bausch and Lomb) had significant minority employment. Alinsky, like Florence, thought sit-ins were not going to work, so he employed more unconventional tactics to confront Kodak such as a bean dinner before a stockholder meeting to create a fart in. Kodak, as you might imagine was very hesitant to change. Executives feared the loss of hiring power and the effect of "quotas" on its corporate culture, its products, and its reputation—familiar complaints of conservatives who failed to acknowledge claims of social equity. After disrupting a stockholder meeting and getting some shareholders to assign their proxies to FIGHT, Kodak relented and started recruitment and training for minorities. Though FIGHT was effective in getting some changes not all community activists shared the views of FIGHT and Alinsky.

Still the actions taken after the uprising was far from a complete success. Substandard housing was demolished and replaced by housing projects and parts of the downtown area in which African Americans lived were torn down for an expressway. These projects had the effect of breaking down whatever sense of neighborhood and community that existed. This was especially the case in the Clarissa street area. Going back as far as the 1820s Clarissa Street had been a center of African American commercial and cultural life. It was also a melting pot where different populations mixed. By the mid-twentieth century, it was the major business district of the community. One writer compared it to the Greenwood District of Tulsa, called Black Wall Street, prior to the Tulsa Massacre of 1921. This is an exaggeration; there was not a lot of wealth, but like Greenwood, it was a concentrated business district with many thriving businesses. It also had a jazz scene including the Pythodd room, where rising Rochester musicians like the Mangione brothers, would play along with national artists, like Wes Montgomery and Pee Wee Ellis. It was a cultural center of integration, where well to do and not so well off black and white socialized. The ordinary guy and city Counselman and judges all frequented it.[12] The inner loop project, cut off Clarissa street from the downtown area, shortened it and demolished a number of its houses and businesses. Today what is left of the area is part of Rochester's Corn Hill District home of a suburban style tract.

Rochester never fully addressed the problems that led to the 1964 uprising. Florence observed almost 50 years later, that while the situation is not the same as 1964, there has not been that much change. Things are in many respects the same today. Schools are more segregated than in the sixties, African American unemployment and poverty is high, more minorities than ever are incarcerated, and schools are underperforming. As the Daniel Prude incident illustrated, despite some increase in minority representation on the police force, community police relations are as bad as, or worse than before. While Rochester may no longer be the smug of City of Quality, it still seemed until recently, willing to pretend its racial problems did not really exist.

Smug Rochester however reacted to groups like FIGHT with fear and derision. They were not comfortable with anything that smacked of African American radicalism. Reporter Justin Murphey who has studied Rochester's history of segregation has also noted the inadequate coverage

[12] Robert Bell, "Can memories of Clarissa Street's golden age of Black business inspire a resurgence?," *Rochester Democrat and Chronicle* December 27. 2021. https://www.democratandchronicle.com/story/news/2021/12/27/can-memories-of-clarissa-street-golden-age-black-business-inspire-resurgence-rochester-ny/6454760001/; On the Pythodd Club see Alan Morrell, "Whatever Happened To ... Pythodd Club?," Rochester Democrat and Chronicle June 19, 2015. https://www.democratandchronicle.com/story/news/local/rocroots/2015/06/19/whatever-happened-pythodd-club/28939711/

of racial conflict.[13] He notes that coverage of racial issues was rooted in the "socially conservative nature" of the community. FIGHT for example was criticized claiming its militancy had become abusive and irresponsible. When covering protests over desegregation of Rochester Schools that I discuss in the next section, they failed to recognize the violence against African Americans and instead called for cooling passions. Like many newspapers, they had an institutional approach to news, that is, their sources of information were officials and business leaders. They were separated from the voices of the community which could have told them about racial violence.

The Failure of School Integration

The lack of progress in the wake of the 1964 uprising can be seen in the fight for desegregation of Rochester Schools.[14] Even before 1964, the National Association for the Advacedment of Colored Persons (NAACP) filed a federal lawsuit in Aikens v Board of education claiming that segregation impacted white as well as African American students. As minority population increased, new school boundaries had been gerrymandered so as to concentrate minority students in a few schools. Rather than integrate, classrooms were put in trailers or space in nearby buildings were rented so that white majority schools were not impacted.

The 1963 hiring of Herman Goldberg as school district superintendent was seen as a hopeful sign. Goldberg was Jewish and had grown up and had worked in his father's store in a diverse community in Brooklyn. He made several proposals to address integration, but his proposal was voluntary; minority students could enroll in majority white schools if there was room. This voluntary approach made the situation worse. Segregation actually increased and white city residents organized against Goldberg's initiatives. The African American Community including FIGHT pressed for bolder action.

After a decade of struggle and shifting coalitions, a majority of integrationists elected to the school board in 1970 developed an integration plan for city high schools to be put into place in fall 1971. Within a month, violence broke out. Parents and even their children would throw bricks

[13] Justin Murphy, "Rochester Newspapers During the Civil Rights Era failed the City's Black Community," *Rochester Democrat and Chronicle*. February 22, 2022.

[14] Justin Murphy, "50 Years Ago Rochester tried an experiment with Desegregation, It lasted less than 2 months," *Rochester Democrat and Chronicle*, February 22, 2022.

and rocks at the buses bringing minority students to the schools. African American students sometimes hid on the floors and in the wells of school buses out of fear of these attacks. A three foot high graffiti featuring the N-word was painted on one of the schools. Students fought in and outside of schools and African American students hid brass knuckles in their books to defend themselves. The real opposition came from the parents. Many of them took their students out of schools and formed illegal schools. They were fiercely opposed to integration and feared the loss of control of their schools. After two months of violence, the plan was rescinded and integration was never addressed again. As white flight continued, the point of an integrated city school district became moot. Some 30 years later, then Mayor William Johnson, while running to become county executive, proposed a county wide school system. The racial animus still present in the white community was harnessed by the republican party in a racially tinged smear campaign against Johnson that assured his defeat.

While FIGHT no longer exists, there are still several organizations which are concerned with social justice. Some of the main ones, however, take a less confrontational approach. The one exception was metro justice which evolved out of the White supporters of FIGHT. The main African American Organizations take a more liberal equal opportunity approach and none of these organizations exerts great influence over policy. With the defeat of the integration plan, a lot of the initiative for activism was lost.

Rochester Reacts to Deindustrialization

The Rochester area did not suffer the effects of deindustrialization as quickly as other manufacturing centers. It benefitted from the fact that until the 1980s Kodak, despite challenges from Japanese camera manufacturer Fuji, continued to expand, reaching a peak of over 60,000 workers in the Rochester area alone in 1982 and 145,000 worldwide in 1988. After that, Kodak employment rapidly and precipitously declined.[15] Less than 6000 people worked for Kodak worldwide in 2017 and it ranked 16th among Rochester employers with around 2000 workers.

[15] Mike Dickinson, "Kodak's decades of decline: Shrinking market leads to 19-month bankruptcy, less lucrative landscape," *Rochester Business Journal* September 13, 2017, https://rbj.net/2017/09/13/kodaks-decades-ofdecline/#:~:text=Kodak%27s%20global%20employment%20topped%20out,during%20its%2030%2Dyear%20decline.

From the beginning, Rochester leadership did not react with a sense of urgency to the changes brought about by neo-liberal deindustrialization and globalization. Kodak's paternalism and virulent anti-union stance resulted (though not completely) in a passive work force and a business culture of entitlement. Kodak has successfully socialized many workers to accept the Kodak conservative outlook. The result was a corporatized culture in which workers tended to believe that corporations should be the basis of economic security and not unions or the government.[16] This paternalistic outlook permeated much of Rochester civic life. Kodak was certainly a decent employer; it paid high wages in an attempt to avoid union organization and gave a substantial yearly bonus in addition to retirement and health benefits. Kodak workers were by and large well off. It was however, a very confining conformist environment. Little deviation was allowed. The situation changed as the economy transitioned, and like other companies, its policies were dictated by return on investment. New management stepped in and as it faced greater losses, Kodak became less of a paternalistic employer and more like a neo-liberal one. Yearly bonuses shrunk and benefits were pared. Health insurance once guaranteed to retirees were pared back and eventually ended. Kodak also successfully reduced the assessments on its properties, which meant that parts of the city and several suburbs lost important school tax revenue. Cutting jobs was good for the stock options the new leadership held. The sagging price of Kodak stock always got a boost when jobs were cut.

Without any strong union or any other support and a conformist attitude, workers had little to fall back on when Kodak and other large Rochester corporations no longer prospered. There was little solidarity between Kodak workers and others in the Rochester work force. Kodak workers thought they were a labor aristocracy—better than ordinary workers were. Eastman strove to hire only the "best" workers; even in the early days, they had to have a high school diploma. Still workers from Kodak had little support once the social contract between Kodak and the community was broken.

Thus, while there was a great deal of dissatisfaction behind the scenes, disorganized Kodak workers lacked a worldview that allowed them to protest. Many of the first workers laid off were older and many took early retirement incentives. They were not young enough to undergo extensive

[16] Sanford Jacoby, *Modern Manors: Welfare Capitalism Since the New Deal* (Princeton: Princeton University Press, 1997). Chapter 3.

job retraining. Most if they needed work ended up in lower paying service sector jobs. Later, as property and school tax revenues declined in several suburbs, there were tax revolts and defeated school district budgets, which reflected the loss of trust between its working-class residents and authorities whom they felt had let them down.

Instead of thoughtful consideration of the challenging economic situation, and the formulation of a solid recovery plan leaders waged a big PR campaign to reassure locals that things were going to be okay. Massive layoffs at Kodak Xerox and other plant closings were met by media campaigns like Positively Rochester which highlighted all the good things about Rochester, or the good deeds of others.[17] Resting on tired clichés, like when one door closes one opens, it would routinely highlighted some ex-Kodak employee, usually one from a research or management position, who started up a new business hiring a handful of people. Civic Boosterism can have a place, but when it based on covering up a bad reality, it becomes a destructive force. Positive thinking without any viable program merely denied the reality of decline rather than facing it. Incomes were declining. A 2008 study noted that the average income of town of Greece residents the town with the heaviest concentration of Kodak employees saw their average incomes decline almost 12 percent in a decade.[18] The figures were not much better in the city or other suburbs where Kodak workers frequently lived. Happy thoughts were not going to pay bills.

The loss of Kodak jobs meant the loss of Kodak benefits. During the post war Kodak was a major participant in what has been called the private welfare state. Distinct from the privatization of the welfare state in neoliberalism, it was Keynesianism without the state. Many jobs provided health care, pensions, and other benefits which allowed a reasonable standard of living. According to Michael Katz, 74 percent of Americans received their health insurance via work in 1979.[19] This was especially true of Rochester which through the influence and economic power of Kodak and Xerox had a robust regional health care system, in which almost everyone had reasonably priced health insurance. It was considered the envy of

[17] Rochester Television Channel WHEC still runs a segment, "Positively Rochester" it "celebrates all things positive in Rochester. We have so many positive things going on in our community, and News10NBC wants to recognize the people who make this such a great place to live." https://www.whec.com/article/13035

[18] See "Incomes," *Rochester Democrat and Chronicle* December 28, 2008, p 10.

[19] Michael B. Katz, *In the Shadow of the Poorhouse: A Social History of Welfare in America* (New York: Basic 1996) : 319.

many. In Rochester as elsewhere, the loss of industrial jobs not only meant jobs that provided less income but also fewer often no benefits. There was a new social contract which did not include commitment to a decent standard of living or health care as a condition of employment. While these changes had a big impact on the middle class increasing their vulnerability to the risks of everyday life, it also impacted the poor.

Rochester media rarely provided incisive discussion of Rochester's problems. One often had to look to out of town newspapers for critical articles on Rochester. Local papers stressed the resiliency of the workforce who after layoffs or buyouts started their own successful business. But the *New York Times* interviewed those with more sanguine views—people who observed the almost total loss of morale after a recent round of layoffs.[20] I can confirm this attitude from numerous discussions with friends and acquaintances who worked for Kodak. The ones who were not laid off were unhappy and simply hoping to hold out until retirement age. As Rochester shed a massive amount of Kodak jobs, one ex-Kodak executive noted you saw little about it in the papers, certainly no in-depth analyses in the major papers. Local TV stations sometimes asked for reactions from workers, usually those just leaving work after learning about layoffs, but only broadcast those who were philosophical about losses or accepted the changes as inevitable. Viewers never saw a worker who said her life would be devastated by job loss or follow ups on families who were negatively impacted. They never questioned the morale of existing workers either. While a good reporter would start to investigate these suppressed attitudes, reporters never acknowledged it was their duty to get beneath the surface and find the truth. They said that was not their job. Many years ago, writer Curt Gerling author of the well-known book *Smugtown* asserted that Rochester businessmen treated workers as children.[21] He was right.

A retrospective article in the *Wall Street Journal*, written when Kodak approached bankruptcy discussed the toll on the factory workers and laborers, not the professionals the Rochester media focused on. "As Kodak

[20] Claudia H. Deutsch, "Kodak to lay off 10,000 employees in a 10% cutback," *New York Times* Nov 12, 1997. Compare a contemporaneous article in the Gannett owned Baltimore Sun (Gannett is the parent of the Rochester papers). Craig Timberg, "In Kodak's town, life after layoffs: With the loss of 26,000 jobs since 1982, Kodak has taught hometown residents a lesson in Survival," *Baltimore Sun* November 21, 1997

[21] Curt Gerling, *Smugtown USA* 2nd edition (Webster: Plaza Publishers; 1993), (original publication 1957).

slashed its workforce, it was the company's factory workers and laborers in its film labs who had the most trouble finding new jobs."[22] Those who had only a high school education were at a disadvantage when they re-entered a job market where even a college degree isn't a secure job guarantee. The *Journal* interviewed one worker who after a recent layoff ended up driving a shuttle bus making a third of what he made at Kodak. The article also noted the fears of many retirees about the stability of their pensions and retirement benefits. Similarly, a story in the *Toronto Star* in 2003 "Rochester: Smug no More," traces the conditions that lead to the dissolution of the self satisfied Rochester outlook but shows how they still had a head in the sand attitude toward Rochester's problems.[23]

By the time of the article in the *Toronto Star*, Rochester leaders were beginning to grasp the impacts of deindustrialization. Tom Richards, then head of the newly formed Greater Rochester Enterprise (GRE), a private business group hoping to bring new businesses to Rochester, and a future Mayor of Rochester, noted, "now that Kodak and Xerox are fighting for their survival, we have to take responsibility for the success of our economy."

The GRE's strategic plan was more candid. It conceded that "the region is quickly falling behind the nation's top seventy-five metropolitan areas in economic standing … This stagnation marks the continuation if a 30-year decline in relative economic performance and outlook." However, another business leader Tom Mooney whom the article describes as stoic about Rochester claimed that Rochester had an advantage over other upstate areas since it did not have such a serious poverty problem. This claim seems incredulous—the problem was certainly known. A 2003 *New York Times* article on the high crime rate in the downtown triangle area of Rochester, notes that at that time 93 percent of public-school students lived in poverty "It's an area of great poverty and high consumption rate of drugs which fuels an incredibly high number of homicides," says Rochester police chief, Robert J. Duffy another future mayor of Rochester,

[22] Dana Mattioli, "Their Kodak Moments, Career Snapshots: Workers Take a Look Back as Many Struggle With Uncertainties About Family Finances, Retiree Benefits," *Wall Street Journal* January 6, 2012.

[23]. David Olive, "Rochester Smug no more: Marquee firms pay high price for complacency," *Toronto Star* Nov 15, 2003. Accessed at http://www.nativecanadian.ca/Native_Reflections/Smug_No_More1.htm.

"It's like a cancerous tumor, and it's growing."[24] A Brookings Institute Study on persistent pockets of poverty singled out the Northern Crescent area of Rochester as among the nation's worst.[25] Rochester did not benefit from the economic recovery of the 1990s and instead experienced continued and deepening economic distress and population loss. The poverty rate increased from 24 to 26 percent in the decade of the nineties and over a third of its census tracts were areas of highly concentrated poverty. It is difficult to see how leaders like CEO Mooney failed to grasp the problem.

Entertaining Adventures

In the wake of Kodak's decline, Rochester, like other cities tried to become entrepreneurial. It had its adventures with the creation of an entertainment district. In the 1990s, the city hired the firm that had helped develop Baltimore's successful harbor front development, to develop the historic High Falls area on the Genesee River.[26] With its scenic views and historical significance in Rochester's early development, it certainly seemed to hold promise. However, the developer pulled out of the project early on and another had to be brought in to complete the project. It was a dismal failure. Despite the significant investment—20 million dollars was put into the area—and some initial success, the project failed in little more than a decade. To be sure, the area has seen an influx of architectural firms and office space is well occupied; but as an economic engine of tourism, it must be judged a failure. It was plagued with poor planning from the beginning, relying on several large bars and restaurants not a variety of smaller ones which would have encouraged more return visits. Lack of parking proved another limit. It also was out of the way according to some and not near residential areas where locals gather. But perhaps the biggest problem is that there is a limit to the amount of dollars that tourism and entertainment can bring, especially in area with shrinking income like

[24] Michelle York, "Mean Streets of New York? Increasingly, They're Found in Rochester," *New York Times* Dec. 24, 2003. https://www.nytimes.com/2003/12/24/nyregion/mean-streets-of-new-york-increasingly-they-re-found-in-rochester.html

[25] Brookings institute, *The Enduring Challenge of Poverty in America: Case Studies from Communities Across the US, 2008.* https://www.brookings.edu/wp-content/uploads/2016/06/1024_concentrated_poverty.pdf

[26] Pierre Clavel, "Rochester's Two Faces of Regionalism: 1993-2006, "in Michael I. J. Bennett and Robert P. Giloth eds., *Economic development in American cities: the pursuit of an equity agenda* (Albany: SUNY Press 2007).

Rochester. More recent attempts like the Parcel 5 area left over from the demolition of parts of Rochester's Midtown Plaza has proved difficult to develop.

Floating in a Sinkhole of Debt

The most notorious attempt to create an entertainment venue in Rochester, however, was the fast ferry project.[27] The idea of creating a ferry service between Rochester and Toronto was floated in the 1990s. Certainly there was enthusiasm in Rochester. Toronto was a popular destination with upstate residents. It had cultural amenities, a bustling downtown area, abundant entertainment, fine restaurants, as well as major league sport teams. Canadians also spent quite a bit of money in the US. At the time, there were about 41 million trips to the States per year by Canadians. Western New York was a gateway for much of this travel. For Rochester proponents the Ferry promised to cut time out of usual car travel and greater saving over rail or bus travel.

When the project was being considered in 2000, the city solicited proposals for operating the ferry and running the Port of Rochester. They sent out requests to 39 groups but only 4 were interested. They asked two of these for full proposals but only one responded, Canadian American Transport Systems (CATS), and they received the contract. CATS was headed by two former Rochesterians who had made their money at the investment bank Lehman Brothers. They had no experience in transportation. This led some local politicians and businessmen to question their ability to carry out such a large project. George Conboy head of a Rochester investment firm, who reviewed their plan, called them better deal makers than businessmen and implied that they had snookered leaders anxious for the project. The mayor, whom Conboy specifically had in mind, was enthusiastic. He thought it would change the gloomy and desperate image of post-Kodak Rochester. However, Conboy saw a lack of transparency. "Taxpayers" he noted "had very little access to the records." Bill Nojay a prominent local politician, who later had his own criminal problems, was, at the time of the proposal, head of the Rochester-Genesee Regional Transportation Authority (RGRTA). The RGRTA was asked to be the lead authority to coordinate and administer public funds; but after

[27] For the fast ferry story see Dick Halsey, "The Short History of the Rochester Fast Ferry." http://mcnygenealogy.com/book/rochester-fast-ferry.pdf

discussing the proposal with CATS, Nojay declined the offer. He felt that the operators did not have sufficient capital and would not reveal even basic financial information.[28]

Still there was a lot of pressure from the city to proceed. The price estimates seemed competitive to the city. After the city approved the project in 2001-02, a ferry was purchased for $43 million from an Australian operator, who delivered the boat in early 2004 but the project ran into immediate and innumerable difficulties. Before it even got to Rochester, the ferry had an accident in New York City opening a 24-foot gash in the hold that required repair. When it arrived in Rochester, further problems were discovered with the engines. When repairs could not be done in Rochester, it had to go to Canada, causing further delays, and the discovery of a customs problem would ultimately sink the project.

Far from being enthusiastic, Toronto authorities and the Toronto elite were indifferent if not downright hostile to the project. Apparently, Rochester authorities had not made airtight prior arrangements for a Toronto site. It took until well into 2003 to get approval for a site to put up a terminal. No one from Toronto even showed up when the boat finally had its maiden voyage. At the same time, *The Toronto Globe and Mail* (paper of record for the well to do and the business class) published an article savaging Rochester as a tourist destination. The *Globe* article viewed Rochester and its barren downtown from the viewpoint of Toronto's haute bourgeois. No doubt, it was a shocking experience for anyone accustomed to Toronto's bustling and vibrant central city, but elements of it smacked of a hit job. The author makes sport of Rochester's Nick Tahoe's restaurant and its well-known garbage plate. There were many good quality restaurants she could have sampled. She also wandered Rochester's empty and dangerous downtown which even Mayor Johnson thought was careless. Had she gone a bit further east she would have discovered the Eastman theater Eastman House (with extensive film history and archives) and several other significant museums and tourist attractions as well as better dining. Later on, she visited Rochester grocery chain Wegmans which by the time this is being written has expanded and positively received throughout the northeast. Still, she was not entirely wrong

[28] Michele York, "From the First, Rochester Ferry was Burdened by Failings in Fine Print," *New York Times* October 26, 2004; Michele York "After a Ferry Venture Fails: Criticism and Questions," *New York Times* August 21, 2006. https://www.nytimes.com/2006/08/21/nyregion/after-a-ferry-venture-fails-criticism-and-questions.html

is her view of Rochester's dismal downtown and the damage had been done at least in Toronto.[29]

The worst mistake among the many bad decisions on the ferry was the registering of the ferry as a Bahamian vessel, a common process in the US. When this was discovered by the Canadians during repairs, its foreign status meant that the ferry needed a pilot to enter US waters at $6000 a trip and Canada added on $2500 in customs fees. Due to its foreign registration, the ferry was also unable to carry commercial trucks across the border. These made a crucial difference in revenue from the ferry.

At its inception, the Ferry appeared popular. It sold out its initial runs, but ridership declined quickly and soon the ferry service was hemorrhaging money. Less than three months after starting in September 2004, CATS ceased operation. Eventually it declared bankruptcy. By the end of September, the boat was seized for owing $370,000 to a fuel company. In an attempt to save the service, the City of Rochester in early 2005 moved to buy the boat at the bankruptcy auction and operate it as a municipal corporation. The City borrowed $40 million to buy the ferry at auction, probably an excessive price. A new operator with extensive experience, Bay Ferries out of Prince Edward Island in Canada, was found and the service resumed at the end of June 2005. Like the earlier service, it was plagued by more mechanical malfunctions and not enough customers. It hit a dock and broke windows. Later, a fuel line burst and after that, it had propulsion system problems. But the worst problem was a lack of customers. It suspended service in December when it ran out of funds and the Mayor asked for an emergency 10-million-dollar loan. This funding never materialized as a new mayor took over in 2006 and decided to end the service, with the city absorbing the debt. Counting both incarnations, it ran less than a year. A subsequent investigation and audit by New York state comptroller Alan Helvesi, criticized the city administration and CATS for mismanagement. The audit found extensive missteps. The city ignored obvious red flags. They did not pay close attention to the financial problems others had identified. The city not only gave CATS the project without soliciting other bids, but it also gave a CATS related company a 40-year lease at one dollar a year to run the terminal built for the ferry project. The City of Rochester failed, the comptroller found, to do

[29] Jan Wong, "Ferry Bad Place: The good news is that Torontonians are getting an exciting new car ferry. The bad news is it's going to Rochester." *Toronto Globe & Mail* November 29, 2003. This article is reprinted in its entirety in Halsey "Short History."

sufficient planning to protect public monies.[30] As I noted in the last chapter, many of these projects were speculative. In the end, the city and state spent $30 million in public money, in addition to the loss of revenues involved in the terminal project with no visible return. The net effect of these failures was to fuel skepticism about the ability of government, especially city government, to carry out large projects and instead looked to private solutions.

Soccer Bails

A third failed entertainment project was the construction of a soccer only stadium on land in downtown Rochester. With a large Italian American population, a significant Ukrainian one, and other immigrant populations, soccer has found widespread interest in Rochester. Back in 1963, the Italian American Sports Club sponsored team won the United States National Amateur Club championship and almost repeated in 1966. In 1967, a local ownership group bought a franchise in the American Soccer League and the Rochester Lancers were born. After some initial success, it moved to the North American Soccer League, which was a division one soccer league on a par with European ones. The Lancers were a good team and won the league championship in 1970. The league had moderate success averaging upwards of 15,000 fans per match, but this average was unrepresentative since in the big franchises such as New York could draw up to 40,000 fans. Smaller franchises could not afford the salaries given to aging world soccer stars. In the eighties suffering from declining attendance, perhaps a result of recession and labor problems, the Lancers disbanded in 1980, and not far behind the league folded in 1984.

The second incarnation of soccer in Rochester came with the formation of the Rochester Raging Rhinos later simply called the Rochester Rhinos, in the Professional Level A-League. Soccer was again an immediate success; the Rhinos made the league finals in their first year and won the championship in 1998. The Rhinos drew well sometimes filling the 13,000 seats at Frontier field, home of the triple A baseball team, the Rochester Red Wings, averaging over 10,000 per date. Soccer owners, however, were not satisfied with the arrangement and wanted their own stadium. Rochester was considered the jewel of minor league sports towns both in baseball and in soccer. The owners had ambitions of moving back up to

[30] York, "Ferry Venture fails."

the National Professional Soccer League, the top tier soccer league in the country. A downtown site was secured, an empty area that was once part of the Rochester subway system. With support from some local legislators $15 million in state aid was obtained although the stadium itself would be privately owned, The city also kicked in $3.5 million in infrastructure support.

This project however, like the others was plagued with poor planning and lack of foresight. It was quickly discovered the site was a brownfield. It had water table and hazardous material disposal problems which caused delays and extra costs. Second, it had funding problems. The Rhino ownership had vastly overstated its ability to provide the private funding the project required.[31] The Rhinos ownership had originally proposed a $44 million stadium including amenities and had pledged to raise $26 million for the project. This proved unworkable and the project was scaled back several times; finally, it became a much leaner $23 million dollar version. That would have required $8 million from the Rhino investors. They could not even reach this goal and only pledged $1.5 million. The rest of the money was kicked down the road to be obtained somehow from loans and unnamed private investors. When one dissenting state legislator raised questions about the ability of the ownership group to pay for the stadium, he was told that the state had seen the Rhino ownership financials in the original proposal for the $15 million state funding and determined they were solvent. I do not think this was probably true. Some of the state legislators supporting the project relied on the ethnic voters who supported the project for their reelection. Despite the popularity soccer enjoyed in Rochester, leagues were unstable. and individual franchises were always dissolving and reforming. Attendance had ebbs and flows. If not, a red flag this ought to have been a yellow card cautioning municipal leaders to proceed carefully. A dedicated soccer stadium in a medium sized city like Rochester was hardly a safe bet.

The stadium finally opened in 2006 as Paetec Park and housed the Rhinos and women's Rhinos as well as the Rochester Rattlers lacrosse team. The latter two teams went through numerous iterations and ownership changes and the women's soccer team was sold and moved to North Carolina in 2017. In the same year, the Rattlers moved to a Dallas suburb.

[31] Christine Carrie Fien, "Is PaeTec Park on solid ground?," *CITY Newspaper* September 6, 2003. https://www.rochestercitynewspaper.com/rochester/is-paetec-park-on-solid-ground/Content?oid=2128037

Repeating a well-worn pattern, attendance was good at first, but soon after began to decline significantly threatening the viability of the stadium and the Rhinos. While its average attendance was over 10,000, by 2010, attendance was around 6000 and it dropped to 2000 by 2017.[32] There may be several reasons for this including economic recession in the years after the stadium opened, but most observers think that a major issue was its location in a deteriorating part of town. Blighted areas had moved north to the stadium area itself. Suburban residents, a major part of the soccer fan base, became increasingly uncomfortable attending games. The downtown stadium today has a few events and low-level soccer teams but generates little revenue to justify the almost $20 million dollars in public expenditures.

For metropolitan areas like Rochester becoming an entrepreneurial city turns out to be risky businesses. Municipal leaders in Rochester did not seem well positioned to assess the viability of business ventures, and often at least in the case of Rochester, employed political or even an emotional considerations to decide on projects. There was rarely a well thought out economic plan. They did not pay attention to red flags or take the time to get solid advice. It was speculative investment. Rochester was gambling with public money and like any betting the odds are stacked for the house. Local citizenry not the project creators paid the price for these failed projects.

Eds and Meds in Rochester

Rochester was somewhat more successful in following the second Ed and Meds model of redevelopment. It had several excellent universities and Colleges including University of Rochester and the Rochester Institute of Technology, and a state university college on the outskirts of the county in Brockport and several small colleges. Monroe Community College was also recognized as high quality. Strong Memorial Hospital, associated with the University of Rochester, had a good medical school and research and other hospitals had areas of excellence in cancer and cardiac specialties. Rochester General Hospital now part of Rochester Regional Health has a long-standing relationship with the Cleveland Clinic and is one of its designated Heart Surgery centers with a record of excellence. It clearly had some resources to draw on.

[32] List of Rochester Rhinos seasons, https://en.wikipedia.org/wiki/List_of_Rochester_Rhinos_seasons

Employment from medical and educational expansion did go part way to cushioning the blow of Kodak downsizing. The University of Rochester when combined with its medical facilities became the area's leading employer with close to 29,000 employees and another hospital system Rochester Regional Health was second. Wegman's food market was third, with about 13,000. Business and Manufacturing were further down the list, payroll business Paychex and Xerox with about 4000 each. Kodak dropped all the way to 16th with only 1600 workers.[33] This illustrates how fully Rochester transitioned from a manufacturing to a service sector economy. Spending for health care has increased at a much higher rate than the general economy. The per capita spending on health care quadrupled between 1980 and 2018, and health care employs about 11 percent of American workers.[34] Substituting jobs in the health care sector for those in manufacturing does not mean equal rates of pay. While medical specialists can make good salaries, many of the staff do not. According to the Bureau of Labor Statistics, "Healthcare support occupations (such as home health aides, occupational therapy assistants, and medical transcriptionists) had a median annual wage of $29,960 in May 2020, lower than the median annual wage for all occupations in the economy."[35] It by no means stemmed the increasing poverty and economic inequality in our area.

While Rochester was struggling economically, several of its suburbs were prospering. According to the *Buffalo Business Journal*, seven of upstate New York's 15 most affluent suburbs are in the Rochester Metro Area[36]—compared to two for Buffalo. The economic gap between in the suburbs and the city is large indeed.

Though the strategy of emphasizing the technological/intellectual base of Rochester in optics and related areas, has brought in a few

[33] "Rochester's Top 20 Employers," *Rochester Democrat and Chronicle* https://www.democratandchronicle.com/story/money/2017/11/09/rochesters-top-20-employers/849683001/

[34] Ryan Nunn, Jana Parsons, and Jay Shambaugh, "A Dozen Facts about the Economics of the US Health Care System," *Brookings Institute* March 10, 2020 https://www.brookings.edu/research/a-dozen-facts-about-the-economics-of-the-u-s-health-care-system/

[35] Healthcare Occupations: Occupational Outlook Handbook: U.S. Bureau of Labor Statistics (bls.gov)

[36] "Upstate New York's Most Affluent Communities," *Buffalo Business Journal* June 26, 2014, http://www.bizjournals.com/buffalo/gallery/48031

high-tech startups and other businesses the idea that the Rochester area is rebounding does not stand up. Most of these businesses do not produce many quality jobs. For example, Excellus a company that has built on Kodak technology to build lenses and parts occupies 16,000 feet in Kodak Park, but only employs 80 people. [37] Most of the work is done by machines. An expensive and ambitious tech center was announced with fanfare at a local industrial park but the state administrator in charge, SUNY-Polytechnic president Alain Kaloyeros, was dismissed over corruption and bid rigging charges of which he was ultimately convicted, so the project came to naught.[38] The good blue-collar jobs of the past are not being created by these startups. On the contrary, the ACT report contended that economic security in our regions is declining.

Industrial Devlopment Authority (IDA's) and Local Favoritism

Another one of the major responses of local government has been to provide tax breaks as an incentive to industries to start up, relocate, or make improvements which add jobs through the local agency COMIDA (County of Monroe Industrial Development Agency). The grants were supposed to be closely tied to job creation, but in many cases, few jobs were created, and money not recouped. Many times, COMIDA grants allowed companies to move within the Rochester area, but not to create new jobs. These grants were more of a rearguard action to prevent companies from fleeing that pitted the City and Suburbs against one another, A good example of this was a COMIDA grant given to The *Rochester Democrat and Chronicle* to move its printing operations from the City to the Town of Greece. While the new plant is no doubt more modern, it actually led to a reduction of jobs due to the new technologies as well as lost income for the city. It worked to shrink an already declining city property tax base.

There is much debate whether these grants work under the best conditions, but in Rochester, the situation is even clearer. COMIDA has often

[37] David Greene, "Rochester Focuses on A New Picture of American Manufacturing," *NPR* Sept 29, 2014. http://www.npr.org/2014/09/29/351522788/rochester-focuses-on-a-new-picture-of-american-manufacturing

[38] Jon Campbell, "Alain Kaloyeros, SUNY Poly founder, gets 3 1/2 years in prison in Buffalo Billion case," *Rochester Democrat and Chronicle* Dec 11, 2018. https://www.democratandchronicle.com/story/news/politics/albany/2018/12/11/alain-kaloyeros-suny-poly-sentence/2207459002/

operated as a slush fund to reward friends without oversight. Exemptions were given to large wealthy companies like Wegmans, one of Rochester's largest employers, which do not need tax breaks. Other projects like granting tax breaks to the promised redevelopment of the empty Irondequoit Mall have been boondoggles. The developer bailed on the project after a few years, and the mall went into bankruptcy. Today it is being redeveloped as a community center by the town itself. Few projects have much to do with industrial development. A database of grants compiled by the Rochester Democrat and Chronicle several years back illustrated this problem.[39] Because these projects include reductions of property taxes over several years, they have negative effects on the tax base of already struggling local school districts and municipalities. Residents bear the burden of COMIDA breaks in increased school tax rates. The Democrat and Chronicle notes "for every dollar in net IDA tax exemptions awarded in 2011, according to the advocacy group Getting Our Money's Worth, schools lost 52 cents." [40] Given the decline in economic security in our area at a time when COMIDA awarded over 221 million dollars in grants (2004-13), it is hard to see any benefit for most area residents.

Still some Rochester boosters believe that Rochester has emerged from the period of job loss from the big 3 (Kodak, Xerox, and Bausch and Lomb). The newest version of Rochester's just so story is as an emerging center of a new "knowledge based" economy. Rochester's highly educated work force and research centers combined with its spirit of innovation and entrepreneurialism have absorbed the impact of deindustrialization. Even the business friendly Rochester Beacon failed to find solid evidence of the success of this transition. Citing a New York Times article, they point to the widening gap between a few successful cities located on both coasts which attract highly educated workers and high-tech companies "and pretty much everybody" Midsize cities like Rochester are not catching up with these cities.[41] Comparing Rochester with other midsize cities such as the research triangle, the Beacon found that Rochester and other cities are lagging. Any metro area, with Rochester's level of poverty cannot be seen as a prosperous new economy.

[39] "Comida Projects" http://rochester.nydatabases.com/database/comida-projects

[40] "Editorial: Comida must shore up public trust," *Rochester Democrat and Chronicle*. February 12, 2014. http://www.democratandchronicle.com/story/opinion/editorials/2014/02/12/comida-must-shore-up-public-trust/5402609/

[41] Paul Ericson "Rochester and the 'superstar' Cities," *Rochester Beacon* July 31, 2019.

Poverty Comes to the Fore

For the last 30 years, the idea of the entrepreneurial city (or in some cases region) has been Rochester's characteristic response to its economic woes. These strategies, while they may have helped keep some suburbs prosperous, have not been able to curb the rise of poverty in Rochester. Poverty rose from the 20 percent to over 30 percent. In the mid-2010s, Rochester's Poverty problems finally became an issue of more urgent concern for Rochester area leaders and power brokers.

After years of inaction on the problem, Rochester area leaders called attention to the scope of the problem. ACT and the Rochester Area Foundation issued a report in 2013 *Poverty and the Concentration of Poverty in the Nine-County Greater Rochester Area* [42] that documented the problem. Rochester Area Foundation CEO Jennifer Leonard stated, "It is time for us to acknowledge greater Rochester's poverty so that we can begin to address and reverse its insidious effects on our education, economy and future as a region."[43] Foundation Vice President Ed Doherty went on to note: "it became apparent that conditions of poverty in Rochester are extraordinary and not just reflective of typical urban patterns," A 2015 update of the 2013 Special Report by ACT *Rochester Benchmarking Rochester's Poverty,*[44] notes that Rochester was the fifth poorest city among the nation's 75 largest urban areas, and the second poorest among cities of comparable size. Only Detroit was worse. 32.9 percent of Rochester residents live in poverty. Rochester also had the highest rate of extremely poor families with annual incomes under $11,000 a year. The rate of childhood poverty was also one of the highest in the nation.

Not surprisingly, Rochester's crime rate was also one of the highest in the nation for cities of comparable size. It had the highest rate of incarceration in New York State and most of the incarcerated were male and African American. The School to Prison pipeline was running overtime in Rochester, with many incarcerated for non-violent drug crimes. This too

[42] Edward Doherty, Principal Researcher, "Special Report: Poverty and the Concentration of Poverty in the Nine-County Greater Rochester Area," 13 https://www.actrochester.org/tinymce/source/2013%20Poverty%20Report.pdf

[43] Act Rochester, *Poverty*

[44] ACT Rochester. *Benchmarking Rochester's Poverty Rochester Area Community Foundation,* 2015

has a direct link to poverty. Once one receives a felony conviction it becomes virtually impossible to qualify for good jobs, housing, and services.

The effects of deindustrialization on the Rochester area and of its transition to lower paying service jobs were still being felt. Overall incomes in the area were in decline. The ACT report notes, "the median household income in our region was $52,200 in 2009-13, a decrease of 14% from 2000.[45] This was lower than the $58,800 in the state and $53,000 in the nation. The City of Rochester was far below the regional median, It had the lowest median income in the region just over $35,000 and the highest rate of poverty, with 33% of its residents living below the poverty line." Young people were leaving the area. The number of residents in the region under 20 decreased 13 percent, and those 20-39 2 percent and 6 percent in the whole region, according to ACT Rochester. While the population of the metro area is stable, the city population has undergone a precipitous decline. Between 1950 and 2000, Rochester lost 34 percent of its population. Since then ACT Rochester notes it has lost another 4 percent to about 210,000 residents, dropping out of the top 100 US cities.[46]

Poverty has been linked to poor educational performance, and as such, much concern in Rochester in recent years has been on its underperforming schools. City schools rank at the bottom or near the bottom of the nation's school districts. Among those with over 2000 students, the City of Rochester School District was ranked the worst in the country in 4th grade math, second worst at 4th grade English, and has the lowest percentage of students who passed the New York State regents exams in Global History and The Living Environment. Although graduation rates have risen some since the report and reached a 58 percent graduation rate in 2019, this is still among the lowest in the State of New York. Another study found that Rochester City Students on average advanced only 2.9 years of academic achievement in the years between 3rd and 8th grades,[47] Most analysts argue that the combination of serious poverty and

[45] Act Rochester, *Poverty*

[46] "American Cities that are Running out of People," *Wall St.* January 2, 2011 https://247wallst.com/investing/2010/12/27/american-cities-that-are-running-out-of-people/

[47] Justin Murphy, "Why are Rochester Schools America's Worst? Study Kodak Park School 4," *Democrat and Chronicle* June 8, 2018.

resegregation of schools were a body blow to successful schools. The city had the poorest school district in New York State.[48]

Federal legislation compounded the problem. Punitive legislation like No Child Left Behind meant that many Rochester schools landed on the state's list of poor performing schools and were in danger of being closed.[49] A number of schools were closed or forced to restructure. The situation became so desperate that a New York State distinguished scholar was appointed to examine the district. While there have a been a few small improvements, there was little progress made in addressing significant problems. The distinguished scholars report listed 84 specific recommendations for improvement.[50] Many of these had to do with organization: the district has had seven superintendents in recent years all with different programs (several more since the report), leading to fragmentation and a seemingly dysfunctional and ineffective school board. However, the biggest problem was financial. Not only does the city have a limited tax base, but it had also not done well in the competition for state funds. It has not received the support it needs. Recently the district discovered a 30-million-dollar budget hole which had led to mid-year teacher dismissals and layoffs.[51] While there is no doubt some serious oversight issues involved, equally to blame is a skewed school state aid programs that favors well off downstate districts, over the neediest ones.[52]

While Rochester avoided the fate of Detroit in becoming subject to an austerity driven state takeover, it had according to a 2013 New York State

[48] Justin Murphy, "Rochester Graduation Rate Up Slightly," *Rochester Democrat and Chronicle* December 18, 2014. http://www.democratandchronicle.com/story/news/2014/12/18/rochester-graduation-rate/20585707/

[49] Jon Campbell, "Some New York Schools Could Face Takeover." *Rochester Democrat and Chronicle* April 6, 2015. http://www.democratandchronicle.com/story/news/2015/04/06/school-takeover-new-york-state/25382697/

[50] *Rochester Distinguished Educator Report: 84 Recommendations to Improve Student Learning and District Operations* (New York State Education Department Nov 14, 2018). http://www.nysed.gov/news/2018/rochester-distinguished-educator-report-84-recommendations-improve-student-learning-and

[51] Justin Murphy, "Sources: RCSD short by up to $50 million; layoffs coming," *Democrat and Chronicle* Sept 21, 2019. https://www.democratandchronicle.com/story/news/education/2019/09/21/rcsd-rochester-school-district-short-50-million-budget-layoffs-warren-layoff/2402982001/

[52] Joseph Spector, "Why NY's school-aid formula is flunking," *Poughkeepsie Journal* Aug 25, 2018. https://www.poughkeepsiejournal.com/story/news/local/new-york/2016/08/25/nys-school-aid-formula-flunking/89314776/

report, a high debt level and a moderately reduced credit rating.[53] However, austerity did lead to in effect a soft take over of schools by the state and its appointed overseer.

Like other areas in which white flight has been significant, the greater Rochester area is highly segregated. A study identifying the nations' most segregated school boundaries found that five of the adjacent suburban school districts that border the Rochester School district, are among the most segregated in the country including the most segregated border in the country between Rochester and the Town of Penfield. [54] Penfield schools had a poverty rate of 5 percent and a median household income of over $80.000. In contrast, the City of Rochester schools had a 47 percent poverty rate and a median income of $32,000. Ninety percent of Rochester School Children are nonwhites, the figure is 16 percent in Penfield. As the authors note, Penfield was able to achieve this end through exclusionary zoning, banning new construction of multifamily homes, and setting minimum sizes for homes and yards. As noted before Monroe county has a history of restrictive covenants through the first half of the twentieth century.[55] Heavy reliance on property taxes to fund schools also played a role. Keeping property values high while they declined in the city meant Penfield was able to keep money flowing for schools and keep out needier students. Observers have noted that segregation in areas like upstate New York,

[53] Thomas Dinapoli, 2013 Fiscal Profile City of Rochester, Office of the New York State Comptroller, 2013, https://www.osc.state.ny.us/files/local-government/publications/pdf/rochester.pdf. By 2021 the rating was further restored Justin Murphy, "City of Rochester credit outlook restored after RCSD gains", *Rochester Democrat and Chronicle* March 30, 2021. https://www.democratandchronicle.com/story/news/2021/03/30/rochester-ny-moodys-credit-rating-restored-rcsd-monitor/7052826002/

[54] Lauren Camera, "Report: Rust Belt, Deep South Home to Most Economically Segregated School Districts," *US News and World Report* Jan. 22, 2020. https://www.usnews.com/news/education-news/articles/2020-01-22/report-rust-belt-deep-south-home-to-most-economically-segregated-school-districts?fbclid=IwAR28WW-04xEV31iG-gw8JIWyzOCXlf5hyM_fcVcdWzCkfEj0LevEvIwt8__A, For the report see EdBuild, *Fault Lines America's Most Segregating School District Borders* https://edbuild.org/content/fault-lines A brief Newspaper article on segregation in Rochester is Justin Murphy. "Decades of legal segregation shape Rochester city schools today," *Rochester Democrat and Chronicle* June 7, 2018.

[55] Justin Murphy, "Use of racial covenants in Monroe County property deeds was pervasive and encouraged," *Rochester Democrat and Chronicle* August 5. 2020. https://www.msn.com/en-us/news/us/use-of-racial-covenants-in-monroe-county-property-deeds-was-pervasive-and-encouraged/ar-BB17y2jj

parts of Pennsylvania, Northern Ohio, and other rust belt areas are as bad as, or worse than the south.[56]

Local agency Action for a Better Community also held a symposium in 2014 on Poverty and Economic Security to address these issues.[57] Poverty was also linked to larger issues of economic power, immigration, the school to prison pipeline, and police treatment of minorities. Relations between the police and community were also important.

The long-standing tension between the police and community seen in the 1964 riots has never been satisfactorily addressed. For many years, activists have sought an independent police review board. In 2019, after decades of struggle, they finally succeeded. Voters passed a ballot initiative approving a Police Accountability Board in which citizens seek redress against overzealous police actions. However, the ballot victory has not settled the problem. The police union waged a vigorous court battle trying to limit the review boards authority. Like most police unions across the country, they think of themselves as the "thin blue line," the guarantors of order in a disordered world. They are adamantly opposed to any form of citizen control.[58]

At the beginning of 2013, the centrist Gannett-owned newspaper, the *Democrat and Chronicle* organized a response to Rochester's racial and poverty crises that it called ***Unite Rochester***. Like most Rochester efforts, it smacked of the elitism of Rochester leadership. Unite Rochester was a group of politicians and notables from the city with some ambitious republican suburban politicians and community members, which set out to create a dialogue between city and suburbs on race and poverty. As noted, the Rochester area is rife with racism and social media discourse that was very nasty. Mayor Lovely Warren an African American woman

[56] "New York State's Extreme School Segregation," *The Civil Rights Project March* 2014, https://www.civilrightsproject.ucla.edu/research/k-12-education/integration-and-diversity/ny-norflet-report-placeholder/ES_NY_CRP_031014.pdf ; Mark Keierleber, "Haves and have-nots: The borders between school districts often mark extreme segregation. A new study outlines America's 50 worst cases," *LA School Reporter* January 22, 2020. http://laschoolreport.com/haves-and-have-nots-the-borders-between-school-districts-often-mark-extreme-segregation-a-new-study-outlines-americas-50-worst-cases/

[57] Action for a Better Community "Symposium on Poverty & Economic Security" Summary of Proceedings October 14, 2014.

[58] Brian Sharp, "Rochester voters approve Police Accountability Board, setting stage for court battle," *Rochester Democrat and Chronicle* November 6, 2019. https://www.democratandchronicle.com/story/news/2019/11/05/police-accountability-board-rochester-ny-election-results-passes-referendum-vote/4171703002/

was a special target of this hateful discourse. When she spoke out about racial isssues she was herself accused by right wingers of using the race card to foment division in the community (a trope common in the right wing media). These however, were little more than projections of their own racist motives.

However, the Democrat and Chronicles version of dialogue shared the flaws Justin Murphy highlighted. They still shivered at the rise of militant or critical positions.

The newspapers' idea of dialogue was heavy with a moralistic tone. From the beginning, this group stressed the need for civility and treated the interconnected problems of race and poverty as if they were questions of disrespectful treatment alone. The limits of this approach were even acknowledged by President Obama when he noted in an interview that racism would not be cured by polite language or by avoiding the n-word.

However, this civility often only extended to those who agreed with its moderate politics of the center and right center. Instead of trying to understand the voices of discontent, some of whom wanted to discuss structural and systematic racism and had a justified anger at the decades of inaction, such voices were simply not included in and banned from the discussion.

In the wake of the Ferguson riots, the leaders of Unite Rochester sprang into action—to combat mean language. "When the conversation turned mean and ugly in social media, on local talk radio and in letters to the editor after the Ferguson grand jury decision," the *Democrat and Chronicle* stated in a December 7, 2014, editorial: "it became obvious that something needed to be done. Quickly. Unite Rochester's newly organized Community Crisis Response Team mobilized"[59] The result of this mobilization was a civility pledge "crafted" by 25 elected officials including the mayor of Rochester, the Monroe County Sheriff, and head of the police union. The pledge does not address the manifest injustices raised by the Ferguson incident but only the anger felt and its potential for incivility; it asks us to engage in constructive discussion with others and to pledge to "overcome our differences and disagreements in a way that unites us." Without a clear diagnosis of the ills of our society, there is little chance of insight into injustices, and little chance of understanding the depth of anger that many felt. Real dialogue is more than this bland model of civil discussion. Discussion can be unruly and disruptive when confronting fixed and repressive patterns of understanding; this was something

[59] Editorial, *Rochester Democrat and Chronicle* December 7, 2014.

Reverend Florence understood long ago. Dialogue has to incorporate less organized but still vital forms of informal opinion formation that exist in society.[60]

A New Map for Fighting Poverty

By the end of 2014, it was clear that Rochester's poverty problem needed a more serious and substantial approach. In early 2015, Lieutenant Governor Kathy Hochul came to Rochester to announce Governor Andrew Cuomo's formation of an Anti-Poverty Task Force as part of a broader "Opportunity Agenda."[61] It was further elaborated in Governor Cuomo's announcement on March 15 of 2015.[62] Chaired by Joe Morelle, the then state assemblyman and Monroe County Democratic Party chairman, Rochester Mayor Lovely Warren, and the then Monroe County Executive and Republican Party leader Maggie Brooks, this bipartisan political group was given a $500,000 grant to establish a group to produce solutions to Rochester's persistent poverty problem. The initial formulation was stacked with local elites who often represented business interests and it was light on community involvement.

The governor's press release spoke of the need for economic security, family stability and the creation of opportunity for all as a condition of a more just society. It speaks of creating greater empowerment for the worst off in our society. The key to the approach can be found in the proposal submitted to the governor in November 2014. The proposal takes off from persistent problems of poverty in the Rochester area and asserts, "Despite an array of traditional anti-poverty programs and investments to raise families out of poverty, this community still faces a devastating and accelerating poverty crisis." They proposed a wide ranging "public-private partnership to address this issue, including government, the Rochester Business Alliance, major foundations, universities, human service agencies, and others." It was this large-scale alliance of diverse interests that was

[60] The notion of wild publics is developed in Jurgen Habermas. *Between Facts and Norms* (Cambridge MA: MIT Press 1993).

[61] Patti Singer, "Task force to address Rochester poverty," *Rochester Democrat and Chronicle* January 18, 2015. https://www.democratandchronicle.com/story/news/2015/01/18/task-force-address-rochester-poverty/21981175/

[62] Governor Andrew M. Cuomo, "Governor Cuomo Announces Rochester Anti-Poverty Task Force Holds First Meeting March 5, 2015," https://www.governor.ny.gov/news/governor-cuomo-announces-rochester-anti-poverty-task-force-holds-first-meeting

going to put a big dent into poverty. It can't escape notice that this was an alliance of elites, not a community based grass roots program. It was another version of what Fraser called progressive neo-liberalism.

With great fanfare, a new organization RMAPI (Rochester Monroe Anti-Poverty Initiative) was created to coordinate and oversee these efforts. Political cleavages were apparent from the start. It was never clear in what way the republican leadership was on board. Immediately Mayor Warren made demands. She stated that she wanted a director who was "authentic" and a voice of the community. If she perceived the initiative to be "Politics as usual" she would withdraw from RMAPI. There needed to be a transparent selection process.[63] The director of the program, Leonard Brock, was hired at the insistence of Mayor Warren as a condition of her participation.[64]

If Warren had withdrawn, the project would have lost most of its credibility. Brock fit the bill. He had grown up poor in Rochester and experienced the effects of poverty firsthand. His mother and other relatives turned to drugs and as a teen, he had dealt drugs. He was a father at 19. He managed however to get a degree at the local state university (SUNY-Brockport) and later a masters and doctorate.[65] He also had several years of experience in Rochester area community organizations. After a brief search, he took the helm in May 2015 with a salary of about $95,000 and several additional staff. Mayor Warren was locked-in to participating in RMAPI and praised Brock as having the drive to lead the initiative due to his life experience. He would be the public face of the initiative.[66] He took the directorship after the formation of the group, and he was saddled with a set of expectations difficult to realize. He was also placed in a political situation that was shaky from the start.

[63] Patti Singer, "Mayor: Anti-Poverty leaders need to be 'authentic.'" *Rochester Democrat and Chronicle* May 7, 2015.

[64] Patti Singer and David Riley, "Anti-poverty initiative leader named," *Rochester Democrat and Chronicle* May 26, 2015. https://www.democratandchronicle.com/story/news/2015/05/26/leonard-brock-anti-poverty-initiative-rochester-members-leadership/27957545/

[65] Patti Singer, "Leonard Brock's journey out of poverty," *Rochester Democrat and Chronicle* January 2, 2016.

[66] Singer and Riley, "Leader Named"

RMAPI set out some high expectations. The original RMAPI report set the goal of reducing poverty in Rochester 50 percent in 15 years.[67] It began with some organizational discussion groups based on list of readings provided by organizers and proceeded to enact several programs and initiatives.

After five years into the project, Director Brock announced his intention to step down in 2020. He has since been replaced by a new director. After five years under his leadership, little seems to have changed. Poverty remains as serious as ever in Rochester. The poverty rate has not significantly changed. What happened with this ambitious program? It has shown few results from its efforts and mostly in recent years, it has tried to enact a set of much lowered expectations. The original target for poverty reduction was unrealistic. According to Brock, "The communications around RMAPI, the public splash, was wrong, and that led to many false expectations and what some people have seen as failure."[68]

Brock was correct in his assessment of the inflated expectations RMAPI proposed, but it was only one element in a series of public errors it made. The secretive approach taken by RMAPI to the larger public was a PR calamity from the start. Many Rochester area residents were skeptical about its original goal. As I noted above in addition to the public reservations about government projects in a conservative post-Reagan era, the City of Rochester as well as Monroe county had a history of failures within the memory of most residents. Many doubted Rochesterians had the skill or the will to solve its problems.

Typical of the reservations of the educated Rochester class was Mary Ann Towler, editor of *CITY* Newspaper, Rochester's Alternative Weekly (though by 2015 it was no longer very alternative). Towler observed that Rochester has known about its poverty problem for a long time and has done little about it. While she applauded the idea of a bold vision, she notes that it was not as bold as it seems. Referring to features that would

[67] RMAPI, *Guiding Principles: Mobilizing our Community to Achieve Self-Sufficiency* (March 2016): 3.

[68] David Andretta, "Rochester Poverty Czar to Step Down," *Rochester City Newspaper* December 12, 2019. https://www.rochestercitynewspaper.com/rochester/rochester-poverty-czar-to-step-"down/Content?oid=11160471 For an earlier article where he also talks about misunderstanding see Christine Carrie Fien, "Anti-poverty group leader: It's time to act," *CITY Newspaper* November 30, 2016. https://www.rochestercitynewspaper.com/rochester/anti-poverty-group-leader-its-time-to-act/Content?oid=2928054

become part of the collective impact model, she notes that RMAPI aims to improve the system of delivery by integrating services and better targeting and coordinating resources. Seeking to make the system more efficient it does not propose radical reform at all.[69]

Towler was also critical of the organizational structure of RMAPI. It seemed to her cumbersome and excessively bureaucratic. Looking at the first interim report in late 2015 she noted, "this seems like a whole lot of preparation and committee-forming to tackle something that has been studied multiple times."[70]

Others were concerned about the transparency of the initiative. Participants at a December 2015 meeting expressed concern about way RMAPI would communicate to the public as did then Mayoral Candidate Rachel Barnhart. The *Democrat and Chronicle* urged Brock to "be transparent. Publish goals, report progress, answer questions, provide information, listen, and respond every step of the way."[71]

But one of the most persistent concerns was the need to show results to the public. As early as August 2015 the Democrat *and Chronicle* warned of the need to show progress and results. They were unhappy that the program did not hit the ground running and had taken too long to appoint staff and roll out a plan. Critics were concerned that the program would lose the initiative if they did not move quickly and avoid getting caught up in organizational issues.[72]

Leadership never sufficiently comprehended the force of this objection. They asked the public and the media to be patient. The public was not, nor was it going to be, patient. One of the main responses took the form of asking people to take the pledge to avoid the racially biased policies of the past and acknowledge the effects and persistence of racism. By

[69] Mary Anne Towler, "Are We Really Willing to Tackle Poverty?," *CITY Newspaper* February 10, 2015.

[70] Mary Anne Towler, "Rochester's anti-poverty report: An uninvited skeptics review," *CITY Newspaper* November 29, 2015.

[71] Editorial Board, "Good luck to anti-poverty director Leonard Brock," *Rochester Democrat and Chronicle* May 30, 2015. https://www.democratandchronicle.com/story/opinion/editorials/2015/05/30/good-luck-anti-poverty-director-leonard-brock/28172163/

[72] Editorial Board, "Anti-Poverty initiative slow to demonstrate progress," *Rochester Democrat and Chronicle* August 8, 2015. https://www.democratandchronicle.com/story/opinion/editorials/2015/08/08/anti-poverty-initiative-slow-demonstrate-progress/31328723/

promoting the awareness of racism, they hoped to keep the problem in the public eye.

Like the Unite Rochester program, this was a very ineffective and individualized approach to the structural problems RMAPI hoped to address. It was no more effective than for example the pledges by large corporations in the wake of the murder of George Floyd in Minneapolis, to withdraw support for racially biased policies and police reform. These quickly passed by the wayside when the political climate shifted. The pledge had no real force.

RMAPI also did little at the beginning to clarify the organizational model they used. Collective Impact was often presented as nothing more than a method of cooperation or collaboration. Even those involved did not fully understand it. One participant in the early discussion groups characterized it as 'odd' and had no knowledge of its character. Collective impact is much more than collaboration, which already occulted between groups in many areas. It was a new model of non-profit governance, which operated with a good deal of unaccountable authority.

RMAPI took a limited approach to poverty. In its first few years at least, it did not pursue the linkage of poverty to larger social issues like immigration policing and even the structure of the economy.

How Did RMAPI Operate

Starting with an unrealistic set of expectations to eliminate poverty, which had little chance of success, Brock and RMAPI failed to communicate to the public exactly what its structure was or how it was to operate.

RMAPI was to be governed by a steering committee described as a "who's who of labor. Faith health, education, business, and philanthropy leaders:" The committee had a "leadership team" consisting of then State Senator Joe Morelle, Mayor Warren, both democrats and former County Executive and Republican Maggie Brooks as well as the at that time United Way CEO Fran Weisberg. Brooks was replaced by the newly elected County Executive Cheryl Dinolfo.[73] It had over two hundred local organizations as supporters. Still despite the claims by leadership that RMAPI included the public, its governance structure is clearly elite driven and top down. It originally formed around six working groups, They were to report to leadership and provide proposals for programs. These did include

[73] Patti Singer, "Task force to address Rochester Poverty," *Rochester Democrat and Chronicle* January 18, 2015.

citizen participants. But what became clear is that they had little authority or control over the initiative. Soon these different groups coalesced into 3 major interests.

Another issue concerned the conflicts between equity issues and managerial outlooks. One of the working groups on structural racism stressed equity perspectives. They noted that they would measure initiatives by their contribution to equity. Another of its major initiatives in contrast stressed entrepreneurialism as the basis of community development. These are not necessarily compatible. There was a disconnect between the justice perspective and many of the initiatives, pilot projects, and the system change of collective impact. None of the latter provided a robust notion of justice. At best, the entrepreneurial model provided a notion of equity as "self-sufficiency." The latter meant adopting the perspective of a better competitor in the economic system. The lack of a well-defined notion of social justice hampered the achievement of goals that would both reduce poverty and realize racial and social justice.

As he departed, Brock tried to lower expectations and give a more modest goal for progress against poverty: he sought a 10 percent reduction in poverty in 10 years. Yet even that might be hard to achieve within the RMAPI auspices. There is scarce evidence of any impact of RMAPI policies on poverty. Some surveys showed a slight increase in poverty in 2018 and a recent one in 2019 showed a small one percent decrease.[74] These small changes could be statistical anomalies or due to a variety of other factors. In short, RMAPI has little to show for five years of work.

Brock gave several reasons for the lack of progress in fighting poverty. One reason centered on the lack of coordination and cooperation between levels of government. By this he means the tension between the republican dominated county government and the overwhelmingly democratic city of Rochester government. They have often failed to agree on goals and strategies. There was no bipartisan consensus from the start. He thought the recent election of a Democratic County Executive, Adam Bello. for the first time in a generation, would be a positive development. Unfortunately, Democratic Caucus behind the new county executive, which was one short of a majority, had within 7 months, already split into two factions.

[74]For the 2018 figures, see Act Rochester, *U.S. Census Data Show Rochester Poverty Rate and Child Poverty Rate Increases* December 18, 2018. https://www.actrochester.org/tinymce/source//Census%20Update%202018.pdf For the 2019 figures see Smriti Jacob, "Rochester's poverty rate declines slightly," *Rochester Beacon* December 23, 2019. https://rochesterbeacon.com/2019/12/23/rochesters-poverty-rate-declines-slightly/

Political interests may well have impeded some of its progress, but the problems with RMAPI were not based primarily in the external environment that RMAPI faced. They were internal to its own organization. The elite character of its organization and its status as a kind of private governance reflects more a top down agenda than one driven by those individuals and groups directly affected by poverty. While RMAPI touted the participation of community members on RMAPI committees, they were clearly juniors partners at best, playing a subordinate role or often no role whatsoever.[75] Greater standards of accountability needed to be built into its structure from the beginning. Besides its failure to clarify its mission, internal RMAPI documents obtained by a local paper claim that RMAPI also suffered from "an inability to control anti-poverty spending, slow program implementation, poor branding and concern over future funding to sustain itself."[76]

Bibliography

"American Cities that are Running out of People." *Wall St.* January 2, 2011. https://247wallst.com/investing/2010/12/27/american-cities-that-are-running-out-of-people/

"Comida Projects." http://rochester.nydatabases.com/database/comida-projects

"Editorial." *Rochester Democrat and Chronicle* December 7, 2014.

"Editorial: Comida must shore up public trust." *Rochester Democrat and Chronicle* February 12, 2014. http://www.democratandchronicle.com/story/opinion/editorials/2014/02/12/comida-must-shore-up-public-trust/5402609/

"Incomes." *Rochester Democrat and Chronicle* December 28, 2008.

"New York State's Extreme School Segregation." *The Civil Rights Project March* 2014, https://www.civilrightsproject.ucla.edu/research/k-12-education/integration-and-diversity/ny-norflet-report-placeholder/ES_NY_CRP_031014.pdf

"Rochester's Top 20 Employers," *Rochester Democrat and Chronicle* https://www.democratandchronicle.com/story/money/2017/11/09/rochesters-top-20-employers/849683001/

"Upstate New York's Most Affluent Communities." *Buffalo Business Journal* June 26, 2014. http://www.bizjournals.com/buffalo/gallery/48031

1939 NYS Commission on Colored Urban Population.pdf—Google Drive

[75] Patti Singer, "Poor to get seat in groups addressing poverty," *Rochester Democrat and Chronicle* April 7. 2015.

[76] Patti Singer, "Internal Documents reveal early challenges to Rochester anti-poverty initiative," *Rochester Democrat and Chronicle*, Dec 30, 2017.

Act Rochester. *Benchmarking Rochester's Poverty Rochester Area Community Foundation*, 2015.

Act Rochester. *U.S. Census Data Show Rochester Poverty Rate and Child Poverty Rate Increases.* December 18, 2018.

Action for a Better Community. "Symposium on Poverty & Economic Security." Summary of Proceedings October 14, 2014.

Andretta, David. "Rochester Poverty Czar to Step Down." *CITY Newspaper* December 12, 2019. https://www.rochestercitynewspaper.com/rochester/rochester-poverty-czar-to-step-"down/Content?oid=11160471

Bell, Robert. "Can memories of Clarissa Street's golden age of Black business inspire a resurgence?," *Rochester Democrat and Chronicle* December 27. 2021. https://www.democratandchronicle.com/story/news/2021/12/27/can-memories-of-clarissa-street-golden-age-black-business-inspire-resurgence-rochester-ny/6454760001/

Brookings institute. *The Enduring Challenge of Poverty in America: Case Studies from Communities Across the US,* 2008. https://www.brookings.edu/wp-content/uploads/2016/06/1024_concentrated_poverty.pdf

Camera, Lauren. "Report: Rust Belt, Deep South Home to Most Economically Segregated School Districts." *US News and World Report* Jan. 22, 2020. https://www.usnews.com/news/education-news/articles/2020-01-22/report-rust-belt-deep-south-home-to-most-economically-segregated-school-districts?fbclid=IwAR28WW-04xEV31iGgw8JIWyzOCXlf5hyM_fcVcdWzCkfEj0LevEvIwt8__A

Campbell, Jon. "Alain Kaloyeros, SUNY Poly founder, gets 3 1/2 years in prison in Buffalo Billion case." *Rochester Democrat and Chronicle* Dec 11, 2018. https://www.democratandchronicle.com/story/news/politics/albany/2018/12/11/alain-kaloyeros-suny-poly-sentence/2207459002/

Campbell, Jon. "Some New York Schools Could Face Takeover." *Rochester Democrat and Chronicle* April 6, 2015. http://www.democratandchronicle.com/story/news/2015/04/06/school-takeover-new-york-state/25382697/

Christenberry Jr, Charles, Director. *Rochester City of Quality.* Rochester Gas and Electric, 1963. https://www.youtube.com/watch?v=2yLKkxq0dH0

Clauss, Ty. "Rochester Race Riots: Unemployment and Unrest." *Reporter* (RIT). https://reporter.rit.edu/features/rochester-race-riots-unemployment-and-unrest

Clavel, Pierre. "Rochester's Two Faces of Regionalism: 1993-2006." in Michael I. J. Bennett and Robert P. Giloth eds. *Economic development in American cities: the pursuit of an equity agenda.* Albany: SUNY Press 2007.

Cuomo, Andrew M. "Governor Cuomo Announces Rochester Anti-Poverty Task Force Holds First Meeting March 5, 2015." https://www.governor.ny.gov/news/governor-cuomo-announces-rochester-anti-poverty-task-force-holds-first-meeting

Dinapoli, Thomas. *2013 Fiscal Profile City of Rochester*. Office of the New York State Comptroller, 2013, https://www.osc.state.ny.us/files/local-government/publications/pdf/rochester.pdf

Deutsch, Claudia, H, "Kodak to lay off 10,000 employees in a 10% cutback." *New York Times* Nov 12, 1997.

Dickinson, Mike. "Kodak's decades of decline: Shrinking market leads to 19-month bankruptcy, less lucrative landscape." *Rochester Business Journal* September 13, 2017, https://rbj.net/2017/09/13/kodaks-decades-ofdecline/#:~:text=Kodak%27s%20global%20employment%20topped%20out,during%20its%2030%2Dyear%20decline.

Doherty, Edward, Principal Researcher. "Special Report: Poverty and the Concentration of Poverty in the Nine-County Greater Rochester Area." *ACT Rochester* 2019:13 https://www.actrochester.org/tinymce/source/2013%20Poverty%20Report.pdf

EdBuild. *Fault Lines America's Most Segregating School District Borders*. https://edbuild.org/content/fault-lines

Editorial Board. "Good luck to anti-poverty director Leonard Brock." *Rochester Democrat and Chronicle* May 30, 2015a. https://www.democratandchronicle.com/story/opinion/editorials/2015/05/30/good-luck-anti-poverty-director-leonard-brock/28172163/

Editorial Board. "Anti-Poverty initiative slow to demonstrate progress." *Rochester Democrat and Chronicle* August 8, 2015b. https://www.democratandchronicle.com/story/opinion/editorials/2015/08/08/anti-poverty-initiative-slow-demonstrate-progress/31328723/

Eison, Carvin Director. *July 64,* ImageWordSound, 2006. https://vimeo.com/349946856;

Ericson, Paul "Rochester and the 'superstar' Cities." Rochester Beacon July 31, 2019.

Fien, Christine Carrie. "Anti-poverty group leader: It's time to act." *CITY Newspaper* November 30, 2016. https://www.rochestercitynewspaper.com/rochester/anti-poverty-group-leader-its-time-to-act/Content?oid=2928054

Fien, Christine Carrie. "Is PaeTec Park on solid ground?," *CITY Newspaper* September 6, 2003. https://www.rochestercitynewspaper.com/rochester/is-paetec-park-on-solid-ground/Content?oid=2128037

Gerling, Curt. *SmugtOwn USA* 2nd edition. Webster: Plaza Publishers; 1993, (original publication 1957).

Goodman, James. "1964 riots revisited: 3 days that shook Rochester." *Rochester Democrat and Chronicle* July 20, 2014. https://www.democratandchronicle.com/story/news/2014/07/19/roberta-abbott-buckle-rochester-riots/12855941/

Greene, David. "Rochester Focuses on A New Picture of American Manufacturing." *NPR* Sept 29, 2014. http://www.npr.org/2014/09/29/351522788/rochester-focuses-on-a-new-picture-of-american-manufacturing

Habermas, Jurgen. *Between Facts and Norms*. Cambridge MA: MIT Press 1993.

Halsey, Dick. "The Short History of the Rochester Fast Ferry." http://mcnygenealogy.com/book/rochester-fast-ferry.pdf

Jacob, Smriti. "Rochester's poverty rate declines slightly." *Rochester Beacon* December 23, 2019. https://rochesterbeacon.com/2019/12/23/rochesters-poverty-rate-declines-slightly/

Jacoby, Sanford. *Modern Manors: Welfare Capitalism Since the New Deal*. Princeton: Princeton University Press, 1997.

Katz, Michael. *In the Shadow of the Poorhouse: A Social History of Welfare in America*. New York: Basic 1996

Keierleber, Mark. "Haves and have-nots: The borders between school districts often mark extreme segregation. A new study outlines America's 50 worst cases."

LA School Reporter January 22, 2020. http://laschoolreport.com/haves-and-have-nots-the-borders-between-school-districts-often-mark-extreme-segregation-a-new-study-outlines-americas-50-worst-cases/

List of Rochester Rhinos seasons, https://en.wikipedia.org/wiki/List_of_Rochester_Rhinos_seasons

Macaluso, Tim Louis. "Franklin Florence on Rochester and Racism: Little has changed." *CITY Newspaper* September 28, 2018.

Mapping Inequality: Redlining in New Deal America https://dsl.richmond.edu/panorama/redlining/#loc=14/43.147/-77.621&city=rochester-ny

Mattioli, Dana. "Their Kodak Moments, Career Snapshots: Workers Take a Look Back as Many Struggle With Uncertainties About Family Finances, Retiree Benefits." *Wall Street Journal* January 6, 2012.

Morrell, Alan. "Whatever Happened To … Pythodd Club?." Rochester Democrat and Chronicle June 19, 2015. https://www.democratandchronicle.com/story/news/local/rocroots/2015/06/19/whatever-happened-pythodd-club/28939711/

Murphy, Justin. "1930s Rochester redlining maps show discrimination." *Rochester Democrat and Chronicle* October 26, 2016. https://www.democratandchronicle.com/story/news/2016/10/20/rochester-ny-redlining-map/92456536/

Murphy, Justin. "50 Years Ago Rochester tried an experiment with Desegregation, It lasted less than 2 months." *Rochester Democrat and Chronicle*, February 22, 2022a.

Murphy, Justin. "Decades of legal segregation shape Rochester city schools today." *Rochester Democrat and Chronicle* June 7, 2018a.

Murphy, Justin. "George Eastman's Complicated Legacy of Race Relations and Philanthropy." *Rochester Democrat and Chronicle*, June 7, 2021a. https://www.democratandchronicle.com/in-depth/news/2021/06/07/george-eastman-kodak-rochester-ny-legacy-black-race-relations-philanthropy/4755198001/

Murphy, Justin. "Rochester Graduation Rate Up Slightly." *Rochester Democrat and Chronicle* December 18, 2014. http://www.democratandchronicle.com/story/news/2014/12/18/rochester-graduation-rate/20585707/
Murphy, Justin. "Rochester Newspapers During the Civil Rights Era failed the City's Black Community." *Rochester Democrat and Chronicle.* February 22, 2022b.
Murphy, Justin. "Sources: RCSD short by up to $50 million; layoffs coming." *Democrat and Chronicle* Sept 21, 2019. https://www.democratandchronicle.com/story/news/education/2019/09/21/rcsd-rochester-school-district-short-50-million-budget-layoffs-warren-layoff/2402982001/
Murphy, Justin. "Use of racial covenants in Monroe County property deeds was pervasive and encouraged." *Rochester Democrat and Chronicle* August 5. 2020. https://www.msn.com/en-us/news/us/use-of-racial-covenants-in-monroe-county-property-deeds-was-pervasive-and-encouraged/ar-BB17y2jj
Murphy, Justin. "Why are Rochester Schools America's Worst? Study Kodak Park School 4." *Democrat and Chronicle* June 8, 2018b.
Murphy, Justin. "City of Rochester credit outlook restored after RCSD gains." *Rochester Democrat and Chronicle* March 3o, 2021b. https://www.democratandchronicle.com/story/news/2021/03/30/rochester-ny-moodys-credit-rating-restored-rcsd-monitor/7052826002/
Nunn, Ryan, Jana Parsons, and Jay Shambaugh. "A Dozen Facts about the Economics of the US Health Care System." *Brookings Institute* March 10, 2020. https://www.brookings.edu/research/a-dozen-facts-about-the-economics-of-the-u-s-health-care-system/
Olive, David. "Rochester Smug no more: Marquee firms pay high price for complacency." *Toronto Star* Nov 15, 2003. http://www.nativecanadian.ca/Native_Reflections/Smug_No_More1.htm.
RMAPI. *Guiding Principles: Mobilizing our Community to Achieve Self-Sufficiency.* March 2016
Rochester Distinguished Educator Report*: 84 Recommendations to Improve Student Learning and District Operations.* (New York State Education Department Nov 14, 2018). http://www.nysed.gov/news/2018/rochester-distinguished-educator-report-84-recommendations-improve-student-learning-and
Second Report of the New York State *Temporary Commission on the Condition of the Colored Urban Population to the Legislature of the State of New York* February, 1939.
Sharp, Brian. "Rochester voters approve Police Accountability Board, setting stage for court battle." *Rochester Democrat and Chronicle* November 6, 2019. https://www.democratandchronicle.com/story/news/2019/11/05/police-accountability-board-rochester-ny-election-results-passes-referendum-vote/4171703002/

Singer, Patti, and David Riley. "Anti-poverty initiative leader named." *Rochester Democrat and Chronicle* May 26, 2015. https://www.democratandchronicle.com/story/news/2015/05/26/leonard-brock-anti-poverty-initiative-rochester-members-leadership/27957545/

Singer, Patti. "Leonard Brock's journey out of poverty." *Rochester Democrat and Chronicle* January 2, 2016.

Singer, Patti. "Internal Documents reveal early challenges to Rochester anti-poverty initiative." *Rochester Democrat and Chronicle*, Dec 30, 2017.

Singer, Patti. "Mayor: Anti-Poverty leaders need to be 'authentic.'" *Rochester Democrat and Chronicle* May 7, 2015a.

Singer, Patti. "Poor to get seat in groups addressing poverty." *Rochester Democrat and Chronicle* April 7. 2015b.

Singer, Patty. "Task force to address Rochester poverty." *Rochester Democrat and Chronicle* January 18, 2015c. https://www.democratandchronicle.com/story/news/2015/01/18/task-force-address-rochester-poverty/21981175/

Spector, Joseph. "Why NY's school-aid formula is flunking." *Poughkeepsie Journal* Aug 25, 2018. https://www.poughkeepsiejournal.com/story/news/local/new-york/2016/08/25/nys-school-aid-formula-flunking/89314776/

Timberg, Craig. "In Kodak's town, life after layoffs: With the loss of 26,000 jobs since 1982, Kodak has taught hometown residents a lesson in Survival." *Baltimore Sun* November 21, 1997.

Towler, Mary Anne. "Are We Really Willing to Tackle Poverty?." *CITY Newspaper* February 10, 2015a.

Towler, Mary Anne. "Rochester's anti-poverty report: An uninvited skeptics review." *CITY Newspaper* November 29, 2015b.

Wiegand, Shane. "History of Segregation and Racial Policy in Greater Rochester." Landmark Society Web Site https://www.landmarksociety.org/wp-content/uploads/2019/05/ShaneWiegand_Redlining-Segregation_web.pdf

Wong, Jan. "Ferry Bad Place: The good news is that Torontonians are getting an exciting new car ferry. The bad news is it's going to Rochester." Toronto Globe and Mail. November 29, 2003.

York, Michele. "After a Ferry Venture Fails: Criticism and Questions." *New York Times* August 21, 2006 https://www.nytimes.com/2006/08/21/nyregion/after-a-ferry-venture-fails-criticism-and-questions.html

York, Michele. "From the First, Rochester Ferry was Burdened by Failings in Fine Print." *New York Times* October 26, 2004.

York, Michelle. "Mean Streets of New York? Increasingly, They're Found in Rochester." *New York Times* Dec. 24, 2003. https://www.nytimes.com/2003/12/24/nyregion/mean-streets-of-new-york-increasingly-they-re-found-in-rochester.html

CHAPTER 5

Reading Poverty

The approach of RMAPI as outlined in Governor Cuomo's statement and their early formulations can best be called progressive neo-liberalism, As noted in Chap. 1, this combines commitment to neo-liberal economic organization with a program of civil rights and equal opportunity. This combination cannot be effectively combined especially in the case of poverty. It leads to neo-liberalism by default. Addressing problems of poverty requires a vision of social rights exiled in neo-liberal thought.

The discourse of neo-liberalism permeated the RMAPI initiative. It defines the problems, provides a diagnosis, and shapes the agenda for discussion. Many of the solutions adopted by RMAPI employ neo-liberal ideas. Thus, no matter how often RMAPI embraces an emphasis on structural racism or justice, these aims conflict with their neo-liberal solutions. An economic program that inherently increases inequality cannot be combined with claims for greater equality. I want to look at some of the works on the reading list used by the study groups at the start of RMAPI's work in order to show their connection to neo-liberal discourse. While my look is selective, it indicates the diagnosis of the problems with what they see as failed approaches to poverty. Like many, they have adopted the "common sense" of the neo-liberal project, as a set of taken for granted assumptions that go unquestioned.

B. Caterino, *The Failure of the Neo-Liberal Approach to Poverty*,
https://doi.org/10.1007/978-3-031-10606-4_5

Prelude: The Policy Environment

The Johnson era Great Society and earlier Kennedy's New Frontier had ushered in a new role for social scientists in the formation of social policy. Social Scientists thought of themselves as neutral experts, technocrats, who would be able to solve difficult social problems with their advanced knowledge of social organization, and to provide policies which would serve desired ends. Expertise was beginning to be detached from political process of policy and consensus formation. This was in a way compatible with the democratic elitism of the time, which placed little emphasis on processes of public deliberation. These were challenged by participatory approaches, but that challenge was defeated.

However, the participatory model did provide an important criticism of the social scientist as technician. Neutrality was little more that loyalty to the existing social order and avoiding structural problems. By the end of the Johnson era and the rise of social protest, many social scientists and policy makers were skeptical of the power of social science to solve recalcitrant problems like poverty, even as the poverty industry grew larger. Disenchanted liberals who formed the core of the neo-conservative movement employed the left critique of the ideology of neutralism but did not take up the need for structural change. They felt that social life was too complex to change. Neo-conservatives were skeptical of the unruly character of democratic demands for participation.[1]

A second approach to policy arose in reaction to the fiscal crises of the welfare state. Neo-liberals broke from the consensus of the post war period and organized to promote a new political agenda. The new agenda did not share the neo-conservative skepticism about change. They no longer tried to work through government but began to create independent organizations in order to win the "war of ideas." Conservative foundations such as the American Enterprise Institute, the Cato Foundation, and the Heritage Foundation were privately funded by wealthy conservatives who aimed to develop explicitly conservative policy. They linked donors in business law and politics in a network that aimed at changing social policy. While there

[1] For the classic critique of neutrality, see Charles Taylor, "Neutrality in Political Science" in *Philosophical Papers 2: Philosophy and the Human Sciences*, (Cambridge: Cambridge University Press, 1985): 58-90.

are still certainly are think tanks on the liberal and even a few on the left politically they are not as effective and overtly political.[2]

As foundations became centers of policy, the power of political parties to form independent platforms declined. The grand platforms of the past that were debated by participants were outsourced to the foundations. Without platform debates, the new policy locus in foundations made policy formation largely detached from any democratic accountability. Using the networks of power that conservatives formulated, they were able to get legislation passed and policies formulated that had little popular support. The development and formulation of social policy both in its conservative and liberal variant became more and more a privilege of the well-off.

The centrality of conservative foundations in shaping the agenda for policy is undeniable. Even liberal foundations have adopted the notion of individualized solutions. Yet, the formation of such policies is rarely the result of any public discussion. In addition to conservative and liberal think tanks, a new generation of policy entrepreneurs who have made fortunes in digital technology and finance have come to prominence. Often steeped in the free-market ideology they have driven a marketization of financialization of social services and policies.

How to Read Poverty

While these readings do not represent final policy of RMAPI nor do they follow every idea presented, they are significant because they represent the range of legitimate alternatives the initial participants were to consider. As the reading list guidance notes, "The intent of this reading material is to help establish a foundational base of common language, concepts and ideas that would serve as helpful input to workgroup activities."[3] This common agenda reflected the neo-liberal outlooks of the past forty years. When RMAPI did undertake pilot programs, they followed ideas in the readings.

[2] Frank Fischer, "Policy Discourse and Think Tanks," in Frank Fischer and John Forester eds., *The Argumentative Turn in Policy Analysis and Planning* (Durham: Duke University Press 1993): 21-42. For a detailed analysis of the funding of public choice economics at George Mason University and the Heritage Foundations see Nancy McLean, *Democracy in Chains: The Deep History of the Radical Rights Stealth Plan for America,* (New York: Viking, 2017).

[3] Reading List RMAPI Secondary research on poverty (Version 5/1/2015)

What's also of note is the prominence of policy proposals from the think tanks and also individual poverty entrepreneurs in RMAPI readings. Not all, to be sure, are private groups or individuals; but I am going to focus on these proposals in order to illustrate how think thanks, foundations, and poverty entrepreneurs, which are illustrative of privatized poverty discourse and which focus on neo-liberal solutions, have an important influence on its discussion. These readings are elements of the privatized welfare state critics have noted.

Transparency was a constant problem for RMAPI, and this extended to the readings. The reading list for the working groups at the start of RMAPI was not open to the public. I had to obtain the list surreptitiously. My "informant" told me they would get into serious trouble if word leaked out. Such a reading list should hardly be a state secret.

Many of the approaches to poverty on the list view the poor as deficient or pathological in their cognitive, emotional, and moral capacities. The way to approach poverty issues is to correct these problems, through guidance by leaders who know better. Other programs sought to cushion the effects of neo-liberal privatization but did not challenge its structure. They combine this with a conservative critique of welfare dependency. This leads to a diagnosis of contemporary welfare state that is at odds with its actual structure.

There are few, if any, progressive economic approaches in this list, and too little about democracy. There are no critical approaches that analyze the macro political economy of neo-liberalism and little about the destructive effects of deindustrialization. There is no discussion of the changing role of non-profits, nor are there any historical approaches to welfare.[4]

A second concern is the way that family structure is treated. Not just individual dependency but family structure (i.e., unstable, and single parent mostly female headed families) is seen as a major cause of the

[4] Susan Greenbaum, *Blaming the Poor: The Long Shadow of The Moynihan Report on Cruel Images About Poverty*, (Rutgers: Rutgers University Press, 2015); Michael B. Katz, *The Undeserving Poor: America's Enduring Confrontation with Poverty:* Second Edition, (New York: Oxford, 2013); Richard Cloward and Frances Fox Piven, *Regulating the Poor: The Functions of Public Welfare, (*New York: Vintage, 1993); Sanford Schram, *Welfare Discipline: Discourse, Governance and Globalization, (*Philadelphia: Temple. 2006). Adolph Reed Jr., *Stirrings in the Jug: Black Politics in the Post Segregation Era,* (Minneapolis: University of Minnesota Press, 1999). Thomas J Sugrue, *The Origins of the Urban Crisis: Race and Inequality in Postwar Detroit* - Updated Edition, (Princeton: Princeton University Press, 2014).

persistence of poverty. While families are important, we must avoid the trap of the culture of poverty theories especially when they speak of family structure as a generational problem. There was little mention of the new social risks and of changes in family structure. Even within the family, it takes an individualizing approach.

One persistent line of concern among throughout the initiative was that the old approaches have failed to solve Rochester's problem. Poverty persisted at a high rate. What exactly the old approach consists of is not specified. Is it the persistence of programs from the welfare state era that are at fault, or is it the 30+ years in which a neo-liberal welfare regime has been established? From the readings given, it appears that the failed programs are largely the former. The older programs create dependency, and need to be replaced by programs that promote self-sufficiency.

Are the Poor Deficient?

A number of these readings take what has been called the deficit approach to poverty. Rather than seeing poverty as a structural problem, they see the cause as deficient qualities either in the personal behavior of individuals or a culture of poverty. Such accounts tend to see the poor as an underclass. They are a source of pathologies that generate poverty. The transition from Daniel Moynihan's earlier version of the culture of poverty to a neoliberal one requires a further move made in the Reagan era, that is, a diagnosis that subjects lack the moral outlook that fosters an obligation to work. Government officials and private welfare practitioners thus came to accept the role of the state in of disciplining welfare recipients and creating entrepreneurial subjects.

The reading list gets off to a problematic start when it recommends two books which set the agenda for its work, Ruby Payne's *A Framework for Understanding Poverty—A cognitive approach*, and *Toxic Charity* by Robert Lupton.[5] Neither of these books provides a serious sustained analysis of poverty. Payne provides a bowdlerized version of positive thinking with a culture of poverty twist. She contends that poverty is caused by cognitive frameworks, sets of behavioral expectations and rules that are often implicit. She calls these hidden rules. These cultural frameworks

[5] Ruby Payne, *A Framework for Understanding Poverty,* (Baytown TX: RFT, 1995); Robert Lupton, *Toxic Charity: How Churches and Charities Hurt Those They Help (and How to Reverse It),* (New York: Harper Collins, 2011).

prevent members of a culture of poverty from adopting values that promote economic success. Poverty then is a result of the failure by the poor to adopt the middle-class expectations that guarantee success. One of the problems teachers have according to Payne is their inability to understand the differing cognitive frameworks the poor employ. She wants to bring these frameworks to the fore as well as show how to change them.

However, Payne's understanding of these frameworks is itself problematic. She employs extensive stereotypes about the poor: they are disorganized, their homes are noisy and unkempt, and they come to school with lower vocabularies. In contrast, she takes an uncritical view of middle-class life as inherently valuable. It becomes a standard to which all should conform. Payne is quite explicit about this approach: only if the poor adopt middle class norms and behaviors (patterns of speech and decorum etc.) will they succeed. Similarly, educators and others who deal with the poor must also teach and enforce middle-class norms. It is the responsibility of educators and others who work with the poor to "teach the differences and skills/rules that will allow the individual to make the choice [to adopt the culture of the middle class]"[6] This approach supports a "deficit" theory of the poor. The poor are inadequate, because of their moral, spiritual, or intellectual deficiencies. Like some other approaches that we will discuss shortly, Payne also advocates a "Bridges" approach to poverty framework that enables people to buttress their strategic thinking skills and to follow through on their goals in the face of daily life challenges that would normally throw them off-course. In practice, these challenges are largely economic. Mentors are supposed to work to lead the poor out of their condition. The individual, however, must pledge to follow the guidelines and become a new person. This new person is modeled after the entrepreneurial self that neo-liberal's desire.

Payne's work has become influential in schools across the country, selling well over 800,000 copies of her book. Since 1996, she and her associates have run up to 200 workshops a year for teachers, reaching up to 25,000 on her method of teaching students in poverty.[7] Payne has extensively marketed and sold her approach especially to educators. Critics contend that she seems to be more interested in marketing her work to clients rather than engaging in public policy discussion of her ideas. Like

[6] Payne, *A Framework*.

[7] Gorski. Paul C.,"Peddling Poverty for Profit: Elements of Oppression in Ruby Payne's Framework," *Equity & Excellence in Education*, 41(1), 130–148

proponents of self-help programs, Payne runs her workshops as a for-profit enterprise. She reportedly makes millions of dollars on a program with a shaky intellectual foundation.

Her work has been the subject of extensive criticism for her use of the deficit approach, for the lack of evidence she adduces, as well as for profiting off poverty.[8] Susan Greenbaum for example, criticizes Payne for commercializing the culture of poverty. The orientation to individualized and therapeutic solutions has led to the rise of a poverty industry in which Payne is a major player. She notes, "With the expansive growth of private nonprofit agencies and foundations, and the increased privatization of social welfare and penal functions, entrepreneurism has blossomed."[9] Payne is the most successful of those who have capitalized on stereotypes of poor people to monetize poverty.

Significantly, Payne's approach had previously been examined in the context of the Rochester City Schools.[10] Jennifer Rogalski critically examined her method and argued that Payne used a misguided perception of students' culture as a culture of poverty. It should be corrected through "geo-literacy projects that would elucidate children's perception of their local environment and the role of their parents." She holds that such projects would reject the paternalist assumptions of writers like Payne and establish more equitable relations between teachers, students, and parents.

Payne, however, has little commitment to social justice. In an exchange with Paul Gorski who criticized Payne's lack of concern with social justice, she argues, "Gorski states that his lens is critical social theory. My theoretical lens is economic pragmatism. The two theoretical frames are almost polar opposites"[11] Payne's work represents commitment to a conservative political agenda like that of George Bush whose no child left behind received her strong support.

Payne's framework reflects paternalist assumptions with a clear class bias. Simply being a member of the lower class is pathological. In some cases, she employs ludicrous stereotypes of class and racial experience. For

[8] Gorski "Peddling Poverty, Greenbaum, *Blaming the Poor.* Randy Bomer, Joel E. Dworinm, Laura May, and Peggy Semingson, "Miseducating Teachers about the Poor: A Critical Analysis of Ruby Payne's Claims about Poverty," *College Record* Volume 110, Number 12, (December 2008): 2497–2531.

[9] Greenbaum, *Blaming the Poor*: 116.

[10] Jennifer Rogalsky, "Mythbusters: Dispelling the Culture of Poverty Myth in the Urban Classroom," *Journal of Geography* vol 108:4-5 (2009): 198-209.

[11] Cited in Gorski, "Peddling Poverty"

example, she says "The poor simply see jail as a part of life and not necessarily always bad. Local jails provide food and shelter and, as a general rule, are not as violent or dangerous as state incarceration"[12] Her adaption of the culture of poverty approach places responsibility solely on these character factors, to the exclusion of the other factors such as resources and opportunities effecting both poverty and education.

The second book is critical of current charity policies although its focus is on the private sphere.[13] For Lupton, private charity, especially that given from a Christian point of view, is problematic. Most of it fails or is wasted. It harms people instead of helping them. Its primary aim is to make the charity giver feel good. Lipton rejects aid based on notions of care and compassion. He thinks that continuing to give people charity creates an expectation of entitlement that reinforces dependency and suppresses initiative. He thinks that we ought to give charity that helps people. One of Lipton's targets is international charity in which much of the money never reaches the intended populace. Certainly, some domestic programs do that too, as do the charities that advertise heavily in the media. I think Lipton also has in mind religious based outlooks in which pity is really a thinly veiled form of disgust for the poor and others. Some of his objections to waste are true. However, compassion is not the problem but politics. The idea that the market which causes dire poverty is going to be the remedy for it lacks credulity.

One of Lipton's arguments makes sense. He believes that we ought to create coops in which the poor work and they also manage and have a stake in the outcome. To the extent that such coops are truly worker run, they might be a good thing. But a true cooperative model would have a decommodifying aspect. It would detach cooperation from private property and the market. Lipton's ideas are based less on the cooperative model than on the idea of promoting free trade and entrepreneurial values. His notion of agency is rooted in the entrepreneurial self and economic self-sufficiency. One element of his Oath for compassionate service stresses "empowering the poor through employment saving and investing" and rewarding achievement. But isn't this assumption paternalistic. The wise charity giver guides the recipient to be a good capitalist. His model of reform is allied with the approaches of moneyed interests like Warren Buffet and Bill Gates whose reforms are based in privatization. While

[12] Gorski, "Peddling Poverty": 22-3.

[13] Lupton, *Toxic Charity*.

Lipton is critical of churches as other religious based social work, he seems to think that these financial and information science leaders have benign intent. Lupton's ideas seem aligned with these projects. If there is any group of Americans that embody the idea that charity is used as an instrument of self-esteem it is the wealthy.

Since Lipton focuses on an asset building approach which encourages entrepreneurial behavior and self-help, he lacks sufficient appreciation of reciprocity and mutuality. Real autonomy requires integrating these values, not just economic self-sufficiency. He does not address deep seated economic inequalities which destroy and suppress mutuality.

Another reading that stands out on the list is an article by former Republican House Speaker Paul Ryan. He is well-known for arguing that the war on poverty has failed.[14] The latest version of Ryan's position avoids the "makers and takers" rhetoric of his earlier view, but it still largely argues that government programs create and maintain poverty. The safety net discourages people from finding work. Not only do such problems restrict individual initiative, they also promote pathological and undesirable expectations. There is still a remnant of the right-Nietzschean critique employed by libertarians in this view. The poor are a resentful lot. Give them money and they will expect it as their right. Ryan disapproves of single mothers and single mother families he thinks they are pathological. Instead, he holds up the ideal of a middle-class two-parent family with a good education as the basis for reducing poverty. One of Ryan's (like Payne's) proposals is to create opportunity grants which assign a social worker to an individual to help the individual get out of poverty. This idea appears in a different form in several other proposals discussed. However, Ryan here views government action as the cause of pathology as much as deficient culture. Governmental activity encourages pathological behavior. Yet his solution seems to create a huge social work bureaucracy, Like others, he sees the solution as the creation of entrepreneurial subjects.

In his criticism of Ryan's plan economist Steven Menendian, argues that his research shows that Ryan has fundamentally misrepresented the role of government:

> opportunity is really best understood as a series of collective resource inputs, and that government plays a critical — if not central — role in generating

[14] Paul Ryan, "Expanding opportunity in America," The full plan from 2014 can be found at https://republicans-budget.house.gov/uploadedfiles/expanding_opportunity_in_america.pdf

human capital, in providing education for citizens and preparing students for civic, cultural, and economic life.[15]

Like Lupton, Ryan's solution is more paternalist and creates more administrative intervention than the condition he wants to replace. But the larger problem is his assumption that poverty is an individual pathological condition that can be overcome by individual therapeutic intervention and remedial action. People in poverty do not just need, market oriented mentors; they need good jobs. There are not enough jobs with wages sufficient to lift individuals and families out of poverty. Here the problem is not the government as much as the market. Most welfare recipients are working poor. The market fails them. Their dependence on government aid is induced by market deficiencies.[16]

The Cato Institute paper "The work versus welfare trade-off 2013" included in this list, also repeats the view that government programs create dependency.[17] They provide a disincentive for work. While they too shy away from the view that the poor are lazy and do not want to work, they still argue that government welfare programs provide too much money to motivate people to work. (a cliché repeated again and again during the debates for COVID relief) Despite the "reforms" of the Clinton administration, they claim many states still offer benefits that exceed the minimum wage! At the time of the article, not only was the federal wage only $7.25 an hour but it was much lower in some states (prior to more recent initiatives to raise it to $15 in some states). CATO rejects any increase the minimum wage. They claim that raising minimum wages costs jobs. There is a lot of evidence to the contrary on this point, but the Cato report does not discuss these.[18] Even if their claim were to be true, one might ask the ques-

[15] Stephen Menendian, "Opportunity in America: The Problem with the Paul Ryan Plan" https://belonging.berkeley.edu/opportunity-america-problem-paul-ryan-plan

[16] Leaving aside children, nearly three quarters of adults who received snap benefits either worked or had recently worked. "Policy Basics: The Supplemental Nutrition Assistance Program (SNAP)." Center on Budget and Policy Priorities updated 2019. https://www.cbpp.org/research/food-assistance/the-supplemental-nutrition-assistance-program-snap

[17] Michael Tanner and Charles Hughes, "The Work versus Welfare Tradeoff, 2013," (Washington DC: *Cato Institute* 2013) https://www.cato.org/sites/cato.org/files/pubs/pdf/the_work_versus_welfare_trade-off_2013_wp.pdf

[18] Sarah Jones, "There's More Evidence That Raising the Minimum Wage Won't Cost Jobs," *New York Magazine* July 2, 2019; Ben Zipperer, "Gradually raising the minimum wage to $15 would be good for workers, good for businesses, and good for the economy," *Economic Policy Institute* February 7, 2019. https://nymag.com/intelligencer/2019/07/new-evidence-says-raising-the-minimum-wage-wont-cost-jobs.html

tion what kind of economy pays a minimum wage so low that no one can afford to live on it? How would work at the abysmally low federal minimum reduce poverty? Do market imperatives take priority over basic needs? Workers, especially the working poor, are clearly subordinates in the Cato playbook. They must be induced to work, by coercive means if necessary, to maintain the profitability of markets for the rest.

The Family Revisited

The work of the Annie E Casey Foundation, *Creating Opportunities* follows on the theme of the stress of poverty but emphasizes its deleterious effects on the family.[19] Poverty works in unobtrusive ways to undermine family stability and the lives of children. Parents who work multiple jobs or jobs at odd hours cannot always devote the time they need to their children. They cannot attend school conferences and functions, and they do not always have access to quality health care or day care. They cannot always get the jobs to obtain the income they need because they lack either the education or the transportation. Affordable safe childcare is a constant problem. Stable families with secure incomes are a necessary feature of childhood success. While the culture of poverty approach has even been employed by some progressives, it has not held up well to examination. Its central premise is that even with political reform many will not get out of poverty because of their cultural outlook. Yet many studies of the matter over the years seem to yield the conclusion that there is no distinct culture of poverty or mindset, but more a set of oppressive political conditions that disproportionately affect the poorest people, such as a lack of access to quality healthcare, housing, nutrition, education, political power, clean water and air, and other basic needs.[20] Culture of poverty approaches ignore questions of social power and dominance.

Family stability, according to the Foundation, is an intergenerational one. Any process of change must include parents and children to break the cycle of poverty. The Casey foundation proposes a two generational approach that addresses both the needs of parents who need jobs and

[19] Annie E. Casey Foundation, "Creating Opportunity for Families: A Two-Generation Approach," November 12, 2014. https://www.aecf.org/resources/creating-opportunity-for-families/

[20] Paul C. Gorski. "Peddling Poverty for Profit: Elements of Oppression in Ruby Payne's Framework," *Equity & Excellence in Education*, 41(1), 130–148: 135.

stable incomes, as well as the needs of children. They too see the establishment of a support network to help parents get access to educational and other resources. Workshop programs and mentoring are important in this view.

The Casey foundation, however, also downplays the political economic context of family problems. The problem is an organizational one. There is a lack of coordination and isolation of services. Often services are so specialized that they are not integrated. They recommend an integrated approach where individual can be followed and an all-access policy in which access to one service automatically allows access to all. Finally, they think that government alone cannot provide sufficient services. They advocate a process in which programs combining federal resources with non-profits or business groups, work together in preparing people for jobs and for obtaining the correct attitudes and skills for financial success. For example, "In California, United Way of the Bay Area is working with several community schools to embed programs that link parents with financial coaching, job readiness assistance and other tools, other programs stress the use of community colleges as job training grounds." This version of the deficit approach is a little kinder and gentler, and no doubt identifies some problems associated with poverty, but still, like the other approaches I have discussed, aims to make individuals more like entrepreneurs. The Casey proposal is another example of wrap around services which individualizes poverty.

Poverty and Therapeutic Intervention: Trauma as a Cause of Poverty

Trauma had been designated as a special area of concern for RMAPI. Several articles focus on this issue. They seek to identify the individual pathologies of poverty that are the result of trauma. Here deficits are not the result of poor character, but poor character and bad judgment is the result of psychic violence. It is an example of the ways that social issues are converted to neo-liberalism by default. While trauma has a potential link to larger social issues, this approach retains an individual psychological focus and proposes an individualized remedy focused on creating self-sufficiency, an individualized entrepreneurial self, and better management. In an article that leaders singled out as read first, Elizabeth Babcock in "Rethinking Poverty" argues that the stress of poverty often undermine an individual's decision-making skills.[21] She argues that "new developments in Brain Science" can show us what these difficulties are and how to change them. In order to get out of poverty with limited resources, however, the individual must act strategically and make all resources count. Reinforcing the deficit theory approach, these executive decision-making skills, she claims are lacking in poor people. They are often overwhelmed by stress. This kind of trauma is especially damaging to children and can decisively affect their learning capacities. It can have a permanent effect on brain development.

She proposes to follow a program developed at Harvard called the Bridge to Self-Sufficiency that addresses these ills. It proposes a five-step program to promote self-sufficient behavior. She also wants to employ mentoring programs aimed at helping individuals and improve their decision-making skills in the face of the daunting life challenges they face. Babcock states this "framework that enables people to buttress their strategic thinking skills and to follow through on their goals in the face of daily life challenges that would normally throw them off-course." This framework "is an EF-informed 'scaffold' structure that helps participants concurrently attain progress in the five areas that our research has shown to be pivotal to fostering economic mobility: family stability, well-being, education, financial management, and career management." The author claims this approach has showed success in getting individuals out of poverty and into jobs that pay substantial wages, upwards of $45,000.

It is no doubt true that poverty negatively impacts mental health, as does the general precarity that most Americans are beginning to face; but under the guise of new thinking, this proposal seems to rely heavily on old conceptions of individual achievement.

Babcock recognizes that the situation that the poor face involves other factors. The question of poverty is a collective one, not merely an individual one. Her solution, however, still revolves around teaching individuals economic values like self-sufficiency and proper thinking and not around changing the broader conditions that caused it. There is a tenuous link drawn between individual psychology and their basis in social structure. Babcock still thinks the remedy requires correction of individual behavior.

[21] Elizabeth Babcock, "Rethinking Poverty," *Stanford Social Innovation Review* Fall 2014. https://ssir.org/articles/entry/rethinking_poverty

It is notable that Babcock's proposal while it claims that traumatized individuals lack planning skills, nonetheless, imposes extraordinary burdens on the poor. They have to be exceptionally smart and resilient to get out of poverty, and to be more dogged and determined to become upwardly mobile. They must exemplars of economic rationality be virtuoso entrepreneurs of the self. How can they both have and lack these qualities?

The lack of proper impulse control is not exclusively applicable to the poor. Leaving aside the realm of psychopathology it is well-established that Americans of all stripes are poor savers, and many have excessive credit debt. Certainly, that is part of deliberate strategy to privatize debt, but it is debt all the same. It is hard to see how "poor executive decision making" is the major factor in poverty. Nor can we say that the rich are economically virtuous. They just begin with better life chances than the rest of us and have more resources to cope with risks. There are studies which in fact show that the wealthy are more ruthless and less ethical than middle classes or the poor. Yet corporate crime is barely prosecuted while African Americans are jailed for simple drug offenses (the double standard Wacquant noted). Few, if any, corporate leaders were prosecuted for the financial meltdown of 2007-08 in which many lost homes or savings.[22]

Babcock's optimism about the possibility of mentoring the poor into upward mobility also seems contradicted by the social trends of the last 40 years. The possibility that a child will earn more income and be better off than their parents has declined dramatically.[23] Even education, which still has a positive impact, has a lesser impact on income growth. This feature can be attributed in part to the lower wages that many Americans earn in service sector jobs. Wage growth has stagnated over the last four decades. The increasing maldistribution of wealth toward the top brackets has also limited the growth of incomes in the middle and lower class.

[22] The well-off are less ethical and more ruthless than those who are lower on the economic ladder. Greenbaum, *Blaming the Poor*: 109-114 for a discussion of white-collar crime.

[23] Raj Chetty has shown that less than 50 percent of 30-year- olds make more than their parents do. See Raj Chetty. David Grusky, Maximillian Hell, Nathaniel Hendren, Robert Manduca, and Jimmy Naran, "The Fading American Dream: Trends in Absolute Income Mobility since 1940," Working Paper 22910 *NBER Working Paper, (National Bureau of Economic Research* December 2016). Also published in *Science* 356 (2017): 398-406.

A report from the National Child Traumatic Stress Network elaborates the effect of trauma on "family systems."[24] They argued that families in poverty are subject to multiple traumas over a long time span and are less likely than the more affluent to have access to resources that allow then to "negotiate" these traumas, instead leading to "maladaptation" of families in poverty. This seems especially true for children. They have fewer internal psychological resources to deal with trauma which means that such traumas result in a greater sense of insecurity danger and anxiety. The lack of control over their environment disrupts social relations as well as generating individual pathology. Like the Casey Foundation, they stress the intergenerational character of these pathologies which work through families. Individuals who are subject to abuse and family violence have problems with emotional regulation, aggression, social competence, and interpersonal relationships, leading to functional impairments in parenting which transmit to the next generation. Social and family trauma leads to disorganized lifestyles, inconsistent relationships, and crisis coping styles.

They draw a depressing picture of poor families which documents what they see as the extent of violence. They contend that 83 percent of children in poverty report experiencing trauma as found in family violence, child abuse, or interfamily crime. Those who end up in trouble with the law or have mental health issues have higher levels of abuse and violence in their family history.

Some have proposed extending the notion of trauma to racism and its effects. According to its proponents, racial trauma can be a specific incident such as workplace discrimination or a hate crime or police harassment or brutality, or it can be a series of small cuts and micro aggressions and the effect of everyday discrimination and similar effects. While these generally do not seem to fit the classic definition of trauma, M.T. Williams, and colleagues argue that the latter can cause traditional symptoms of PTSD, such as anxiety, mood disturbances, flashbacks, avoidance

[24] Kathryn Collins, Kay Connors, Sara Davis, April Donahue, Sara Gardner, Erica Goldblatt, Anita Hayward, Laurel Kaiser, Fred Strieder, Erica Thompson, *Understanding the impact of trauma and urban poverty on family systems: Risks, resilience, and interventions,* (Baltimore, MD: *Family Informed Trauma Treatment Center,* 2010). http://nctsn.org/nccts/nav.do?pid=ctr_rsch_prod_ar or http://fittcenter.umaryland.edu/WhitePaper.aspx

behavior, and hyperarousal.[25] Sometimes specific causal events may not always come to light in therapeutic settings. While ordinary trauma is easy to grasp, microaggressions are more subtle. "These can be brief remarks, vague insults, or even non-verbal exchanges, such as a scowl or refusal to sit next to a Black person on the subway. When experiencing microaggressions, the target loses vital mental resources trying figure out the intention of one committing the act."[26] They provoke anxiety and can lead to a chronic sense of vigilance fear and paranoia. As a result, people with PTSD-like syndromes are more likely to react when other traumatic events or even conflicts occur. They sometimes see situations as more threatening than they really are. Williams notes that such experiences are not confined to a racial context, but she wants to focus on what she knows. She notes the obvious fact that African Americans suffer more incidents of prejudice than other groups and that about 9.1 percent can be said to have been traumatized, compared to close to 7 percent in the total population. Although she also notes that African Americans have less clinical anxiety than other groups, they do have higher rates of alcoholism and other stress related problems, and have less faith in the benevolence of the world.

There is little doubt that racial prejudice, along with other forms of stigmatization can generate long-lasting stress and individual psychological problems, but I wonder whether an overextension of the category of trauma really explains all the harms that the poverty and racial prejudice create. Once we extend the notion of trauma beyond the scope of specific events of violent or other singular life experiences, we risk substituting individualistic explanation for harms that are social in nature. Individual pathology displaces social issues.

Trauma theory plays a major role in the RMAPI's approach to poverty. However, as a psychological theory it is controversial. The provisional unproven nature of these ideas can be found in the above-mentioned report. At one point the authors state "There are no instruments designed to assess the influence of trauma and urban poverty on families" they recommend using other measures. Further most children exposed to trauma the report

[25] M. T Williams, I. W. Metzger, C. Leins, & C. DeLapp, "Assessing Racial Trauma within a DSM–5 framework: The UConn Racial/Ethnic Stress & Trauma Survey," *Practice Innovations*, 3:4, 2018 242–260. https://doi.org/10.1037/pri0000076. Cited in Discovering the Trauma of racism APA

[26] Monica T. Williams, 'The Link Between Racism and PTSD," *Psychology Today*. https://www.psychologytoday.com/us/blog/culturally-speaking/201509/the-link-between-racism-and-ptsd

states adapt some degree of coping strategies and function within what might be considered "normal." Other times, the report over generalizes trauma and engages in some stereotypes. The report notes that up to 90 percent of all adult's experience trauma. Whether or not this figure is correct, it leads to explanatory problems. Critics of trauma theories in psychology have pointed this out: If trauma is ubiquitous throughout the population, there ought to be far more mental illness than currently exists. While trauma can be a factor in many mental illnesses, it is fair to wonder whether more than trauma is involved in the pathology of poor families. Many people have traumatic experiences without suffering debilitating PTSD. None of this is meant to minimize the effect of trauma or the psychological effects of racism, but only to an over-extension of the use of trauma. A more careful analysis of the social and political psychology of racism is required along with an systematic approach to the sources of child abuse, violence against women and economic exploitation.

Asset Building Approaches

Several of the readings suggest another alternative with neo-liberal roots, the asset building approach. It was already touched upon in the discussion of Lupton's Toxic Charity. This approach was first articulated in the early 1990s by Michael Sherraden in *Assets and the Poor: New American Welfare Policy.*[27] Like other critics read here, Sherraden finds that the welfare system has failed the poor and failed the nation. While he notes that welfare transfers have reduced poverty to a limited extent, this reduction is superficial. When we take away the effects of welfare transfers, we find that the pretransfer poverty rate in 1984 was not 14 percent but almost 23 percent. This was up slightly from 1965. From this Sherraden concludes that while welfare transfers can mitigate some of the effects of poverty, and perhaps avoid extreme deprivation, it does nothing to help people get out of poverty. To do so requires a different approach.

Sherraden does not employ a classical deficit approach. He is at pains to avoid the view that the poor lack motivation, or a work ethic. He rejects the views of Murray and others that welfare benefits reduce the motivations to work. There is simply no good evidence for this view. A 2015 study by the Harvard Poverty Lab undertook a cross cultural study of welfare programs in several nations. It found "no systematic evidence that

[27] Michael Sherraden, *Assets, and the Poor: New American Welfare Policy,* (New York: Routledge, 2015) (originally 1991).

cash transfer programs discourage work." Nor does Sherraden seek to eliminate welfare transfers as a whole. Many recipients are unable to work or are aged. They need these transfers to live in at least some security. Thus, he represents a more moderate version of neo-liberalism. It is one however, one that still employs neo-liberal premises.

Even prior to the Clinton reforms, he notes, many welfare recipients worked or lived in households where at least one person works. Sherraden identifies the problem with welfare programs in the demand side approach of Keynesian welfare policies. These policies, he argues, are based on increasing the income of welfare recipients. To be sure, the transfer payments can have a positive economic effect, especially in economic downturns. They exert a counter cyclical effect on the economy because they increase consumption of produced goods and services. However, if our aim is to lift the poor out of poverty, programs cannot focus exclusively on income but have to look at assets. The latter indicate the basic wealth that an individual or more often a family owns. Wealth refers to a more long-lasting stock of wealth. In order to get out of poverty families have to accumulate wealth.

The asset building approach like other approaches stresses inducing market like behavior among the poor. Saving, investment, and asset accumulation are emphasized rather than income, consumption, and spending. It is impossible, Sherraden argues to spend one's way out of poverty. While income maintains consumption, assets change the way people think.[28] They take long-term perspectives and pursue long-term goals. Too often welfare policies discourage asset accumulation. Means testing punishes those who have assets or try to save money. According to Sherraden, the asset approach which is part social welfare and part financial planning will reduce economic inequality and ultimately, asymmetries in political power as well. Asset building advocates a stakeholder approach. It empowers the poor to take control of their own lives. In this way, the asset building approach is seen as an alternative to the deficit approach.

Some versions of asset building look to the formation of community resources and suggest self-sustaining models. However, most versions retain the neo-liberal emphasis of Sherraden. They are not forms of mutualism. In the hands of the Paul Allen foundation on the reading list, the cooperative model of asset building in self-sustaining communities

[28] Sherraden, *Assets and the Poor:* 6.

becomes exclusively market driven.[29] Assets are used to build capacities for accumulation and not for seeking sustainable cooperative communities. As in the mainstream view, the emphasis is on the capacity to be frugal and to save money and manage it better. The Allen foundation also looks to families but primarily in terms of building economic capacities. In their chamber of commerce vision, asset building consists of helping small businesses with planning and finances and helping individuals to save and be savvy economic actors.

For example, such approaches have in the past supported individual development accounts (IDAs) which encourage individuals to start savings. IDA's then are seen along with some changes in housing laws to encourage homeownership. But it says little or nothing about the banking and credit policies which have put many into debt in the first place. Adolph Reed Jr. points out:

> These red flags confirm that the agenda at work here stems from a concern to create competitive individual minority agents who might stand a better fighting chance in the neoliberal rat race rather than a positive alternative vision of a society that eliminates the need to fight constantly against disruptive market whims in the first place[30]

Like other approaches on the list, the asset building one holds that the market alone can provide a solution to poverty, if it works as it should. But in creating systematic inequality, the market is doing exactly what it was designed to do. As analysts like Piketty have indicated and as the historical record shows, a free market, unregulated and left to its own devices, produces inequality. All of these approaches ignore the larger political economic structure if neo-liberalism which contains deep seated power asymmetries.

One version that seems to provide an alternative like the one Reed suggests that has some potential to escape the neo-liberal market mold is John Kretzman and John McKnight's version of asset management.[31] The asset

[29] Paul G. Allen Foundation, "Disrupting Poverty: Coming Together to Build Financial Security for Individuals and Communities," March 2014. https://www.pgafamilyfoundation.org/MediaLibraries/PGA-Foundations/Documents/PDFs/DisruptingPoverty.pdf

[30] Adolph Reed Jr., and Merlin Chowkwanyun, "Race, Class, Crisis: The Discourse of Racial Disparity and its Analytical Discontents, *Socialist Register* (2012): 149-175 at 166.

[31] John P. Kretzman and John L. McKnight, "Building Communities from the Inside Out: A Path Toward Finding and Mobilizing a Community's Assets." https://resources.depaul.edu/abcd-institute/publications/Documents/GreenBookIntro%202018.pdf

building approach sees itself as an alternative to the deficit approach stressing building capacity versus repairing damage. Kretzman and McKnight take a strong anti-statist stance that is familiar to radical critics of society. Taking a cue from critical theorists, they think the problem with these programs is the fact that are citizens are converted into clients. Here it is not economic dependency that is the result, but subordination to experts. Thus, Kretzman and McKnight are also skeptical of the helping professions including social work and medicine. Using ideas that suggest the critiques of Lasch and Foucault, each of these professional groups use their authority to shape individuals through expert knowledge.

In contrast to this bureaucratic vision, Kretzman and McKnight want to shift reform process in a community-oriented direction, where individuals and their community are self-directing. They are skeptical in the current political context about the possibility of government funding to reconstruct communities and look to ecologically self-sustaining models of community and for forms of self-organization. Sometime this emphasizes locally owned cooperatives. They employ a version of an asset building model that takes up the skills of the community and uses them in self-organizing sustainable ways. This asset building model is rooted less in the model of the large-scale market system but cooperatives which would bypass larger markets.

In a radical ecological iteration, the community asset building approach might approach the ideas of an autonomous association of cooperatives with a decidedly socialist or mutualist orientation. The nature of property would be transformed. Again, much depends on the way such coops promote decommodification. At the least, the idea might come close to those of Rousseau or Jefferson, who formulated ideas of property-owning democracy which was composed of small landholders. They both had in mind the primarily agricultural economy of their times. Such a version could present a distinct challenge to neo-liberalism and its notion of property. However, such communities in contemporary global economies, a community Jefferson conceived of could hardly be self-sustaining. This version of community ignores the way critics like Peck and others have noted the linkage of cities to the neo-liberal order. Pursuing this alternative would involve more radical social change.

Asset Building in Practice

While the version of self-sustaining communities which focus on the creation of public life has some merit, the main line of asset building approaches promotes a more neo-liberal agenda. Guy Feldman and Sanford Schram's study of an asset building program in Philadelphia has illustrated how these programs induce a neo-liberal mindset both in clients and in social workers.[32] They shape expectations to conform to neo-liberal assumptions. In their view, asset building is aimed at ending the "dependency" on the welfare state and encouraging personal responsibility by promoting market-like behavior. Such programs are especially directed at poor women who are viewed as exemplifying the dependency mentality and most in need of direction. "Asset-building discourse rests on the assumption that poverty can be reduced through savings and asset accumulation that are essential to promoting families' long-term financial wellbeing"[33]

Feldman interviewed a number of poor black women in the program, in order to determine in what way, they adopted or failed to adopt aspects of the neo-liberal entrepreneurial outlook. This interpretive approach allows us to examine the elements of shaping of the self that neo-liberal theory requires. I suggest based on this research that the aim of the program is not primarily with economic success, but with the identity of the poor. Feldman follows a discourse theory in his analysis, looking at the ways in which the structure of discourse shapes the self. It selects the elements of action that are seen as important and it influences what can be said and what cannot be said, what counts as a reason, and what is irrelevant. It seeks to change expectations, rather than reform macro socio-economic processes. In so doing, it establishes a set of acceptable norms of behavior to which the participant must conform (middle-class norms). Social workers too must adopt the discourse of the market. They have accepted this role and seek to convince and influence participants to adopt the perspectives of entrepreneurs.

Participants generally take up the view of entrepreneurial subjects and come to believe this will better them. Such acceptance is not always rooted in the success of action. Participants are induced to accept the individualist

[32] Guy Feldman and Sanford Schram, "Entrepreneurs of Themselves: How Poor Women Enact Asset-Building Discourse," *Journal of Social Policy*, Volume 48, Issue 4, (October 2019): 651—669.

[33] Feldman and Schram, "Entrepreneurs of Themselves": 652.

standpoint even when it is not actually in their economic interest, and even when they get contradictory economic advice as they did in his study.

The attribution of personal responsibility for the economic fate of the individual however, is problematic even for the individuals if they encounter the structural barriers to asset accumulation. Then the confidence of individuals wanes due to lack of success building assets.

Predatory Inclusion and Formal Equality

The problem with an individualizing approach is apparent when structural barriers are considered. One of the structural barriers the new entrepreneurs might encounter involves the financial sector. The standard story of the lack of financial success and wealth building on the part of minorities, stressed the effect of redlining and past discrimination. If one can make these practices illegal, the story goes, then the free market will take care of the rest. While it is obviously true, that redlining and other discriminatory practices have kept African Americans from accumulating wealth, it does not always follow that formal equality and the "free" market will remedy the problem. Such accounts assume that participants in market transactions have equal power or at least sufficient power to avoid unfair or exploitative treatment. But just as the pluralists assumed that citizens or groups had roughly equal power, this assumption is unfounded.

Many of the articles in the reading list suggest, at best a form of racial liberalism. It contends that African Americans (and other excluded groups) can be successfully integrated into American democracy through the combination of legal protections and the free market economy. Certainly, some version of this idea of racial liberalism is at play in the RMAPI program. I want to use the example of what was called predatory inclusion to show formal equality can lead to increasing inequality.

During the Johnson era, there were initiatives to expand minority home ownership. The Fair Housing Act of 1968 banned discrimination in the rental, sale, and financing of housing. Discrimination on the basis of race, sex, religion, and national origin were declared illegal, with the aim of promoting integration. While the legal commitment to equality and inclusion should not be minimized, it proved insufficient. It failed to promote greater integration instead generating predatory inclusion.

Though its legal intention was clear, politically speaking the motivation behind the law was not always equality, but the blunting of protest potentials in minority communities.[34] Insufficient attention was paid to existing real estate practices that took advantage of poor and minorities, and which were able to circumvent formal laws. Instead of promoting real equality, they gamed the laws. Financial institutions and Real Estate interests were able to take advantage of the new situation. They made extensive profits off the new rules of housing, while further impoverishing black families. According to Taylor

> The suggestion that African American's equality in the real estate market could be achieved by the formal end to housing discrimination failed to take into account the very ways that racial inequality was structured and embedded within the architecture of the system of buying and selling real estate in the United States.[35]

When HUD was transformed from an agency that sought to provide public housing to one that looked to provision for needs through the market, it engaged in a number of the private public partnerships prevalent in neo-liberalism. One effect of these public private partnerships was regulatory capture. The latter refers to a process in which regulatory agencies come to be controlled by the very business interests they were meant to regulate. As a result of its capture, HUD did little to prevent discriminatory practices. The fact that loans to lower income clients were guaranteed by the federal government meant that there was an incentive to provide mortgages to low-income buyers with little or no risk to financial or real estate interests. Thus, loans to low-income groups often saddled them with substandard houses and they often had insufficient financial resources to repair them and pay mortgages at the same time. The result was a series of foreclosures in the seventies which further impoverished minority households. Obviously, this pattern repeated itself several times most notably in the housing bubble created by the extensive use of derivatives in the first decade of the 21st century. Once again, minority homeowners were particularly vulnerable to market crashes.

What racial liberalism as exemplified in formal equality of opportunity, fails to acknowledge is the way in which social power can circumvent

[34] Keeanga-Yamahtta Taylor, *Race for Profit: How Banks and the Real Estate Industry Undermined Black Homeownership*, (Chapel Hill: University of North Carolina Press, 2019); also, Gene Slater, *Freedom to Discriminate: How Realtors Conspired to Segregate Housing and Divide America*, (Berkeley: Heyday, 2021).

[35] Taylor, *Race for Profit*: 7

formal legal guarantees. Just as formally democratic decision making can be distorted by power that sets agendas or excludes important problems, in this case financial and real estate interests are able to accumulate power in neo-liberal arrangements. Formal democratic arrangements for example, were unable to stop the flow of big money into campaign processes. So, the larger power interests got to dictate the agendas of housing policies. To be sure, such social power has existed in capitalist societies for a long time, but it has intensified under neo-liberalism. Asymmetries in social power including wealth without being effectively regulated by considerations of justice, can override formal political rights.

But more than this, discrimination remained because it was good business for real estate and financial interests. Profit and not equality drove the real estate industry and there were no effective legal barriers. In the suburbs, implicit segregation was good business; it increased property values and the desirability of such housing to white buyers. The effects of housing segregations, including the impoverishment of certain urban areas through loss of services and amenities, are well-known. To be truly effective, formal equality requires substantial equality in social power. It has to address more forcefully structural elements of racism.

I want to return to the assumptions of asset building in the previous section. Because proponents restrict their analysis to the working of the markets and shaping the behavior of market compliant subjects, they do not or do not want to consider social power. The neo-liberal asset building approach produces a distorted understanding of the social world that ignores the effect of social power. The inability to accumulate financial resources is not the result of the lack of personal economic behavior but the result of systemic accumulation of social power (including the structural racism that concerns RMAPI) which reinforces discriminatory policy, However it is likely that given the continued existence of these asymmetries in social power that, short of any new federal initiatives which currently seem stymied, the economic security that these programs promise will remain unachievable to many. How will participants act when these expectations are not fulfilled due to structural constraints? The poor are not cultural dupes. Participants' can interpret the dominant discourse through their own experiences and could even reject it. Agency always implies the ability to do (and think) otherwise.

While racial liberalism assumes that the subject suitably equipped with, the right motivations and drive will find no barriers to success. It is more likely that such a person will run into many of the systematic barriers that still exist. Are they going to maintain the view that they are at fault or that individual effort overcomes all barriers, or are they going to reflect on dissonant experiences in which the norms of economic entrepreneurial subjectivity do not meet expectations?

Structural Racism

The questions raised by predatory inclusion bring structural racism, another point of emphasis in RMAPI, to the fore. Though there is no one fully agreed upon definition, most would include the idea that structural racism, consists of forms of prejudice that are embodied in laws, institution, and policies and not simply a prejudice held by an individual. For the Aspen Institute whose paper is on the reading list:

> The term structural racism refers to a system in which public policies, institutional practices, cultural representations, and other norms work in various, often reinforcing ways to perpetuate racial group inequity. It identifies dimensions of our history and culture that have allowed privileges associated with "whiteness" and disadvantages associated with "color" to endure and adapt over time.[36]

The existence of structural racism is often tacit and unacknowledged. We can sometimes enact structural racism without deliberate prejudice or malice. We take for granted a world in which Caucasian people hold positions of power and authority without much reflection. Only when individuals are confronted with a situation that violates these taken for granted assumptions (e.g., an African American president) that conflict may arise. Yet while this tacit understanding no doubt exists, the line between structural racism and individual prejudice is not always clear. In the previous example, banks and real estate enterprises knew quite well that redlining, racial compacts, and other practices, were racially motivated. In the current cultural moment, it has become difficult to maintain these tacit assumptions without dissonance.

The analysis of structural racism seems to require a break with the individualizing approach of neo-liberalism. The sources of racism and poverty are found in social structural barriers to equality and not in individual

[36] Aspen Institute, *Structural Racism and Community Building,* (Washington DC Aspen Institute 2004) Glossary https://assets.aspeninstitute.org/content/uploads/files/content/docs/rcc/aspen_structural_racism2.pdf

behavior. The remedy then would seem to require structural change, including the embedded inequality that generates prejudice and economic subordination. However, in the Aspen Institute definition, structural racism is reduced to a cultural framework that can be transformed by individual action or asset building approaches.

The Aspen Institute conceives of the analysis of structural racism within the bounds of racial liberalism. It seeks a race neutral society in which "racial equity can only be achieved if whites and Americans of color are equally likely to have positive or negative experiences in employment, education, homeownership, criminal justice, and all the other arenas that determine life outcomes in the United States." [37]

Though the Aspen Institute paper puts major emphasis on cultural presuppositions in the form of laws or in the form of cultural practices, structural racism is an important issue for any analysis to poverty; but the explanation of why structural racism is prominent is not well explained. Is structural racism merely a question of cultural attitudes or does it have roots in economic structure and the social power that accompanies economic dominance? Racial liberalism can too easily assimilate itself to a cultural approach. The Aspen Institute's paper assiduously avoids any extensive discussion of the systemic production of inequality, economic system to focus on the way culture operates. [38] For example, when it discusses history of slavery, Aspen stresses its origins in the cultural coding of white and nonwhite which justified taking native American lands and later, slavery. Slavery, however, began in economic exploitation around the plantation system and production of sugar. While it is no doubt true that European explorers had a mentality which saw non-Christians as heathens their motives were also largely economic both in the case of the conquest of native Americans and slaves.

While I cannot fully address the complex relations between race and class, I think there is something to be gleaned from the notion of racial capitalism found in Cedric Robinson's work.[39] He contends that racism is not just a cultural add on that has little to do with the structure of capitalism but was essential to its establishment. Capitalism and racism are thus linked if not through necessity at least through elective affinity. Understanding

[37] Aspen Institute, *Structural Racism.*

[38] Aspen Institute, *Structural Racism.*

[39] Cedric Robinson, *Black Marxism: The Making of the Black Radical Tradition* 3rd Edition (Chapel Hill: University of North Carolina Press, 2021)

structural racism requires reference to the economic purposes to which artificial and socially constructed racial distinctions were employed. Anti-racist policies are also policies that challenge the unfettered workings of the market. The Aspen analysis says little about the source of those disparities.

Without reference to racism's connection to economic exploitation, using the notion of equal opportunity does not offer much hope for reducing poverty. If neo-liberalism is an inequality machine, then the best we can hope for is a less racially based distribution of poverty. The poverty rate could still be high but distributed in a more racially equitable manner. There is no discussion of the way in which social power creates greater inequality and whether that too perpetuates racial disparities.

When the Aspen institute does approach economic issues, they employ neo-liberal assumptions. They include social impact investment that supports for profit educational schemes privatization and charter schools. It too endorses making minority groups better investors. It assumes that formal equality within a free market can solve the problem of structural racism.

The attempt to combine racial equity policies with a neo-liberal economic framework has been typical of the "progressive" version of neo-liberalism at least since Clinton. As we saw earlier, attempts by third way politicians to forge a kinder and gentler free market system has often defaulted to a crueler version. It remains another attempt to square the circle. The quest for social equity and neo-liberal economic policies are incompatible. The free market, left to its own devices, produces inequalities and generates disparities in social power which then translate into political power and domination. Not only does it generate inequalities but also vast differences in wealth and social power which are corrosive to democratic institutions. They are not compatible with the commitment to social equity. Formal equity under the law is not necessarily genuine equity in the face of significant asymmetries in social power. The Keynesian welfare state raised claims to social rights and social equity; even if it did so imperfectly, in a way that muted its challenge to the market.

Poverty and Economic Exploitation

The readings presented here reflect a neo-liberal version of poverty knowledge. Even if it is a "progressive" version of the underclass critiques of the Reagan and Clinton eras, it retains other elements of the neo-liberal thought. Many of the readings assume that poor individuals lack either the cognitive capacities or emotional self-regulation to be successful economic actors. They lack the capacity for economic agency. Neo-liberal reforms seek to create entrepreneurial subjects who can achieve "self-sufficiency." They argue that in addition to cultural barriers rooted in underclass status government programs impede the formation of effective agency by providing entitlements, expectations of support that detach them from the economic nexus. In the view of neo-liberalism, economic agency is the core of all other forms of agency. The complex notion of social agency is reduced almost entirely on economic success and carrying your own weight.

Where advocates for the welfare state point to its decommodifying function, the ability to detach some needs from the commodity system, the neo-liberal outlook thinks that the poor are not commodified enough. In order to succeed they must turn themselves into better more marketable and market compliant commodities. But this view is faulty. It equates decommodification in toto with dependence. On the contrary, such transfers can relieve the burdens caused by the pathologies that result from the free market and restore a sense of agency. Someone who is able to pay for rent, food and other bills can have a sense of agency and a sense of choice restored that was in fact threatened by these pathologies. It is the unregulated workings of the free market that cause pathology and dependency. The safety net provides a sense of security that is necessary for basic functioning in society.

Neo-liberal capitalism not only has increased the economic insecurity of the average person especially the poor, but it has also degraded the environments in which many of the poor live. It has fragmented families who cannot afford childcare services and it has robbed central cities and poor areas of needed services. It has created food and banking deserts. Poor areas are much more likely to be closer to sources of pollution and toxic waste (environmental racism). It has resulted in areas in which health is poor and health services are either lacking or unreachable. Tony Judt characterizes some of the effects of inequality thus:

> Inequality, then, is not just unattractive in itself; it clearly corresponds to pathological social problems that we cannot hope to address unless we attend to their underlying cause. There is a reason infant mortality, life expectancy, criminality, the prison population, mental illness, unemployment, obesity, malnutrition, teenage pregnancy, illegal drug use, economic insecurity, personal indebtedness, and anxiety are so much more marked in the US and the UK than they are in continental Europe ... Inequality is corrosive. It rots societies from within ... people feel a growing sense of superiority (or inferiority) based on their possessions; prejudice toward those on

the lower ranks of the social ladder hardens; crime spikes and the pathologies of social disadvantage become ever more marked. The legacy of unregulated wealth creation is bitter indeed.[40]

Bibliography

Annie E. Casey Foundation. "Creating Opportunity for Families: A Two-Generation Approach." November 12, 2014. https://www.aecforg/resources/creating-opportunity-for-families/

Babcock, Elizabeth. "Rethinking Poverty." *Stanford Social Innovation Review* Fall 2014. https://ssir.org/articles/entry/rethinking_poverty

Bomer, Randy, Joel E. Dworin, Laura May, and Peggy Semingson. "Miseducating Teachers about the Poor: A Critical Analysis of Ruby Payne's Claims about Poverty." *College Record* Volume 110, Number 12, December 2008: 2497–2531.

Chetty, Raj, David Grusky, Maximillian Hell, Nathaniel Hendren, Robert Manduca, and Jimmy Naran. "The Fading American Dream: Trends in Absolute Income Mobility since 1940." Working Paper 22910 *NBER Working Paper, National Bureau of Economic Research* December 2016.

Cloward, Richard and Frances Fox Piven. *Regulating the Poor: The Functions of Public Welfare*. New York: Vintage, 1993,

Collins, Kathryn, Kay Connors, April Donohue, Sara Davis, Sara Gardner, Erica Goldblatt, Anita Hayward, Laurel Kaiser, Fred Strieder, and Erica Thompson. *Understanding the impact of trauma and urban poverty on family systems: Risks, resilience, and interventions*. Baltimore, MD: *Family Informed Trauma Treatment Center*, 2010. http://nctsn.org/nccts/nav.do?pid=ctr_rsch_prod_ar

Feldman, Guy and Sanford Schram. "Entrepreneurs of Themselves: How Poor Women Enact Asset-Building Discourse." *Journal of Social Policy*, Volume 48, Issue 4, October 2019: 651—669.

Fischer, Frank. "Policy Discourse and Think Tanks." in Frank Fischer and John Forester eds., *The Argumentative Turn in Policy Analysis and Planning*. Durham: Duke University Press 1993: 21-42.

Gorski. Paul C. "Peddling Poverty for Profit: Elements of Oppression in Ruby Payne's Framework." *Equity & Excellence in Education*, 41(1), 130–148.

Greenbaum, Susan. *Blaming the Poor: The Long Shadow of The Moynihan Report on Cruel Images About Poverty*. Rutgers: Rutgers University Press, 2015.

Jones, Sarah. "There's More Evidence That Raising the Minimum Wage Won't Cost Jobs," *New York Magazine* July 2, 2019 https://nymag.com/intelligencer/2019/07/new-evidence-says-raising-the-minimum-wage-wont-cost-jobs.html

[40] Tony Judt, *Ill Fares the Land*, (New York: Penguin, 2010): 22

Judt, Tony. *Ill Fares the Land.* New York: Penguin, 2010
Katz, Michael B. *The Undeserving Poor America's Enduring Confrontation with Poverty:* Second Edition. New York: Oxford, 2013.
Kretzman, John P., and John L. McKnight. "Building Communities from the Inside Out: A Path Toward Finding and Mobilizing a Community's Assets." https://resources.depaul.edu/abcd-institute/publications/Documents/GreenBookIntro%202018.pdf
Lupton, Robert. *Toxic Charity: How Churches and Charities Hurt Those They Help (and How to Reverse It).* New York: Harper Collins, 2011.
McLean, Nancy. *Democracy in Chains: The Deep History of the Radical Rights Stealth Plan for America.* New York: Viking, 2017.
Menendian, Stephen. "Opportunity in America: The Problem with the Paul Ryan Plan," https://belonging.berkeley.edu/opportunity-america-problem-paul-ryan-plan or http://fittcenter.umaryland.edu/WhitePaper.aspx
Paul G. Allen Foundation. "Disrupting Poverty: Coming Together to Build Financial Security for Individuals and Communities." March 2014. https://www.pgafamilyfoundation.org/MediaLibraries/PGA-Foundations/Documents/PDFs/DisruptingPoverty.pdf
Payne, Ruby. *A Framework for Understanding Poverty.* Baytown TX: RFT, 1995
Reading List RMAPI Secondary research on poverty (Version 5/1/2015)
"Policy Basics: The Supplemental Nutrition Assistance Program (SNAP)." *Center on Budget and Policy Priorities* updated 2019. https://www.cbpp.org/research/food-assistance/the-supplemental-nutrition-assistance-program-snap
RMAPI Reading list 2015.
Reed Jr, Adolph. *Stirrings in the Jug Black Politics in the Post Segregation Era.* Minneapolis: University of Minnesota Press, 1999.
Reed Jr, Adolph and Merlin Chowkwanyun. "Race, Class, Crisis: The Discourse of Racial Disparity and its Analytical Discontents. *Socialist Register* 2012: 149-175.
Robinson, Cedric. *Black Marxism: The Making of the Black Radical* Tradition 3rd Edition. Chapel Hill: University of North Carolina Press, 2021.
Rogalsky, Jennifer. "Mythbusters: Dispelling the Culture of Poverty Myth in the Urban Classroom." *Journal of Geography* vol 108:4-5 2009: 198-209.
Ryan, Paul. "Expanding Opportunity in America," https://republicans-budget.house.gov/uploadedfiles/expanding_opportunity_in_america.pdf
Schram, Sanford. *Welfare Discipline: Discourse, Governance and Globalization.* Philadelphia: Temple. 2006.
Sherraden, Michael. *Assets and the Poor: New American Welfare Policy.* New York: Routledge, 2015.
Slater, Gene. *Freedom to Discriminate: How Realtors Conspired to Segregate Housing and Divide America.* Berkeley: Heyday, 2021.
Sugrue, Thomas J. *The Origins of the Urban Crisis: Race and Inequality in Postwar Detroit* - Updated Edition, Princeton: Princeton University Press, 2014.

Tanner, Michael, and Charles Hughes. "The Work versus Welfare Tradeoff, 2013," Washington DC: *Cato Institute* 2013. https://www.cato.org/sites/cato.org/files/pubs/pdf/the_work_versus_welfare_trade-off_2013_wp.pdf

Taylor, Charles. "Neutrality in Political Science" in *Philosophical Papers 2: Philosophy and the Human Sciences.* Cambridge: Cambridge University Press, 1985: 58-90.

Taylor, Keeanga-Yamahtta. *Race for Profit: How Banks and the Real Estate Industry Undermined Black Homeownership.* Chapel Hill: University of North Carolina Press, 2019.

Williams, M. T., I. W. Metzger, C. Leins, & C. DeLapp. "Assessing racial trauma within a DSM–5 framework: The UConn Racial/Ethnic Stress & Trauma Survey." *Practice Innovations*, 3:4, 2018: 242–260. https://doi.org/10.1037/pri0000076.

Williams, Monica T. 'The Link Between Racism and PTSD." *Psychology Today.* https://www.psychologytoday.com/us/blog/culturally-speaking/201509/the-link-between-racism-and-ptsd

Zipperer, Bem. "Gradually raising the minimum wage to $15 would be good for workers, good for businesses, and good for the economy." *Economic Policy Institute* February 7, 2019.

CHAPTER 6

Following the wrong map: From Social Enterprise to Collective Impact

The Slow Rollout

RMAPI took a while before it came up with a set of clearly defined principles though many of the areas of concern were found in the readings. The lack of early progress was a sticking point with media and the community. One of its earliest statements, *Progress Report: A Roadmap, for Change* in September 2015 lists eight workgroups around areas of concern: Education, Health & Nutrition, Housing, Jobs, Justice System, Safe Neighborhoods, Childcare, and Transportation. They claim to have extensive participation in the project, with over 200 volunteers and another 800 who responded to a survey on community conditions.[1]

By early 2016, they had settled on three guiding principles: Structural Racism, Addressing Trauma, and Rebuilding and Supporting Communities. While the readings examined in the previous chapter show, the problems are often conceived within a neo-liberal framework.

For example, the co-chairs of the Rebuilding Communities Group presented their program emphasizing adult mentoring, encouraging entrepreneurship, and increasing home ownership. They endorse the neo-liberal connected community's program I discuss shortly. This program is based on an Atlanta Program that claimed progress in reducing poverty while mostly gentrifying the area, creating charter schools which

[1] RMAPI, "Progress Report: A Roadmap, for Change," September 2015.

B. Caterino, *The Failure of the Neo-Liberal Approach to Poverty*,
https://doi.org/10.1007/978-3-031-10606-4_6

booted out poor performers, and displaced the poor to other areas of the city.[2] Another unfortunate element of the makeup of this group is co-chair George Moses. In 2021, he was convicted of defrauding three non-profit organizations which aided low-income residents and programs which provided after-school programs in the Rochester City School District while he was Chair of the Rochester Housing Authority.[3]

Co-chairs of the Trauma group think there is a lack of services to deal with traumas in the minority community. Often, authorities are slow to recognize traumas. However, the authors focus on individual pathology rather than addressing the causes of trauma. They give the example of traumatized young women who are subject to violence crime abuse and neglect, Their survival skills make them ill-suited for schoolwork. They want to focus on individualized therapeutic interventions through school and social agencies.[4]

These guiding principles were to be implemented in an action plan. According to the 2016 statement the guiding principles were to be carried out through a multi-generational focus (1) an adult mentoring plan that was meant to connect adults to employment opportunities (2) Early Childhood Supports focused on giving kids and families the best opportunity to succeed; and (3) Systems Integration which includes the design and implementation of more coordinated systems of social support that allow for a more straightforward path to self-sufficiency.[5] Issues of mentoring were to be addressed by pilot programs. While the two of the guiding principles seem to be covered, Structural Racism does not seem to be addressed. The notion of system integration really introduces a different organizational dimension I will discuss later.

RMAPI programs in fact took a while to unfold. By the end of the 2016 year, almost two years after being formed, RMAPI claimed that they would begin to implement some of their pilot programs in the second quarter of

[2] Shaun Nelms and George Moses, "Rochester Anti-Poverty Initiative: Rebuilding Community," *Rochester Democrat and Chronicle* Dec 31. 2015.

[3] "Former Rochester Housing Authority Chair Convicted By A Federal Jury On 28 Counts Including Multiple Fraud Charges, Money Laundering And Lying To The FBI," *US Attorney's Office Western District of New York* December 21, 2020. https://www.justice.gov/usao-wdny/pr/former-rochester-housing-authority-chair-convicted-federal-jury-28-counts-including

[4] Trilby de Jung and Christiana Otuwa, "Anti-poverty initiative: Ending vicious cycle of trauma," *Rochester Democrat and Chronicle* Dec 31, 2015.

[5] Rochester-Monroe Anti-Poverty Initiative, *2016 report.*

2017. However, this was already a postponement of about six months from its first timeline. There was difficulty getting people to sign up for the pilot programs. The early childhood education initiative was even further behind. RMAPI's statement of progress only states that it will "begin planning for coordination, integration and implementation to address these needs by early 2017"[6] It does not state when the public can anticipate implementation. The system integration element is similar slow to start. The end of year report only states that in 2017 they will **begin work** on system change and integration, There are no actual results to report.

RMAPI did report some funding including: $250,000 to support adult mentoring and home visitation services, $370,000 grant to move the RMAPI process to a collective impact model, $4 million for the Strengthening Working Families Initiative (supporting role), $8 million for the Health Professional Opportunity Grant (HRSA) (supporting role). However, the money from the last two did not go directly to RMAPI. What they directly received was just over $600,000.

Obtaining Funding, however, was a major issue in this report. Consistent with the principles of collective impact that I will discuss, the need for secure and continuing funding was central to the long-term existence of a collective impact project. Part of their plan then stresses the need to identify national donors and establish relationships with foundations who may want to assist implementation. They also seek to create a local funder team to meet with the state. Funding priorities are on the one hand to be aligned with state poverty reductions programs and on the other hand individual groups affiliated with RMAPI must align with RMAPIs goals in order to share in funding.

Though it is not mentioned here, these funding concerns illustrate problems with the private public partnerships that RMAPI embodies. They raise questions about who actually controls the agenda for poverty, RMAPI or its funders, The constant discussion of "alignment" also raises questions of whether the need for alignment undercuts any real forms of democratic decision making.

The 2016 reports illustrate some of the weaknesses of the RMAPI program. First, it continued to define and address the problems it seeks to solve in neo-liberal terms. Second the problems involved in the collective impact model, raises questions about the ability of RMAPI to implement its programs.

[6] Rochester-Monroe Anti-Poverty Initiative, *Implementation and Action* 2016 end of year report.

The Public and the Problems

RMAPI continued to have problems articulating their aims to the public. For example, at the 2015 meeting in which RMAPI was introduced no one could answer questions about its funding or organizational structure. During their first years it was hard to find information, and there was not enough effort put into keeping the public informed or to show results. Thus, for much of the public RMAPI was a community organization funded lavishly by the state. It could even be seen as a state organization. When it did try to communicate these expectations, leaders tried to roll back inflated expectations and acknowledge that RMAPI's role was more limited than originally indicated.

A year into its work, a survey conducted by Unite Rochester found that only 22 percent of county residents said they were "somewhat familiar" with the initiative.[7] Many had no understanding of the structure of RMAPI and its "collaboration" of health business education and government leaders. More participants in the city were aware than suburban ones, but the result of the survey highlighted the emerging communication problem that would plague RMAPI. Despite media coverage, it failed to provide either transparency or an easily identifiable program to attract public support. Brock was aware of this and agreed with the survey's finding that RMAPI had its work cut out. One respondent said that RMAPI had no online way to access information casually. It also lacked a way to appeal to suburban residents who were skeptical about claims of structural racism. It was I think concerns like these that led the *Democrat and Chronicle* editorial board to complain that the initiative lacked a charismatic leader to bring its message home to the wider public. Charismatic leadership was unlikely to arise within the managerial and bureaucratic organization of RMAPI.

Media reporting at the time reinforces the idea that RMAPI had not shown much in the way of results and had continued to suffer from poor communication. They failed to address the impatience of the public after years of inaction. Reporting in early 2016, David Riley observed that RMAPI had yet to announce any specific programs. In response, Brock noted that RMAPI had made progress in organizational matters. One of its major projects also remained unclarified and unspecified: the

[7] Patti Singer, "Few Know about anti-poverty initiative poll says," *Rochester Democrat and Chronicle* January 31, 2016.

redesigning of area social services. Riley wondered aloud about its "most potentially massive, complicated" undertaking, and the viability of funding sources.[8]

Many of these issues continued to be problems into 2017. Prior to a community meeting on May 1, organized by the league of women's voters, community members expressed continuing confusion about RMAPI programs. Georgia DeGregorio head of the anti-poverty committee of the League, observed "every time I turn around, there's another agency involved, and I don't know who the lead agency is?" She and her committee members were finding they had more questions than answers. This was especially true in the suburbs, where at a distance from the program knowledge was limited.[9] These issues took on even more relevance in the light of Singer's investigations which I report below.

Given that lack of clarity and the dearth of immediate results, there were legitimate concerns in the community about what RMAPI did and where the money went. Rachel Barnhart an investigative journalist (now a county legislator), attempted to find out exactly how RMAPI operated, how much money it got and where the money went.[10]

When investigative reporter Rachel Barnhart tried to discern RMAPI's organizational structure and funding she found resistance. One Co-Chair was miffed by her request. He criticized her "demanding tone" and asked why they had to cooperate with a "private citizen" Although RMAPI was run similarly to a non-profit they were not in fact a regulated charity organization, not officially part of the non-profit United Way which is subject to public examination. RMAPI rules of organization and their budget were not subject to disclosure. From the view of public relations, an organization like RMAPI which is given the task of addressing the Rochester areas biggest social problem ought to be accountable to the public. Securing the good will of at least a large segment of the public was going to be crucial to its success. Thus, after considering the depth of this controversy in the community, RMAPI director Leonard Brock agreed to clarify the role of RMAPI.

[8] David Riley, "Progress Report What has the anti-poverty initiative accomplished?," *Rochester Democrat and Chronicle* Jan 2, 2016.

[9] Patti Singer, "Why we should all care about anti-poverty efforts." *Rochester Democrat and Chronicle* April 28, 2017.

[10] Rachel Barnhart, "Fighting Poverty in the Cloud RMAPI has a lot of potential, but must address key problems," *Medium* Sept 22, 2017. https://medium.com/@rachbarnhart/fighting-poverty-in-the-cloud-91176a21098f

From the start, confusion reigned as to how RMAPI was funded. RMAPI was funded by an original grant of $500,000, for staff and offices and later by an operating grant of $2.75 million for five years. Later in 2018 -19 it received another $15 million dollar grant though as noted it did not administer those. It's funding however was confused with $500 million in aid given to through The Upstate Revitalization initiative, encompassed a variety of economic development programs in the Rochester/Finger Lakes area and was administered by the Finger Lakes Regional Economic Development Council. Residents thought that money had gone to RMAPI to distribute. Most of these grants had nothing to do with RMAPI or poverty related programs. Only six million went to Rochester area poverty programs, but even that money was granted to and administered by the City of Rochester, not RMAPI. Still, it faced widespread criticism for wasting money it never had. Brock saw that this misperception undermined confidence in the work of RMAPI.

The problem with clarifying the role of RMAPI, he stated, is that it does not actually do anything. It is not a social service agency. It does not carry out any social work or other activity. Nor does it distribute money. It is not a 501(c)(3) corporation and does not administer funds, although it has an influence over funding. According to Barnhart's research, RMAPI did not even have a bank account. So, the key to understanding it was through its organizational role. It was a type of umbrella organization.

The account given by Director Brock to Rachel Barnhart was confusing. It was clarified a bit later in the more business friendly *Rochester Beacon*. Originally RMAPI was under the auspices of the United Way. However, after contracting with the collective impact consulting firm FSG, RMAPI severed this direct relationship. It still retained a close relationship to the United Way.[11] RMAPI is housed in their offices, and employees of RMAPI are United Way Employees. Money from grants went directly to the United Way and grant contracts were with the United Way not RMAPI.

While RMAPI had a certain independence from the United Way, there were clear links between the United Way and collective impact programs. As Dan Duncan noted in a white paper, "The term Collective Impact is now getting a lot of attention in the United Way world."[12] Duncan's paper

[11] Smriti Jacob, "Is RMAPI misunderstood?," *Rochester Beacon* October 25, 2018.

[12] Dan Duncan, *United Way Collective Impact: The Power of RBA and ABCD, https://clearimpact.com/resources/publications/united-ways-collective-impact/#*

stresses, business strategies, like Results Based Accountability (RBA) and Asset Based Community Development (ABCD) reinforce collective impact principles. And a simple internet search yielded numerous United Way Associations across the US employing collective impact models. These included the Greater Lehigh Valley, Southwestern Indiana, Lancaster County, Northern California, Southwest Michigan, New York City, San Antonio and Bexar County, Southwest Oregon, Greater Union County. This list is by no means exhaustive. It does, however, indicate a close connection between RMAPI, the United Way and the Collective Impact model. Whether one thinks that the involvement of the United Way is a good thing or a bad thing, the denial of its central role is an example of the lack of transparency in the RMAPI project. The current web site of the United Way (2021) makes the connection crystal clear. It lists itself as the host and fiscal agent for RMAPI.

There is an organizational structure to RMAPI, but it is elaborate. At the core is a 46-member steering committee (the number at the time of Barnhart's interview) that meets bimonthly and supplies strategic oversight. Then there is an executive committee with two chairs and seven members which oversees day-to-day operation, and four working groups and two councils, one of these is supposedly made up of people impacted by poverty. However, as Brock noted RMAPI is not a social service organization (like the United Way or Catholic Charities) and does not do anything for the public. He sees its work as establishing linkage between these social service institutions. RMAPI serves as backbone organization for a collective effort. It is hard to imagine that such an unwieldy structure leads to fast or effective decision making. However, like many bureaucratic administrative institutions, it lacks transparency.

Here too Brock's assertion that RMAPI does nothing is not true or to be generous ill stated. If in fact RMAPI did nothing there would be little point in the outlays of money to run it. While RMAPI does not carry out welfare programs on its own it is the governing structure of the anti-poverty program in which programs are being carried out. It decides what programs are to be selected under its auspices and decides upon the goals of the organization. It has authority over the direction of the project. It is a structure of (private public) governance. It sets and administers policy.

Despite some nods to those affected by poverty, RMAPI takes on characteristic features of an elite-driven and not a democratically founded project; it is neither transparent, publicly accessible nor is it fully accountable to the public. It's purposes and aims are not chosen or directed by needs and goals defined by those impacted by poverty, but by goals often defined by the interests of social work professionals, foundations and their priorities for funding, business leaders and sometimes federal governments. These elitist elements are a central part of the collective impact model. Repeatedly problems of "alignment" (and not consensus) are seen as its central problems. Throughout its first five years, public accountability remained a problem.

In addition to Barnhart's investigations, a story in the December 31, 2017, *Democrat and Chronicle* by reporter Patti Singer detailed some of the struggles RMAPI had clarifying its program, its aims and implementing them.[13] The story written almost three years after the initiative was announced in Jan 2015 raises the familiar concerns that there were few if any results. Despite the impressive rhetoric of its programmatic statements, poverty in Rochester declined 1 percent in the past few years. but it was still among the highest in the nation.[14] Although City officials and RMAPI claim this as a success there is no real evidence that would lead us to conclude that this small amount of decline is the result of RMAPI programs or if other factors like a steady if slow growth in the economy begun in the Obama years was the cause or some other variation.

Although RMAPI was not forthcoming in its public pronouncements, Singer was able to obtain a progress report from the New York State Office of Temporary and Disability concomitant to a grant that needed periodic report. Groups that obtain such state grants are legally required to provide periodic reports to the state which are public and accessible through the freedom of information act. It outlined some of the difficulties that RMAPI encountered in its first three years. These included not only the public relations problems associated with the inflated aims of the program and the lack of clarity of its nature and funding, but internal organizational ones. RMAPI had major difficulties getting all groups to buy in the collective impact model, with getting partnered pilot programs off the ground (neither program had sufficient participation) with political criticism of

[13] Patti Singer, "Internal Documents reveal early challenges to Rochester anti-poverty initiative," *Rochester Democrat and Chronicle,* Dec 30, 2017. https://www.democratandchronicle.com/story/news/2017/12/30/internal-documents-reveal-early-challenges-rochester-anti-poverty-initiative/984496001/

[14] Steve Orr, "Small drop in Rochester poverty rate offers ray of hope," *Rochester Democrat and Chronicle* Dec 11, 2017. https://www.democratandchronicle.com/story/news/2017/12/11/small-drop-rochester-poverty-rate-offers-ray-hope/937193001/

the project and challenges to the autonomy of the organization, All of these represented significant impediments to progress.

By 2018, some of the frustration of media and no doubt of community leaders was apparent. In an editorial, the Democrat and Chronicle called for a "reboot" of the RMAPI program. They note that from its promising start as a model program for all New York State anti-poverty efforts, the program was entirely absent from Governor Cuomo's 2018 State of the State address a likely indicator of the disappointment with the program. Restating the results of reporter Singer's investigations, the editors state "RMAPI is struggling under the weight of community misperception, political friction, an inability to control anti-poverty spending, slow program implementation, poor branding, and concern over future funding to sustain itself."[15]

RMAPI leaders however, rejected the idea of a reboot. Ann Johnson, leader of ACT Rochester, asserted that a reset would mean that vital progress would be lost, "When you say the word reset, you've got to decide why you're resetting, Anytime you change something that's moving in a certain direction it's disruptive. And often you lose momentum." She also noted that a consultant's report had already examined the need for a reset of the collective impact model. RMAPI in 2016 stated its aim to align different services to the poor. As part of this project, they stated they intended to bring in consulting firm FSG to "help pivot the initiative towards a Collective Impact model that will strengthen and sustain implementation efforts." One of the principals of FSG is Mark Kramer co-author of the original paper on Collective Impact. According to Barnhart's investigation, this report resulted in a new governing structure.

Certainly, there were some non-organizational factors that effected RMAPI's progress, though some were of their own making. Republican county executive Maggie Brooks who had been part of the original group had been replaced by executive Cheryl Daniloff. She and I suspect other republican leaders, rejected the idea that structural racism existed, and thus were out of step with one of the main aims of the initiative.[16]

[15] "Editorial: Time to hit reset button on fighting Rochester Poverty," *Rochester Democrat and Chronicle* January 6, 2018.

[16] Jesse McKinley, "In a Picture-Postcard New York Town, Racist Incidents Rattle Schools," *New York Times* November 27, 2021. https://www.nytimes.com/2021/11/27/nyregion/pittsford-racm.html; Randy Gorbman,"Racist incidents in Pittsford are the focus of a NY Times story," *WXXI News* November 29, 2021. https://www.wxxinews.org/local-news/2021-11-29/racist-incidents-in-pittsford-are-the-focus-of-a-ny-times-stor

The slow rollout of pilot programs and the lack of buy-in by the community also posed problems. Later though, as we will see, Brock and the groups involved later touted these as successes. Although RMAPT hoped to start pilot programs in early 2016, as of the end of 2017 not enough community members had enrolled in these pilot programs to get them started.

Nearly three years after its formation the organizational framework, RMAPI seemed to have great difficulty getting all groups onboard. Singer described this as trying to herd cats. Brock interprets this recalcitrance as a changing of the guard. He claims "Many embrace collective impact—some of the older, more seasoned leaders don't understand collective impact and believe RMAPI should be governed similarly to traditional organizations. They may perceive collective impact as a lack of 'accountability' when it's actually shared responsibility." While Brock could be correct the reason for resistance could just as easily be an example of RMAPI leadership disregarding the past experiences of existing groups in the interests of "alignment," or dismissing legitimate criticisms which have been raised by many critics. Though insider information was extremely difficult to get as Barnhart and others indicate, I did find a couple of former social workers speaking off the record, who said they and the leaders of some groups found the approach untenable. There was no consensus over the value of the collective impact approach.

The organizational status of the project was further called into question. Instead of affiliation with the United Way the leaders of the Finger Lakes Regional Economic Development Council expressed interest in bringing RMAPI into the fold and making it a function of the council. Brock rejected this: He held, no doubt correctly, that such a move would subsume it under an economic development group which had fundamentally different aims. By staying separate they would be better able to respond to the needs of the poor. The one potential advantage of such a merger, a more secure source of funding, touched on a real problem. Brock admitted they had no clear contingency plan if state funding and other foundation sources were discontinued. This was just another indication of the lack of clarity with which RMAPI was founded. Not only were there public relations problems and organizations deficiencies, RMAPI was itself the subject of a turf war.

Brock was also stung by community criticism during elections. Mayor Warren felt there was a "branding" problem. The name itself seems to imply the deficit. He also felt unfairly criticized in the 2017 mayoral campaign opponents of Mayor Warren. Once again however, RMAPI did not take a public role in meeting this criticism.

Part of RMAPI's problem was in the model of collective impact itself. Far from a simple collaborative model, it is really a managerial model. Far from advocating community involvement its membership largely consisted of "leaders" if you will elites who are solving a problem **for** the community not **with** the community.

What Is Collective Impact?

The idea of collective impact is at the core of the implementation of the RMAPI project. Does it in fact provide such a powerful organizational vision that we should adopt it as the model to address poverty? Like many enthusiasts, Brock seems to think the collective impact model is the wave of the future, serving as a model program for all of New York State. Other participants use the language of neo-liberalism to characterize RMAPI. They saw it as an alternative to a "command and control" model of organization used by state socialist societies but often attributed by neo-liberals to the government.[17] It is of little notice that the federal government has been outsourcing social services for almost 40 years. Perhaps it is the outsourcing model that is the problem. It is also ironic since the fragmented nature of outsourcing and not command and control that creates a need for collective impact.

The notion of collective impact is a relatively new organizational philosophy. It was first introduced in a 2011 article by John Kanis and Mark Kramer in *Stanford Social Innovation Review*.[18] Kanis and Kramer begin from a diagnosis of the contemporary state of social change programs. Especially in the case of education, which is their major focus, social reform programs have been failures. Despite efforts to reform it, the US educational system is declining and remains ranked toward the bottom of the developed world. As of 2011 for example, it ranked 18th out of 24 industrialized nations in high school graduation rate. In their view the flaw lies, not in any pathologies of politics, economics or in the vast and savage inequalities of our educational system but in the lack of coordination of

[17] Velvet Spicer, "Anti-poverty agency seeks community's ideas," *Rochester Business Journal* April 21, 2018.

[18] John Kanis and Mark Kramer, "Collective Impact," *Stanford Social Science Review* (Winter 2011). https://ssir.org/articles/entry/collective_impact

helping agencies. The reason that we do not effectively solve social problems is an **organizational one**. Though Kanis and Kramer do not say this directly, the outsourcing and privatizing of social services is a significant cause of this fragmentation as it has resulting in a plethora of individual programs without coordination. These individual agencies have different often conflicting goals, and this defeats the chances of success. Collective Impact is the solution to this problem. It repairs the problem caused by the previous fix to the so-called problem of government inefficiency. The absence of government coordination of programs creates a new problem of coordination which collective impact seeks to solve.

One of the major examples of the success of collective impact cited by Kanis and Kramer is the case of the Cincinnati Strive program. The program has achieved significant increases in student achievement. Here groups give up their individual agendas and collaborate on a "structured process" that focused the whole educational community on a single set of goals. It creates a comprehensive approach to education. According to this idea, to achieve successful change we have to take a holistic approach and address many areas in the educational process at once. This would entail a "cradle to grave" program to improve every stage of a child's life. Such an ambitious goal requires cooperation and collaboration. However, I want to argue that such a notion of shared responsibility is skewed by the organizational framework of collective impact.

Collective impact is a method of collaborative organization that is meant to address difficult social problems. These problems are the result of "system complexity" (not social power) that is from the existence of different and sometime conflicting elements within a larger entity. According to the authors it is "the commitment of a group of important actors from different sectors to a common agenda for solving a specific social problem" Collective impact is meant to be an organizational tool for bringing about change in sectors where older methods have proved ineffective. This is the idea that RMAPI, along with the United Way and others, adopted. Kanis and Kramer state look to a form of organization that is a public private partnership, All agencies and stakeholders including government and business have to be linked under a central directive or coordinating agency behind a common goal. It is supposed to be the centralized infrastructure to serve as what the authors call the "backbone agency." RMAPI is one such backbone agency.

While forms of collaboration are not new Kanis and Kramer think that their version of collaboration is unique. "Unlike most collaborations, collective impact initiatives involve a centralized infrastructure, a dedicated staff, and a structured process that leads to a common agenda, shared measurement, continuous communication, and mutually reinforcing activities among all participants."[19]

These elements are expressed in the five conditions of collective impact as developed by Kanis and Kramer

(1) A common agenda means that, while there will always be some disagreement across a range of issues, all the leaders involved must agree on the primary goals of the collaborative initiative.
(2) Shared measurement means that data are systematically collected and reported on a set of indicators that can be used to continually assess progress and encourage learning and accountability.
(3) Mutually reinforcing activities mean that, while different partners play different roles in the system, their activities are strategically linked to the overarching plan that is determined collaboratively.
(4) Continuous communication is achieved through regular face-to-face and web-based interactions, in which partners in the initiative build relationships, trust, and shared vocabulary.
(5) Backbone support means that an infrastructure exists—including dedicated staff—independent of the project partners to coordinate, facilitate, support, guide, and mediate the collaborative effort.[20]

When these five conditions are present, effective collaboration, according to the authors can achieve "large scale system change." In a later work however, they give further criteria. The collective impact project needs "influential champions" who can make the case for the collective impact model and persuade others to adopt it, as well as the need for sufficient resources (funding) and a sense of urgency.[21] They also stress the idea of creating public will to support it through community engagement.

[19] Kanis and Kramer, "Collective impact."

[20] Kanis and Kramer, "Collective impact."

[21] Fay Hanleybrown, John Kania, & Mark Kramer, "Channeling Change: Making Collective Impact Work," *Stanford Social Innovation Review (2012)*. http://www.ssireview.org/blog/entry/channeling_change_making_collective_impact_work

In the decade following its inception, the wave of collective impact took the non-profit sector by storm. It became the next big thing in the non-profit sector.[22] It was chosen as the number 2 philanthropy buzzword in 2011.[23] Collective impact theories have been adopted for many government programs and some community collaboration efforts. The authors promoted it extensively through their own consulting business (FRG contracted by RMAPI has Kramer as a partner) another example of profiting off social problems. More important, grant makers have come to explicitly require applications require commitment to collective impact to win funding.[24]

Precursors: Business Adopts Social Impact

What's less emphasized in the celebration of collective impact is the importation of business and market models into many collective impact projects. These often aim to financialize and marketize social services. We can see this in what Kanis and Kramer see as their precursors. For Kanis and Kramer collective impact bears some family resemblance to notions of venture philanthropy and social entrepreneurship that gained prominence in the last decades. I mentioned these approaches in my discussion of the transformation of non-profits. Each of these approaches employs business principles and market models to the solution of social problems. Venture philanthropy arose because of a dissatisfaction with standard forms of funding from government or more traditional foundations. It is modeled after the venture capital movement of the 1990s. Unlike the social enterprise model, however they do not seek to gain a profit but promote a social good. In the case of a social good like education, Venture Philanthropy treats giving to schooling as a social investment that, like venture capital, must begin with a business plan, involve quantitative

[22] Rodney Holmes, "Collective Impact": the 'next big thing' for Community Development, or a Neoliberal Trojan Horse?," n.d.

[23] Lucy Bernholz, "Philanthropy Buzzwords of 2011," *The Chronicle of Philanthropy* December 27, 2011. https://www.philanthropy.com/article/Philanthropy-Buzzwords-of-2011/157395

[24] B.D. Christens and P.T. Inzeo, "Widening the view: situating collective impact among frameworks for community-led change," *Community Development*, Vol. 46, 4 (2015): 420–435 at 422.

measurement of efficacy, be replicable, be brought to scale and ideally leverage public spending in ways compatible with the strategic donor.[25]

Though Venture Philanthropy does not seek a profit, it often pursues the transformation of public institutions in a more market-oriented direction. One such attempt in the realm of education was studied by Zeichner and Sandoval. The New Schools venture fund was an attempt to privatize and marketize teacher education. The venture hoped to dismantle the current system of teacher education and replace it with a competitive privatized market. This conversion would open a huge business opportunity in the teacher education market, and the grantee was very explicit about its long-term profit motive. Other charitable groups including the Walton Foundation the Gates Foundation have made extensive attempts to change education in a market-based direction. Venture capitalists then seek to not simply promote a good, but they change the definition of what a social good is in the process.

Social Enterprise and Entrepreneurship (SEE) is a second, related model that has risen to prominence. It also arose in part out of a dissatisfaction with venture philanthropy. SEE also holds that market-based approaches to our social problems produce the best outcomes. However, they often seek to introduce profit making ventures into non-profit operations. "SEE advocates construct social problems as **knowledge problems** that can be solved by technical innovation driven by competition among individual social entrepreneurs, operating through for-profit, nonprofit, or hybrid enterprises."[26] They think that the entrepreneurial firm is the best model for social change with its flexibility, efficiency, and competitive nature. Both of these models then introduce not just market principles but neo-liberal conception of the role of the market into non-profit theory. Claiming that market principles are the best ones for solving social problems, they marketize social services.

The second element mentioned in the quote, however, is a technical managerial one. Interpreting social problems as knowledge problems leaves questions of social power as well as normative ones unthought. It tacitly assumes that the larger social order is desirable as is.

[25] Kenneth. Saltman, *The gift of education: Public education and venture philanthropy*, (New York: Palgrave Macmillan, 2010). Kenneth M. Zeichner and Cesar Pena-Sandoval, "Venture Philanthropy and Teacher Education Policy in the US: The Role of the New Schools Venture Fund," *Teachers College Record* 117 5 (2015):1-44

[26] Jason Spicer, Marshall Ganz, and Tamara Kay, "Social Enterprise Is Not Social Change," *Stanford Social innovation review* February 23, 2018

Like other new buzzwords, there is not a lot of evidence that SEE models work even though such models have gotten a foothold in universities and foundations. To the contrary such initiatives are mostly small scale and largely incapable of being reproduced on large scale systems without the very government intervention they claim to dislike. There are, however, other problems with the idea that we should convert public goods to private ones. It is neither desirable nor completely possible. Economists and theorists, even those based in rational choice models have recognized that public goods cannot always effectively be distributed through a market. Further many SEE initiatives are neither public nor transparent, making them hard to track. Neither Venture Philanthropy nor SEE models provide much in the way of democratic control of these initiatives, as economic imperatives are more important than political ones.

Critics of outsourcing and privatizing the non-profit sphere have been quick to point out the destructive effects of these privatizing and marketizing policies.[27] Eikenberry and Kluwer note, "The outcome [of marketization-bc] is the potential deterioration of the distinctive contributions that nonprofit organizations make to creating and maintaining a strong civil society."[28] Non-profits are concerned with more than just efficiency and effective delivery of services. They are part of the voluntary sphere of social life in which both public discussion of issues and the creation of solidarities are initiated. Thus, social welfare organizations are advocates for social justice.

The imposition of market values onto social welfare is detrimental to democracy. A market consumer-based model fails to provide an adequate notion of democratic accountability or a conception of collective political action in the public interest. Market models with their emphasis on efficiency and cost effectiveness do not have much to say about collective action or social justice. Not only does the constant competition for funding take up an inordinate amount of time, but it also changes the goals of the social service sector to serve the demands of the funders who often serve more middle class and elite aims. These "reforms" are ways of disciplining and shaping social service providers, so they do not get too progressive or too out of line. The neo-liberal outsourcing of services then cannot be seen independent of certain political aims. Power is employed

[27] Angela M. Eikenberry Jodie Drapal Kluver, "The Marketization of the Nonprofit Sector: Civil Society at Risk? ," *Public Administration Review* Vol. 64, No 2 (March/April 2004).

[28] Eikenberry and Kluwer, "Marketization": 140.

to change the goals of social services and takes power away from groups that often have more direct grass roots contact with the poor. Authority is transferred to funding agencies which often have quite different concerns.

A Neo-liberal Trojan Horse?

The shrinking of state services coupled with a distrust of government solutions has often led to the outsourcing and privatizing of social services. On the view of advocates outsourcing saves money and avoids public obligations. The growth in the non-profit sector as a provider of services, however, has unintended consequences. This growth generates increased problems of complexity in the social service sector. On the one hand fragmentation of services occurs as isolated groups are not coordinated or connected. On the other hand, outsourcing leads to a competition in services in which winners and losers are designated and governments and foundations try to guess what agencies will be best to carry out these functions. Thus, there is a "lack of coordination, mutual awareness, and cooperation between organizations in local systems of service delivery and advocacy."[29]

Collective impact understands itself as a solution to the fragmenting of services in neo-liberalism. However, it does not generally challenge the fact of privatization and marketization of services nor the models of venture philanthropy or SEEs. The best way to see it is as a system of private governance of non-profits and others who are now the major providers of social services. It takes over the role that should have been carried out by elected governments.

Collective impact aims to make the operation of social services more efficient and more effective, but not necessarily more just or fair. It can be viewed as a supply side approach that seeks to change the efficiency of services not the source of problems. It addresses the problems of neo-liberal fragmentation with a neo-liberal solution. It takes for granted the fragmentation of services without asking about the desirability of processes of privatization and marketization.

[29] Christens and Izeo, "Widening the View": 423

Private Public Partnerships

One of the main mechanisms collective impact employs to carry out programs is the Public Private Partnership (PPP). This form of partnership is best defined as collaborations between the government and a private entity (or entities) with the aim of financing and operating a project. While these arrangements are not new the extent to which they have been used has broadened in scope.

Public Private Partnerships were often used in infrastructure projects when a government entity contracted with a private entity to construct a project like a road or a bridge or other public infrastructure like a public hospital building. The private company often has to provide financing and takes on the risks for cost overruns and other problems but gets incentives from the government. In theory the innovative spirit and knowledge of the private company yields a superior cost-effective result. The government for its part takes the risk that such a project might not yield the revenue or benefits sought but wins the rewards if they do. PPPs are often thought to be a cost-effective alternative to inefficient government projects that plagued by cost overruns and often seen as pork barrel projects benefitting friends. A second reason for projects in the neo-liberal era is the fiscal weakness especially of state or local governments. They often lack resources to invest in costly infrastructure projects.

The privatizing of risk on such projects, does not always work as conceived, Private companies often blame the government for cost overruns or other problems and attempt to recoup losses.[30] In this case the public pays. Private funding can also raise problems. Because projects employ many of the complicated private financial market funding schemes these projects can be influenced by the demands of funders.

While these partnerships are seen by some as advantageous, they have come under criticism. They often cloud the nature of public purposes shifting the focus of projects in the direction of profit-making activity. Operating on these terms both public officials and private companies act more in their self-interest than the public good. Looking at the results of

[30] Kevin DeGood, "The Limits of Risk Transference Through Public-Private Partnerships," *Center for American Progress* December 11, 2019. https://www.americanprogress.org/article/limits-risk-transference-public-private-partnerships/

these projects in a global context, Smith argues that they have not lived up to their promise.[31]

A second and relatively new role for PPPs is in providing government services, especially in the non-profit sector. Collective Impact theorists hold that because governments have failed to successfully solve problems like educational achievement and poverty, Public Private Partnerships are better suited to address complex system problems. Not only do they provide the flexibility of enterprise they promise to be more accountable for the results of their projects.

In the view of the Brookings institute PPP's show promise for addressing social problems [32] This article is interesting because it illustrates the extent to which neo-liberal assumptions have permeated not just conservative but liberal discourse. Their analysis of the potential of PPP's for solving social problems relies heavily on the use social impact bonds and outcome bonds to achieve public purposes. Benefits are a matter of efficiency. They claim:

> these new PPPs encourage true partnerships with a diversity of stakeholders. By harnessing the technical expertise, approaches, and networks possessed by governments, private-sector organizations, non-governmental actors, and donor agencies, these new PPPs can provide innovative mechanisms and promote collaboration to address challenges that traditional government resources and competing priorities struggle to negotiate. In doing so, they can increase capacity, improve quality, enhance equity, and target poor or marginalized populations for the delivery or financing of services.[33]

Collective Impact models draw on privatized pay for service operation in which groups are paid according to their results that is their success in achieving goals. Such pressures lead to transformation of the non-profit sector into a servant of private interests more than the public good.

The outsourcing of a project with a public purpose does not always lead to the achievement of public purposes or goods. Public Private

[31] Fred L. Smith, "The Problem with Public Private Partnerships," *Competitive Enterprise Institute* https://cei.org/blog/the-problem-with-public-private-partnerships/.

[32] Amel Karboul, Emily Gustafsson-Wright, and Max McCabe, "Partnerships for public purpose: The new PPPs for fighting the biggest crises of our time," *Brookings* May 27, 2021 https://www.brookings.edu/blog/education-plus-development/2021/05/27/partnerships-for-public-purpose-the-new-ppps-for-fighting-the-biggest-crises-of-our-time/

[33] Karboul, "Partnerships for Public Purposes."

partnerships can be vehicles for the monetization and financialization of public goods, like education. These types of private public partnerships, however, do not operate on a community-based system of shared values or a shared conception of social justice. Rather. the goal here is one of getting private non-profits on board with the project of creating entrepreneurial subjects. Nordtveit observed:

> it can be argued that the market-based system has a perverse effect on civil society associations since they are transformed from social capital (trust based networks) into private businesses. Hence, it can be claimed that the very mechanisms that are supposed to create and strengthen civil society (and social capital), corrupt, and weaken it.[34]

Far from standing in opposition to neo-liberal market models, collective impact is at one with the neo-liberal stress on outsourcing problems, using the vehicle of private public partnerships. It just provides a more centrally directed version of the same model. Starting from a notion that system problems stem from the way services are provided and allocated. Collective Impact is compatible with views that treat social services as a market. and citizens who receive these services as mere consumers. LeChasseur suggests that Collective Impact is a supply side model of the market in service delivery. "CI suggests altering the supply chain of services that prevent or intervene in social problems. Service providing organizations are mentioned as having the power to influence or enact change substantially more frequently than individuals."[35]

Critical Views of Collective Impact

Despite some concessions to democratic deliberation and organization collective impact models are largely top down and elite based models. The addressees of Collective Impact are the social and political elite who Collective Impact assumes are the crucial policy makers, not the public or the communities affected. Kramer and Kanis are quite explicit about this.

[34] Bjorn Nordtveit, "Use of Public-Private Partnerships to Deliver Social Services: Advantages and Drawbacks," *Center for International Education* Faculty Publications. 38. (2004). Retrieved from https://scholarworks.umass.edu/cie_faculty_pubs/38

[35] Kimberly LeChasseur, "Re-examining power and privilege in collective impact," *Community Development* 47: 2, (2016): 225–240 at 230. https://doi.org/10.1080/15575330.2016.1140664.

Community leaders and social service agencies are to make up the core members of their collaborative group. When they identify the individuals they want in collective impact organizations, they include funders, nonprofits, government officials, civic leaders, business executives, and other notables, not ordinary citizens. They set the agenda for change. Collective impact establishes asymmetric relation of authority between an "expert" group and the community. Examining this power asymmetry in the collective impact model is an important element in assessing its adequacy.

Critics of collective impact like Tom Wolff have pointed not only to its slim evidential base but to many flaws in its basic approach. [36] It ignores years of evidence that practitioners in the field have accumulated regarding collaboration and community development. Wolfe echoes criticisms commonly given of its top-down structure. One practitioner claims that Collective Impact is about bringing "CEO-level cross-sector leaders together."[37] Other major problems with Collective Impact in his view include its inadequate focus on social justice. The market model seeks efficiency not justice and fails to build community leadership. He wonders whether the five conditions of collective impact are sufficient to create effective cross sector coalitions.

From the view of a practitioner, Vu Le is sensitive to the forms of coercion that can result from the elite oriented structure of Collective Impact. He argues that the top-down structure of collective impact tends to create a herd mentality in which diverse groups are shoehorned into a single model. More colorfully he compares it to the hive mentality of the Borg in Star Trek. Collective impact does not foster a democratic discourse between coalition members rather a situation in which groups are induced to align with Collective Impact aims. Leadership provides the direction and sets the agenda. Groups are told that their funding relies on following this model. As a result, sometimes collective impact projects present the "illusion of inclusion." With this closed institutional structure Collective Impact projects can stifle criticism in indirect ways: they become too big to fail, and feedback from participants can either be ignored or misinterpreted. For Vu Le this is especially true among those of color. Questions of equity are an afterthought in Collective Impact. The end result is a process of trickle-down community engagement that "bypass the people

[36] Tom Wolfe, "Ten Places where Collective impact gets it wrong," *Global Journal of Collective Psychology Practice*

[37] Hanleybrown, "Channeling Change."

who are most affected by issues, engage and fund larger organizations to tackle these issues, and hope that miraculously the people most affected will help out in the effort, usually for free"[38] He wants to incorporate community organizing models to either complement or replace Collective Impact.

Many of the criticisms advanced by Le provide examples of the communicative distortions analyzed in the earlier work of critics of power. The social power and status of elite groups construct and constrict deliberative discourse. They set the terms for "proper" participation. Unwillingness to comply with such restricted discourses results in exile or excommunication and the loss of sources of funding along with the pressure to comply. If groups do not have equal access to or equal ability to participate in authoritative decisions, they are subject to manipulation. If for example a funder requires that the grantee adopt a collective impact framework to obtain funding as many have, the participants in the project have little choice.

The Problem of Implementation

Another potential problem with collective impact concerns the question of its suitability to provide the coordination it claims to present. The aim of collective impact is to produce alignment in the work of many parties around a specified goal, but in practice there is a gap between the idea of coordination and its achievement. The achievement of consensus is so tedious as to dominate other work, As one critic observes "that appears to be a challenge for some groups, taking so much time and effort that little time or energy is left for actual collaborative action"[39] This is a problem that occurred with RMAPI.

This criticism was recognized by collective impact originators. In some later work, Kanis, Kramer, and their associates describe collective impact as a long and sometime arduous process which required years of coalition building.[40] They add that impact requires not only the five

[38] Vu Le, "Why communities of color are getting frustrated with Collective Impact," *Nonprofit AF* website. https://nonprofitaf.com/2015/11/why-communities-of-color-are-getting-frustrated-with-collective-impact/

[39] Jeffrey R. Henig, Carolyn J. Riehl, Michael A. Rebell, and Jessica R. Wolff, *Putting Collective Action in Context: A Review of the Literature on Local Cross-Sector Collaboration to Improve Education,* (New York, New York: Teachers College, Columbia University Department of Education Policy and Social Analysis, 2015): 30.

[40] Hanleybrown, "Channeling change"

conditions but also several preconditions. In the end, however, they note, "As much as we have tried to describe clear steps to implement collective impact, it remains a messy and fragile process." They expand the model longitudinally to include a number of phases which take a long time to implement.

Collective Impact as a Form of Governance

Perhaps the biggest problem with the collective impact theory is that leaves out the major group effected by impact: the people themselves. There is however another alternative. In contrast to collective impact theories community development theories look to organize and empower those who are affected by problems. They not only have to have a seat and the table they must have to power to act to set agendas and propose alternatives. Genuine collaboration also means allowing existing social service groups to make authentic contributions and contribute their experience without having their ideas rendered moot by a clumsy central agency. Collaboration must be a fair process. Wolfe and his cohorts have recently stated this clearly "We believe that efforts that do not start with treating community leaders and residents as equal partners cannot later be reengineered to meaningfully share power. In short, coalitions and collaborations need a new way of engaging with communities that leads to transformative changes in power, equity, and justice."[41] Christens and Inzeo also think that collective impact reduces the influence of community. Instead of a grassroots approach, they use a "grasstops" approach consisting primarily of "established organizational leaders and decision makers."[42]

Other critics have raised similar concerns about limits on democratic deliberation in the collective impact model, but these include both internal and external constraints on democratic decision making. The internal restraints include those barriers within the collective impact organization;

[41] Tom Wolff, Meredith Minkler, Susan M. Wolfe, Bill Berkowitz, Linda Bowen, Frances Dunn Butterfoss, Brian D. Christens, Vincent T. Francisco, Arthur T. Himmelmanand Kien S. Lee, "Collaborating for Equity and Justice: Moving Beyond Collective Impact," *Nonprofit Quarterly* (Winter 2016).

[42] Brian D. Christens and Paula Tran Inzeo, "Widening the view: situating collective impact among frameworks for community-led change," *Community Development* Vol. 46, No. 4, (2015): 420–435 at 428. https://doi.org/10.1080/15575330.2015.1061680

the external ones encompass the relation between collective impact agencies and the broader public. Internal barriers include some of the issues raised by Vu and Wolfe. For example, Holmes is critical of the lack of community engagement and the potential domination by business or other expert cultures. He questions whether Collective Impact Models can meaningfully engage with local communities. Especially given the importance of foundations and local elites, often collective impact takes on the character of an agenda imposed from without which does not represent that of the participants in a local community. "The CI steering committee overseeing the CI backbone organization is not democratically representative of the local community. It centralizes powerful decision-- making about funding."[43] Similarly, others like Levine want to make sure that collective impact doesn't act as a monopoly or a cartel which squeezes out other groups.[44]

Not only internal problems but external one can led to problems in collective impact models. The report *Putting Collective Impact in Context* while sometimes praising collective impact for its ability to create cross sector communication, notes that collective impact models have a negative impact on the public sphere and civil society, a point also made by Eikenberry and Kluwer. The function of making policy and administering it is left to the private sector to carry out.

In addition to restricting the scope of civil society, collective impact models blur the distinction between governance and management. Generally speaking, in government there is a distinction between governance and administration. One body makes policy while another branch administers it. When public functions are outsourced, this distinction is lost; notions of democratic accountability for public policy are also lost. "It threatened the participatory underpinnings of democracy, as decisions that were the provenance of government are transferred to private agencies and actors."[45] This development identified earlier by Soss, Schram, and Fording indicates the outsourcing of public concerns to a privatized form of governance and contributes to the emptying out of the state and its loss of legitimacy.

[43] Holmes, "Collective Impact": 8

[44] Peter Levine, "Questions About Collective Impact". 2014 questions about "collective impact" « Peter Levine

[45] Henig, *Putting Collective Impact in Context*: 40

The Fetish of Data

The use of data to confirm success and refine approaches is a central feature of collective impact. "Evidence based" is one of today's go to buzz words, but often it is just a rhetorical trope and not a serious commitment with a true social scientific function. Because data promises to be quantitative and objective (value free), precise and certain, it creates credibility for a program of reform and gives it legitimacy. Such claims are common in the new non-profit environment. Programs results are to be ascertained through measurable goals and strategies and programs are to be assessed by data that provide feedback on what works and what fails.

There was already a decades long tradition of research on poverty well before collective impact. In the Kennedy era social science was enlisted in the support of government with the belief that social scientists would be able to conquer social problems, a kind of culture of expertise that supported a technocratic outlook. While this hope proved unfounded and liberals like Daniel Patrick Moynihan whose report was central to the war on poverty became skeptical of social science engineering. However, the role of poverty research remained significant. There was a need for data that provided assessment of the results of government programs. Alice O' Connor termed this the poverty research industry.[46] The aims and scope of this research changed however, over the course of a decade. Sociologically oriented research that aimed at the elimination of poverty was displaced by more narrowly considered econometric research. Poverty research developed an analytic approach which aimed more narrowly to measure progress in mitigating poverty. Anticipating later dominant ideas it focused largely on the individual and not social factors or relationships of power. O'Connor notes "In the subsequent Reagan era poverty research was increasingly outsourced to conservative think tanks though a certain amount remained more in the form of entrepreneurial competition for contracts."

At the end of this section, I will raise some objections to the idea of value-neutral social science, but for now I just want to indicate that research on poverty is selective. It is always based on some notion of relevance that reflects the situation and aim of the interpreter. If for example

[46]Alice O' Connor, *Poverty Knowledge: Social Science, Social Policy, and the Poor in Twentieth-Century U.S.* History, (Princeton: Princeton University Press 2001).ch 9.

the researcher defines the important elements to study to be individual, then they will employ as O'Connor notes a certain type of causal account.

Finding effective or adequate measurements is not automatic. Much of the work done on collective impact uses limited or inadequate measuring instruments. Writing in the context of education the authors of *Putting Collective Action in Context* assert:

> Despite the emphasis on data and new kinds of data potentially available for incorporation into multi-indicator systems, at the moment it appears that the data indicators in use by collective impact projects are fairly conventional, and they do not often reflect a theory of action for the process steps needed to produce particular outcomes. That is, a data point around reading competency does not reflect the contributions of family social services or other aspects of a collective impact collaboration that have been marshaled to affect that outcome.[47]

For other critics, an excessive stress on data leads to a tendency to employ data collection without any rigor just for the sake of appearing to be with the program. Schmitz wonders that CI's "relentless focus on short--term data can trap groups into doing the most measurable activities, not necessarily the right ones."[48]

Measurement in the social sciences is not simply a matter of scaling or measuring the objects of nature. They involve interpretation of meaning. Thus, creating a survey or measure is an assessment of the meaning of social action and can reflect that interpretation.[49] They are never value free. Interpretations are always in part evaluations.

Collective Impact and System Theory

One aspect of collective impact theory has not been extensively discussed in critical literature: Its character as systems theory. The exact way that systems theory is incorporated into RMAPI is not always clear or formally

[47] Henig, *Putting Collective Impact in Context: 32*

[48] Paul Schmitz, "The Real Challenge for Collective Impact," *Huff Post* September 27, 2012 The Real Challenge for Collective Impact | HuffPost Impact. Cited in Steve Jones, Sally Latham, Jason Pemberton, Pauline Saunders, Nick Scott "Collective Impact," June 28, 2017.

[49] This was noted in the classic work by Aaron Cicorel, *Method and Measurement in Sociology*, (New York: Free Press, 1964).

correct. Sometimes systems change is used as an analogue to fundamental social change. In the latter case social change entails a movement for greater freedom and agency, through changing norms and practices. The "system" was used negatively to indicate the operation of impersonal forces which exerted malign power and stifled agency. In order to understand what the ideas developed by the theorists of collective action and the implications of the theory a more precise understanding in required.

What Is a System

Social Systems theory had its social scientific heyday in the post war era through the work of Talcott Parsons. Emile Durkheim, one of Parsons precursors conceived his functionalist theory through a biological analogy. A system is a complex entity which is also purposive. That is, it seeks a goal or goal state. A body for example is a complex of organs and organ systems which are coordinated in order to maintain the life system of the body. Similarly, such entities live in an environment itself, a holistic concept that signifies the totality of conditions in which the entity exists. Biological systems at least, have to achieve homeostasis. They have to maintain a state of bodily equilibrium in order to continue to exist in an environment. The loss of this bodily boundary would mean the death of an entity. The emphasis on equilibrium, however, has often led critics to observe that in the context of social sciences, system theory is conservative and prefers stasis to change.[50] More recent versions of systems theory borrow from cybernetics, organizational and information theory but they still employ a holistic system integration perspective.

The second problem concerns the relation between agency and structure. System theorists have difficulties taking account of the agency of participants in the social system. Are they just elements in a system, or do they play an independent role in social change? In recent system theory (Luhmann), this problem is found in the concept of autopoiesis, the idea that systems can be self-reproducing. Agency and communication are just environments for a system.

[50]Among the critics: Ralf Dahrendorf, *Class and Class Conflict in Industrial Society*, (London: Routledge and Kegan, 1959); Lewis Coser, *The Function of Social Conflict*, (New York: The Free Press, 1956); Jurgen Habermas, "Talcott Parsons: Problems of Theory Construction," *Sociological Inquiry*. vol. 51. no. 3–4. 1981; Alvin Gouldner, *The Coming Crisis of Western Sociology*, (London: Heineman, 1970); C.W. Mills, *The Sociological imagination*, (New York: Oxford University Press, 1976).

Collective Impact does not draw directly from sociological analysis but from versions of systems thinking that stress its potential for social change. Some of these influences include recent attempts draw from organizational theory and business administration and problems of management. Some representative works include Donella Meadows *Thinking in Systems: A Primer*; Peter Senge's *The Fifth Discipline* and David Peter Stroh's *System Thinking for Social Change.*[51] Meadows is well known for her work on ecological systems as the lead author of *Limits of Growth*. She was concerned with questions of system dynamics and finding what interventions are most effective in changing system states. She sees system theory as capable of determining points of intervention that are most effective in bringing about goals. The most effective points of intervention are those which change all aspects of system. A change in system goals changes most other aspects of the system. She employed an ecological model concerned with a system that because of human activity is out of equilibrium and in danger of losing its integrity. Changes are meant to restore self-regulation through feedback mechanisms.

In Meadows account, a system is an "interconnected set of elements that is coherently organized in a way that it achieves something." [52] More broadly systems integrate elements into a unit that is oriented to achieving this goal. To the extent that she applies systems theory to human action Meadows employs a theory of purposive rational action. Following Max Weber's characterization, they involve choosing means which are appropriate to the goals or ends. Here agency counts. While these may be achieved unconsciously for biological systems through evolutionary adaption, human systems entail a conscious form of purposive rational action. They deliberately choose means to achieve ends.

System theorists focus on a set of problems that relate failures in policies and programs to insufficient knowledge of systems processes and functions. Following Weber once again theorists speak of unintended consequences when human action that is purposively rational fails to achieve its goal and in fact may impede or negate the goal sought because of insufficient knowledge of system interconnections. To use the oft-cited

[51] Donella Meadows, *Thinking in Systems: A Primer*, (White River Junction: Chelsea Green Publishers, 2008); Peter Senge, *The Fifth Discipline: The Art and Practice of the Learning Organization,* (New York: Crown, 2006*);* and David Peter Stroh, *System Thinking for Social Change,* (White River Junction: Chelsea Green Publishing, 2015).

[52] Meadows, *Thinking in Systems.*

example, the first attempts by urbanists to demolish rundown housing and replace it with new stock often simply created new ghetto areas. Houses were replaced with high rises or fragmented well established communities of residents were moved to areas distant from their original and familiar surroundings often without sufficient transportation or access to services. From a system perspective these unintended consequences are the result of incomplete knowledge of system complexity rather than any malign or other normative component. Elements of a system are interconnected. A change in one element of the system may mean changes in another element but not in a linear fashion. Thus, purposive action may not lead to the consequences desired. In other cases, a different kind of knowledge problem is created. Goals undertaken by actors or groups in different elements of the system may conflict. The analyst and the policy maker require a holistic notion of the social system that includes the way that the different elements interact.

Stroh sees a number of other related problems when systems principles are not applied.[53] In one strategy reformers seek a quick fix or something that addresses the symptoms of a problem instead of addressing root causes. In these cases, he argues they make the situation worse because the social problem deepens, and blame can be shifted to the wrong factors. A variation of this is a case in which goals slip and are modified so as to lose focus on important causes or elements due to the pressure of events. In other cases, the lack of system knowledge and coordination can mean that groups that want system changes find they are at cross purposes. Since they have competing goals they become antagonists. Often, in addition, the current structures of any system can impose limits or constraints on purposive action that require change before they can be transcended. Finally, he sees the well-known notion of the tragedy of the commons as a constraint on system change.[54] Here individuals who have access to a shared resource, and act in a self-interested way without common rules deplete the resource. Borrowing from mathematics and information theory such systems are often seen as nonlinear. A change in condition a does not lead to a corresponding change in B. In a system change may take place in unanticipated ways. Thus, crucial to the solution of systems problems is a mapping procedure which attempts to depict the connections

[53] Stroh, *System Thinking for Social Change.*

[54] Garrett Hardin, "The Tragedy of the Commons," *Science* 162 1968: 1243-1248.

and feedback loops which provide an accurate assessment of the effects of action, but this must be connected to an organizational form which realizes purposes. One of those forms Stroh explicitly considers is collective impact. He interprets it as an organizational model that combines four major elements drawn directly from Kanis and Kramer: mutually reinforcing activities; sharing a common agenda; shared measurement; and constant communication. These elements are supposed to assure success by making an organization into a purposive actor, with common goals and feedback through self-correcting mechanisms. System theorists would argue that once we can achieve a form of organization that is fully purposively rational, we can overcome problems of coordination of self-interested action that are found in the tragedy of the commons and avoid the perverse consequences of action that disregards system effects. A system of action according to this understanding is complex because it takes place in the context of social connections and coordination of different elements of social life. The social world especially in modern societies is differentiated into different subsystems which have to be connected. The economy, administration, the family, education, and vocational systems are just some examples of elements of society that carry out different tasks according to social systems theory and have to be coordinated. Social complexity theories argue that social problems cannot be addressed without accounting for the complexity of social life.

System problems cannot be solved through one institution or sector of society. Schools need attention not just from the educational sector but include families, social work, and psychological intervention the economic and business sphere and governments. Poverty mitigation also requires on this analysis a multisector approach. Without it any solution is bound to create perverse effects or simply fail.

As used by collective impact organizations however system analysis is not simply a way to maintain a social system or explain equilibrium but seeks system change. The notion of social change is not necessarily the same as system change. How system and social change are distinct or connected is the issue I wish to clarify next.

System Change or Social Change?

Social Systems theory relies on a notion of **system integration** to explain its workings. Coordination of its elements is one of the central problem a social system faces. In the system theorists I examined integration is achieved though purposive action that seeks to maintain the conditions for the achievement of its goals. The system failures it identifies concern the inability of systems to achieve goals due to the lack of coordination. However, not all forms of social integration and reproduction can be understood from the standpoint of the goal seeking actor. Social reproduction is also normative; it requires not common goals but common understanding about how we carry out our lives as members of a society. This form of action is what Habermas calls communicative action. The social world is a communicative order; it requires a consensual form of social interaction that seeks mutual understanding. When we speak of social change, we are in fact not just referring to system change but changes in the norms, values and practices we judge to be right or good

In the 1960s as part of disputes with Parsons' system theory a debate ensued over the role of system integration versus social integration in social theory.[55] In contrast to notions of system integration, social integration refers to the binding forces (and sometimes the lack of them) between social actors through the mutual understanding they achieve in interaction. Explaining social change requires reference to social integration (though the latter does not preclude conflict). We regulate out action through norms and values. It only stipulates that the kind of integration, the way society is held together involves consensual rather than purposive action. Earlier critics of systems theory noted that it did not consider social conflict between social actors. The social integration perspective however can encompass both conflict and consensus.

Take for example a social movement seeking anti-discrimination laws. Actors don't seek just to change goals, but to change norms, the way we act in relation to others. Action seeks to change the legitimacy of norms and to conform to norms like equality or equal respect. Problems of social integration are not the result of inefficiencies or unintended consequences, but failure to achieve binding norms or practices which enable a good life.

Questions of social integration also can involve problems of power. Social inequality for example, is not just a problem of inadequate knowledge, but of the existence of unequal power, that is of unjust norms and

[55] David Lockwood, "Social Integration and System integration", in G. K. Zollschan and W. Hirsch (eds). *Explorations in Social Change*, (London: Routledge, 1964). For commentaries see Nicos Mouzelis, "Social and System Integration: Lockwood, Habermas Giddens," *Sociology* 31:1 1997 :111-19; Margaret Archer "Social Integration and System Integration: Developing the Distinction," *Sociology* Vol. 30, No. 4 1996: 679-699 ; Habermas, "Talcott Parsons."

harmful practices. A government could become illegitimate if it is seen to allow severe inequalities and asymmetries of power and if it excluded many from democratic participation. It could also fail to do so if it restricts access to participation or limits communicative practice in a way the excludes reasons and experiences that would challenge its rule. Social power can restrict or direct forms of mutual understanding so as to limit the forms of understanding and acting. Nor would we consider a social order just, simply because it is well-integrated, well-managed or efficient. Social justice requires regulative principles abouts the way needs and benefits can be distributed. These rules are those under an uncoerced condition that members of a society would accept.

To be sure, some system theorists try to incorporate elements of the social integration that characterizes the participants' perspective into their analysis. Parsons talked about normative systems, but he saw them primarily through their functional qualities in providing functional integration and pattern maintenance, adaption, and goal achievement. However, in the most advanced version of social systems theory formulated by Luhmann the social life world disappears as does any idea of social integration.[56] Much is lost from the standpoint of social explanation when an inquirer exclusively employs this observer's perspective. It cannot articulate the normative problems that we face as participants in society, and it cannot explain the very inquiry that it undertakes. But the participants perspective is also employed by those engaged in social science inquiry. The analyst understands fellow humans because they too are participants in the social world who are already engaged in practical processes of mutual understanding.

Stroh's attempt to incorporate a more social integrative perspective is instructive. He introduces the role of narrative in his discussion of "system stories."[57] He begins with the experiences participants have in encountering troubling issues. These stories are first seen from the participants perspective, they are the ways we understand our life histories as member of a social life world. Stories and narratives are caught up with our identity. In our stories we reveal who we are.

For Stroh, stories can be important in shaping understanding. However, he ties these narratives of social life to a system perspective and hence denies their independent status. The narratives provide data but are not sufficient in themselves. The participants' perspective is subordinated to

[56] Jurgen Habermas, *Theory of Communicative Action volume 2 Lifeworld and System: A Critique of Functionalist Reason*, (Boston: Beacon Press, 1987): 129.

[57] Stroh, *System Thinking:* chapter 2 System Stories: 29-43.

the system outlook, as little more than an adjunct. Such stories then link social experience to the system problems he identifies, such as unintended consequences or conflicting goals. These involve knowledge problems, but not questions of injustice. Once participants make this linkage and realize how problems are really problems of system integration, insight replaces a sense of impotency with the knowledge that provides empowerment and motivation for change. The participant then knows how things really work. The way things really work does not however, seem to involve social problems like inequality injustice, subordination or oppression induced by social power.

Problems like poverty are not just system problems but problems of social integration. Whereas questions of system integration earlier are interpreted by collective impact theories as managerial/knowledge problems social and political problems require action concerned with changing norms. Poverty cannot be understood in terms of absolute deprivation, though it can include that, it includes notions of social deprivation and maltreatment that is disrespect taking that term in the broadest sense, and subordination. In advanced affluent societies, poverty is not the result of real lack of sufficient resources to provide all a minimum of decency. Either the poor are judged as unworthy, unlike the rest of us, or the distribution of power is so skewed that the poor are reduced to substandard conditions. Each of these is an implicit notion of justice employed in considering remedies.

The Complexity Problem

The notion of system complexity entered into policy discourse in the late 1970s at the high point of the neo-conservative critique of social science expertise.[58] This version supported a more conservative solution. Since systems are complex, planned change was likely to fail, or at least to encounter unintended consequences, such planned change should not be pursued. Something of this critique was found in the famous or infamous Trilateral Commission report, authored by Samuel Huntington and

[58] Frank Fischer, "Policy Discourse and Think Tanks," in Frank Fischer and John Forester eds., *The Argumentative Turn in Policy Analysis and Planning*, (Durham: Duke University Press 1993): 21-42.

others. Too many demands for democracy create system problems system instability and disequilibrium of the American Political System.[59]

However, system perspectives could be harnessed to different political agendas. Aspects of systems complexity theory could appeal to neo-liberals who saw the model as supporting some market reforms such as the rejection of agencies of central planning as hierarchical and prone to failure. The market was capable of coordinating the discrete forms of information seamlessly. Even on its own terms however, markets can be incapable of dealing with increased complexity.[60] Take for example problems of the supply chain, which have risen to prominence in the COVID crisis. A breakdown in the supply chain in complex economies can have a crippling effect. In social services we saw this in the idea that isolated service systems are incapable of coordination in isolation. Another layer of organization is required to achieve coordination of isolated services. Thus, another version of complexity theory developed in policy analysis, which I am going to call the moderate version because of its appeal to the centrists who see it as striking a balance between a hierarchical central authority and the anarchy the free market fundamentalism.[61]

Here social science takes a more positive view of the ability of a system perspective to solve problems of complexity. This is especially true of problems of governance. The term 'governance' itself is a relatively new one that arose to signify precisely the kind of organization that have been created in contemporary societies where nations are no longer autonomous and national problems no longer solvable by hierarchical central governments. Instead they require the coordination of many groups. Ideally according to proponents such coordination is decentered. Even on lower levels, such problems indicate that state and local governments have lost their autonomy.

One form of this coordination that is close to the RMAPI model has been called interorganizational relations. This has been described as task oriented strategic alliance between organizations based on a perceived

[59] Michel Crozier, Samuel Huntington, and Joji Watenusi, *The Crisis of Democracy: Report on the Governability of Democracies to the Trilateral Commission*, (New York: New York University Press, 1975).

[60] John Dryzek, "Complexity and Rationality in Public Life," *Political Studies* 35 (1987): 424-442.

[61] Bob Jessop, "The Governance of Complexity and the Complexity of Governance: Preliminary Remarks on some Problems and Limits of Economic Guidance," in A. Amin and J. Hausner, eds, *Beyond Markets and Hierarchy: Interactive Governance and Social Complexity*, (Cheltenham: Edward Elgar, 1997): 111-147

confluence of interests under conditions in which resources and control is dispersed, yet coordination of these resources is needed to produce mutually beneficial outcomes. This mode of coordination requires a form of reflexivity. Reflexive self-organization is distinct from what is seen as the automatic coordination of the market. It requires some form of monitoring, communication, and awareness on the part of members of organizations to consciously coordinate action. However, such activity occurs at the organizational level not that of participants. It requires those who have authority in these organizations to commit to common goals. This process, however, raises questions about the linkage of organizations and democratic legitimation. If governments have lost some autonomy what the role of consent is. Is complexity compatible with democracy?

The complexity model, however, still retains the system theoretical conceptions of organizations as goal seeking operation. Interorganizational coordination is a strategic or more broadly instrumental form of coordination. Both of these forms of coordination, while they may include reflexivity, have limited forms of accountability. Strategic actors take account of the actions of others, but they are not accountable to others in a normative sense. Communication between members is a strategic exchange of information. Democratic legitimacy as opposed to strategic reflexive organization in contrast requires mutual accountability.

Even on its own terms, as strategic alliance, such forms of addressing complexity have limited success. If complexity is as significant a problem as theorists claim it is, then governance schemes will be plagued with problems of failure. Such schemes are often unable to master the complexity that they are mean to address. Forms of intergovernmental coordination would need to build flexibility so as to be able to switch to other strategies. Focus on coordinating for a strategic goal may just as easily lead to inflexibility in the face of new contingencies. There are other problems that can limit the effectiveness of these arrangements some of which I have already mentioned, such as the time needed to coordinate action and even competing attempts to solve the same problem.[62]

Bringing a model from the natural sciences directly into the social sciences is problematic. In agreement to an extent with Habermas' formulation, Jessup notes "recognition of growing social complexity, even

[62] Jessop, "Governance." For a Foucauldian view see Jeff Malpas and Gary Wickham, "Governance and failure: on the limits of sociology," *Australia and New Zealand Journal of Sociology* (1995) 31:3.

assuming that this could be measured accurately … does not justify the simple appropriation of models of complexity from mathematics and the natural sciences without regard to the differences as well as continuities between the natural and social worlds. In particular, this may ignore the meaningfulness of the social world and the scope for agents to engage to respond to complexity in different ways."[63]

John Dryzek also questioned the role of complexity in policy studies.[64] He notes theories of complexity conceive of issues in problem solving not normative terms. He looks at problems of system mapping and modeling in the contexts of US air pollution policy. The Environmental Protection Agency (EPA) attempted to map sources of pollution, including those that were changed in nature in the process of entering the environment.

Dryzek argues that problems of mapping complexity can never be purely matters of value neutral procedure. The EPA found it difficult to achieve a common measure of pollution. Standards of health and well-being which are implicated in the analysis of pollution are value laden terms. There is no neutral standard to which to measure well-being. Dryzek argues "Large-scale modelers tend to simplify their own lives by relying on too many questionable assumptions-not the least of which is that the relationships they establish are valid across time and space."[65] A similar problem it would seem is found with questions of measuring poverty. It also requires some standard of the good life or at least a minimum below which there is deprivation. Not only are these based on norms but on the developmental state of a society. What may be deprivation in an industrial society may not be the same in an agricultural one.

The complexity that the system model addresses is non-normative; it does not address the complexity involved in social integration. Thus, even though complexity theories distance themselves from market fundamentalism its organizational managerial framework simply works to make neoliberalism and its tendencies to commodification and financialization run more efficiently. It does not confront questions of democratic organization of power.

Given these considerations, it seems that complexity theories have a limited validity. A participatory approach which used communicative

[63] Bob Jessop, "The Governance of Complexity and the Complexity of Governance, Revisited"

[64] Dryzek, "Complexity and Rationality"

[65] Dryzek, "Complexity and Rationality"

rationality to define problem situations could accommodate concerns with decentered decision networks without defining problems in a way that invite governance failure. But these require replacing the problem of system integration for one of social integration.

Bibliography

Archer, Margaret. "Social Integration and System Integration: Developing the Distinction." *Sociology* 30, No. 4, 1996: 679-699.

Barnhart, Rachel, "Fighting Poverty in the Cloud: RMAPI has a lot of potential, but must address key problems." *Medium* Sept 22, 2017. https://medium.com/@rachbarnhart/fighting-poverty-in-the-cloud-91176a21098f

Bernholz, Lucy. "Philanthropy Buzzwords of 2011." *The Chronicle of Philanthropy* December 27, 2011. https://www.philanthropy.com/article/Philanthropy-Buzzwords-of-2011/157395

Christens, B.D., and P.T. Inzeo. "Widening the view: situating collective impact among frameworks for community-led change." *Community Development*, Vol. 46, no 4 2015: 420–435.

Cicorel, Aaron. *Method and Measurement in Sociology*. New York: Free Press, 1964.

Coser, Lewis. *The Function of Social Conflict*. New York: The Free Press, 1956.

Crozier, Michael, Samuel Huntington, and Joji Watenusi. *The Crisis of Democracy: Report on the Governability of Democracies to the Trilateral Commission*. New York: New York University Press, 1975.

Dahrendorf, Rolf. *Class and Class Conflict in Industrial Society*. London: Routledge Kegan, 1959.

De Jung, Trilby and Christiana Otuwa. "Anti-poverty initiative: Ending vicious cycle of trauma." *Rochester Democrat and Chronicle* Dec 31, 2015.

DeGood, Kevin. "The Limits of Risk Transference Through Public-Private Partnerships." *Center for American Progress* December 11, 2019. https://www.americanprogress.org/article/limits-risk-transference-public-private-partnerships/

Dryzek, John. "Complexity and Rationality in Public Life." *Political Studies* 35 1987: 424-442.

Duncan, Dan. *United Way Collective Impact: The Power of RBA and ABCD. https://clearimpact.com/resources/publications/united-ways-collective-impact*

Editorial Board. "Editorial: Time to hit reset button on fighting Rochester Poverty." *Rochester Democrat and Chronicle* January 6, 2018.

Eikenberry, Angela M., Jodie Drapal Kluver, "The Marketization of the Nonprofit Sector: Civil Society at Risk? " *Public Administration Review* Vol. 64, No 2, March/April 2004.

Fischer, Frank. "Policy Discourse and Think Tanks." in Frank Fischer and John Forester eds. *The Argumentative Turn in Policy Analysis and Planning*. Durham: Duke University Press 1993: 21-42.
"Former Rochester Housing Authority Chair Convicted By A Federal Jury On 28 Counts Including Multiple Fraud Charges, Money Laundering And Lying To The FBI." *US Attorney's Office Western District of New York* December 21, 2020. https://www.justice.gov/usao-wdny/pr/former-rochester-housing-authority-chair-convicted-federal-jury-28-counts-including
Gorbman, Randy. "Racist incidents in Pittsford are the focus of a NY Times story." *WXXI News* November 29, 2021. https://www.wxxinews.org/local-news/2021-11-29/racist-incidents-in-pittsford-are-the-focus-of-a-ny-times-stor
Gouldner, Alvin. *The Coming Crisis of Western Sociology*. London: Heineman, 1970.
Habermas, Jurgen. *Theory of Communicative Action volume 2 Lifeworld and System: A Critique of Functionalist Reason*. Boston: Beacon Press, 1987.
Habermas, Jurgen. "Talcott Parsons: Problems of Theory Construction." *Sociological Inquiry*. vol. 51. no. 3–4, 1981.
Hanleybrown, Fay, John Kania, & Mark Kramer. "Channeling Change: Making Collective Impact Work." *Stanford Social Innovation Review* 2012. http://www.ssireview.org/blog/entry/channeling_change_making_collective_impact_work
Hardin, Garrett. "The Tragedy of the Commons." *Science* 162, 1968: 1243-1248.
Henig, Jeffrey, Carolyn J. Riehl, Michael A. Rebell, and Jessica R. Wolff. *Putting Collective Action in Context: A Review of the Literature on Local Cross-Sector Collaboration to Improve Education*. New York, New York: Teachers College, Columbia University Department of Education Policy and Social Analysis, 2015.
Holmes, Rodney. "Collective Impact": the 'next big thing' for Community Development, or a Neoliberal Trojan Horse?" n.d. https://scholarworks.umass.edu/cie_faculty_pubs/38
Jacob, Smriti. "Is RMAPI misunderstood?" *Rochester Beacon* October 25, 2018.
Jessop, Bob. "The Governance of Complexity and the Complexity of Governance: Preliminary Remarks on some Problems and Limits of Economic Guidance." in A. Amin and J. Hausner, eds, *Beyond Markets and Hierarchy: Interactive Governance and Social Complexity*. Cheltenham: Edward Elgar, 1997: 111-147
Jessop, Bob. "The Governance of Complexity and the Complexity of Governance, Revisited." unpublished https://eprints.lancs.ac.uk/id/eprint/218/
Jones, Steve, Sally Latham, Jason Pemberton, Pauline Saunders, and Nick Scott. "Collective Impact," June 28, 2017. https://static1.squarespace.com/static/547fa984e4b035612a9f5b1c/t/5b19c54188251b8e27a588c1/1528415560488/Collective+Impact+Summary+Resource.pdf
Kanis, John, and Mark Kramer. "Collective Impact." *Stanford Social Science Review*, Winter 2011. https://ssir.org/articles/entry/collective_impact

Karboul, Amel. Emily Gustafsson-Wright, and Max McCabe. "Partnerships for public purpose: The new PPPs for fighting the biggest crises of our time." *Brookings* May 27, 2021, https://www.brookings.edu/blog/education-plus-development/2021/05/27/partnerships-for-public-purpose-the-new-ppps-for-fighting-the-biggest-crises-of-our-time/

Le, Vu. "Why communities of color are getting frustrated with Collective Impact." *Nonprofit AF* website. https://nonprofitaf.com/2015/11/why-communities-of-color-are-getting-frustrated-with-collective-impact/

LeChasseur, Kimberly. "Re-examining power and privilege in collective impact." *Community Development* 47, no 2, 2016: 225–240. https://doi.org/10.1080/15575330.2016.1140664.

Levine, Peter. "Questions About Collective Impact." 2014.

Lockwood, David. "Social Integration and System Integration." in G. K. Zollschan and W. Hirsch eds. *Explorations in Social Change*. London: Routledge, 1964.

Malpas, Jeff, and Gary Wickham. "Governance and failure: on the limits of sociology." *Australia and New Zealand Journal of Sociology,* 1995: 31:3.

McKinley, Jesse. "In a Picture-Postcard New York Town, Racist Incidents Rattle Schools." *New York Times* November 27, 2021. https://www.nytimes.com/2021/11/27/nyregion/pittsford-racm.html

Meadows, Donella. *Thinking in Systems: A Primer.* White River Junction: Chelsea Green Publishers, 2008.

Mills, C. Wright. *The Sociological Imagination*. New York: Oxford University Press, 1976.

Mouzelis, Nicos. "Social and System Integration: Lockwood, Habermas Giddens." *Sociology* 31, no 1, 1997 :111-19,

Nelms, Shaun and George Moses. "Rochester Anti-Poverty Initiative Rebuilding Community." *Rochester Democrat and Chronicle* December 31, 2015.

Nordtveit, Bjorn. "Use of Public-Private Partnerships to Deliver Social Services: Advantages and Drawbacks." *Center for International Education* Faculty Publications. 38 2004.

O'Connor, Alice. *Poverty Knowledge: Social Science, Social Policy, and the Poor in Twentieth-Century U.S.* History. Princeton: Princeton University Press 2001.

Orr, Steve. "Small drop in Rochester poverty rate offers ray of hope." *Rochester Democrat and Chronicle* Dec 11, 2017. https://www.democratandchronicle.com/story/news/2017/12/11/small-drop-rochester-poverty-rate-offers-ray-hope/937193001/

Riley, David. "Progress Report: What has the anti-poverty initiative accomplished?" *Rochester Democrat and Chronicle* Jan 2, 2016.

RMAPI. *Implementation and Action* 2016a.

RMAPI. "Progress Report: A Roadmap, for Change." September 2015.

RMAPI. 2016b *report.*

Saltman, Kenneth. *The gift of education: Public education and venture philanthropy*. New York: Palgrave Macmillan 2010.
Schmitz, Paul. "The Real Challenge for Collective Impact." *Huff Post* September 27, 2012.
Senge, Peter. *The Fifth Discipline: The Art and Practice of the Learning Organization*. New York: Crown, 2006.
Singer, Patti. "Few Know about anti-poverty initiative poll says." *Rochester Democrat and Chronicle* January 31, 2016.
Singer, Patti. "Internal Documents reveal early challenges to Rochester anti-poverty initiative." *Rochester Democrat and Chronicle* Dec 3o, 2017a. https://www.democratandchronicle.com/story/news/2017/12/30/internal-documents-reveal-early-challenges-rochester-anti-poverty-initiative/984496001/
Singer, Patti. "Why we should all care about anti-poverty efforts." *Rochester Democrat and Chronicle* April 28, 2017b.
Smith, Fred L. "The Problem with Public Private Partnerships." *Competitive Enterprise Institute*. https://cei.org/blog/the-problem-with-public-private-partnerships/
Spicer, Jason, Marshall Ganz, Tamara Kay. "Social Enterprise Is Not Social Change." *Stanford Social Innovation Review* February 23, 2018.
Spicer, Velvet. "Anti-poverty agency seeks community's ideas." *Rochester Business Journal* April 21, 2018.
Stroh, David Peter. *System Thinking for Social Change*. White River Junction: Chelsea Green Publishing, 2015.
Wolfe, Tom. "Ten Places where Collective impact gets it wrong." *Global Journal of Collective Psychology Practice*. https://www.gjcpp.org/en/resource.php?issue=21&resource=200
Wolff, Tom, Meredith Minkler, Susan M. Wolfe, Bill Berkowitz, Linda Bowen, Frances Dunn Butterfoss, Brian D. Christens, Vincent T. Francisco, Arthur T. Himmelmanand and Kien S. Lee. "Collaborating for Equity and Justice: Moving Beyond Collective Impact." *Nonprofit Quarterly* Winter, 2016.
Zeichner, Kenneth, and Cesar Pena-Sandoval. "Venture Philanthropy and Teacher Education Policy in the US: The Role of the New Schools Venture Fund." *Teachers College Record* 117, no 5 2015:1-44

CHAPTER 7

Collective Impact in Action

Collective Impact and the Long Rollout 2

In the last chapter, I discussed the collective impact model and some of its weaknesses. It contains theoretical commitments that are not suitable for the construction of a theory of social change that can address questions of poverty because it a managerial approach that lacks a conception of justice. Collective Impact seeks to make systems more efficient or to eliminate conflicts of system elements. Organizationally, it contains undemocratic elements. The theory's focus on higher level decision making lacks democratic accountability and has a deleterious effect on the structure of civil society.

Despite these questions, RMAPI enthusiastically embraced collective impact, even contracting with its originators' consulting firm to conform more closely to its principles. Following the consulting contract with FSG, leaders of RMAPI expressed strong confidence in the collective impact model and strong support of Brock. Co-director McMickel stated, "he's doing a great job."[1] He is burdened by expectations that are not of his making. But they ask the public for patience, especially in light of the reset the FSG recommended. Now according to one board member, it will take at least seven to eight years for the collective impact model to reach full speed. Difficulties in explaining the collective impact model to the public

[1] Smriti Jacob, "Is RMAPI misunderstood?" *Rochester Beacon* October 25, 2018.

B. Caterino, *The Failure of the Neo-Liberal Approach to Poverty*,
https://doi.org/10.1007/978-3-031-10606-4_7

no doubt increased their impatience. Jaime Saunders CEO of Board contended, "The sense of wanting to make a change fast is understandable, but we know that for social change and community change to be effective takes time, takes process, takes buy-ins and communication, communication communication." Others asserted that evaluating RMAPI and collective impact will take up to 15 years. A bit of reflection on this statement yields problems. Since the original article on collective impact was published in 2011, a 10–15-year window for evaluation would mean that there is literally no information on which to evaluate the progress of collective impact during it whole existence. In that case, it would be little more than a social experiment lacking any effective public accountability, with the poor as the unwilling objects of the experiment.

Counseling patience was not an effective strategy. Brock was the victim of high expectations, and was subject like other African American leaders, to harassment in the community. His family was threatened, and he was forced to move from his city residence out of safety concerns. He was chided by many who thought he was flush with money. By 2017, much of the public had come to see the project as a failure. They were looking for indications of success.

None of these reprehensible actions against Brock was justified but the more general skepticism contained a grain of truth. Rochester had experienced deindustrialization in a dramatic way with the loss of better paying Kodak jobs and had seen wages decline. The response in the decades prior to RMAPI was a PR campaign to prop up Rochester's image, and a series of poorly planned projects and handouts to corporate cronies under the guise of Industrial Development. Many residents were discouraged and skeptical and in the suburbs, the politics of resentment so well cultivated by Reagan, then adopted in Fox News and Trump, prevailed. RMAPI leaders operated without successfully addressing these fears. Was this cumbersome organizational framework which even its creators admitted was fragile the best vehicle to address poverty?

The structure of collective impact increased the distance between the initiative and the community. The impetus for adopting a collective impact model was not a result of community consensus, but of institutions like the United Way along with the private foundation and think tank groups on the national level. These groups had their own agendas which were not necessarily those of the local community. Instead on the collective impact model local groups has to be induced to accept a model which sets its own parameters.

IBM and Collective Impact

In addition to the influence of the United Way, an IBM Smart Cities grant was another source of the initiative. IBM gave grants to United Way agencies in places like the research triangle in North Carolina when they adopt the collective impact model of community services. The adoption of the collective impact model was not based entirely on its superiority, little evidence of effectiveness existed in the early days. It was the managerial model it proposed that was congenial to the new brand of foundations that arose in the neo-liberal era.

In 2015, the Rochester United Way also got an IBM Smart Cities Challenge Grant. As part of this grant, the IBM foundation sought to find ways to get cities to address the future by making unban services more efficient. Sometimes these grants concern ways to create greener and more sustainable cities. In other cases, like Rochester, they concern improving social services. As part of the grant, IBM "contributes the skills and expertise of top IBM talent" to study critical challenges facing communities. They made a three week visit to an area and meet with "key stakeholders" to determine areas in which the RMAPI project is held back. Consistent with Kanis and Kramer's formulation, they were most likely political and business leaders, not the people affected by poverty. Most of these recommendations IBM proposed concern questions of efficiency and implementation of collective impact principles. Their recommendations are detailed in the report prepared for the City. the *Rochester USA Smart Cities Challenge Report.*[2] The report has a decidedly technocratic approach drawn from the assumptions of systems theory.

The problems of reducing poverty in Rochester are impeded by the misalignment between services. The report claims that Rochester has sufficient social services; the problem is the way they are delivered and the way that outcomes are measured. Thus, it needs to be addressed through a reorganization of social services. Employing the principles of collective impact, IBM uses the report to promote its own business interests. Data services like those provided by IBM will give a greater idea of where services can be developed more efficiently, and proactive services will address populations before problems arise rather than after. This means providing support and services to those seeking jobs like daycare and other services to make sure that there are fewer barriers to get jobs. Using data services,

[2] IBM, "Rochester, USA Smarter Cities Challenge report 2015." www.cityofrochester.gov

they will not only be able to share services but be able to measure results with data and guide decisions on poverty. Further suggestions include a proactive policy which seeks not just to help those in poverty but also to identify those in danger of falling into poverty.

RMAPI early on made the goals of system integration an important part of its program. In its early 2016 report on implementation and action, it notes, "Phase I Implementation includes Systems Design and Integration at both the macro- and micro-level, to support the overarching goal of 50% reduction in poverty in 15 years." The centrality given to collective impact in RMAPI thus justifies the intensive look I have taken. The organizational structure of RMAPI, however, plays a more significant role in structuring its aims than its leaders claimed.

The IBM report reinforces the notion that collective impact takes a neo-liberal supply side approach to social problems. Poverty is addressed the same way a business might approach a supply chain problem. To continue the analogy for a moment there is little discussion in the IBM report that asks why there is a need for such services in the first place, no analysis of the political economic or social factors that generated poverty, or the causes of inequality or the asymmetries of social power which increase poverty. It assumes that the current economic and political arrangements are suitable to solve the problems of poverty.

The smart cities approach is an expert driven top-down one that imposes a business/technological model onto a social problem that involves questions of social justice. It seeks to influence the powerful to reform supply side weaknesses without disturbing relations of power that generate inequality. Given these limits, it is hard to understand the way in which IBM proposals in fact are examples of system change. The notion of system change is here narrowly conceived. It doesn't really propose a change in systems goals, just a better way to achieve them. They do not propose fundamental change in the principle of the neo-liberal welfare governance, just a plan to make it more efficient. While reform per se is not a bad idea, using the rhetoric of fundamental change while leaving the basic social and political arrangements in place is ersatz revolution that typifies much neo-liberal rhetoric. It is more proper to see this project as system revision not change.

Poverty is not a technical problem but has social and political roots. The IBM version of system change does not have a place for these problems. How then can RMAPI carry out an effective program starting from such limited premises? The workings of the neo-liberal political economy run on the principles of commodification and financialization which can then be used to financialize social life to the profit of large corporations. How does the IBM report provide a solution that addresses these problems?

Self-Sufficiency or Precarity

Rather than addressing the problems of commodification and financialization and the way they colonize the social life world of participants, the neo-liberal version of collective impact and the RMAPI program pursue a program of recommodifying those subjects in poverty under the banner of "self-sufficiency." This program, while it aims to take individuals out of a situation of "dependency" on social services, has a limited notion of self-sufficiency. The stakes involved in questions of self-sufficiency go far beyond those of the neo-liberal diagnosis of "dependency" caused by government programs.

Social Theorists have coined the term "precarity" to designate the increasing risks to individuals that are created by neo-liberal socio-economic arraignments.[3] The decline of the safety net means that social risks are redistributed to those who can least afford it. This is not a problem of government action, but of inaction. Wealth is redistributed upward and risks downward. Someone with a low paying job, poor working conditions can hardly be seen as independent. To the contrary, individuals are subject to contingencies that limit their autonomy. Even the middle class may lack enough money to pay rent or mortgages, and many less affluent do not have sufficient nutritious food. They may lack money for reliable transportation, or medical insurance, or not be able to afford prescription medicine. Increasingly we are aware of the extent to which poor are more subject to environmental harms and suffer the consequences of such exposures. They have poor access to financial services. Thus, financial stresses that a middle-class or upper-middle-class family could withstand can throw the life of the largely working poor into chaos, debt, and perhaps bankruptcy. Most people don't have more than a few hundred dollars to their name to withstand an unexpected financial or medical shock.

Reducing precarity is not a matter of creating better economic subjects. It requires macro-level change which increases market regulation, higher taxes on both income and wealth of the high income brackets redistribution and a reactivation of the social safety net.

[3] See Guy Standing, *The Precariat-The New Dangerous Class* (London: Bloomsbury, 2011).

Autonomy is found in a fulfilling life and active participation in civic life social and political affairs, in short the idea that one can direct one's life according to goals or ideals one chooses. Even the poor have hopes and aspirations, even if their lived experience discourages those goals. Equating the notion of freedom from government programs with the more complex notion of freedom that the notion of autonomy entails is flawed.

Developing Impact in Rochester

Some of the problems with collective impact identified by critics have been encountered by RMAPI. The initiative had a hard time getting started, and creating the organizational framework moved at a glacial pace. Only after five years in existence did RMAPI claim that it had finished its initial phase of creating alignment.

RMAPI remained less than fully very transparent about its work. It is hard to find information about its progress. While there have been periodic reports which one can access on the website, there are no downloadable reports for the years starting in 2019. A web video is available for one year. There is no continuing mechanism for keeping the public informed.

In addition, RMAPI has done little in the way of public outreach in the last few years and it has virtually ignored the imperative to make its policies part of a public debate about poverty. The programs and policies of RMAPI have been decided within the framework of its internal discussions. Such policies are left up to "experts." There is no small degree of irony because it is not really experts but private foundation interests that have driven some of its projects. It is important that these private interests be subject to public-criticism driven decision making.

The role of RMAPI like many collective impact projects remains ambiguous. Is RMAPI simply a technical/managerial organization seeking to craft solutions to predefined problems, or is it involved in policy making that involves public issues. To the extent that members of RMAPI are supposed to share common goals which allow then to choose between projects they would seem to be engaging in creating public policy without any political deliberation or debate. RMAPI's version of collective impact, illustrates the change in what was called public governance under neoliberal political economic organization. Elements of public accountability are either eliminated or restricted, and although it is true that many of our representative democratic institutions themselves have been captured by business interests, they still retain a modicum of democratic accountability. Citizens can vote them out of office or at least demand explanation and information. This accountability is lost when groups such as RMAPI take on quasi-governmental functions. We can see some element of an unaccountable governance structure when we revisit the Borg problem.

RMAPI's Borg Problem: Who Gets Funded

Vu Le colorfully compared collective impact to the Borg Collective in Star Trek. This highlights the ability organizations to operate in a top-down manner to which its membership has to conform to the central directive. Often collective impact leaders talk about the need for communication, but that is quite different from an emphasis on dialogue. In the complex systems model communication is a way of exchanging information and not of discourse aimed at mutual understanding, Reflexive monitoring in this sense means accounting for others in calculation but not deliberating with others. It does not rule out forms of power.

Coercive power can be exercised through control of funding. I mentioned this already in the way national level foundations could stipulate that grantees must adopt collective impact models in order to obtain grants. RMAPI has attempted something similar on the local level, in order to induce community agencies to agree with its definition of priorities, This is one of the ways RMAPI can induce participants to accept a common purpose.

Rev. Marvin McMickel for example stated that he was working with the Rochester Community Foundation to get it to adopt RMAPI priorities. Grantees from the local foundation have to pledge their intention to adopt RMAPI principles: "Let's get all the funders, all of whom have membership on the RMAPI Steering Committee, to say the same thing, so that nobody gets a grant to address quality of life issues Rochester that has not voted to embrace RMAPI principles and goals."[4] This could be seen as a form of reflexive monitoring on the part of RMAPI to ensure that all follow the same plan.

I do not know if McMickel succeeded in his plan but clearly, his idea is one of induced or constrained collaboration. I have used the term 'induce' often in this work deliberately. Inducement is distinct from agreements achieved through discussion. Inducement is a strategic action. Agent A

[4] Smriti Jacob, "Is RMAPI misunderstood?"

gets agent B to help A achieve a goal through rewards and punishments, many of which can be more subtle, but compliance of B with A's purposes is here achieved by controlling the agenda. Agreement in the sense that I have used it means an understanding that is based on moral reasons which can be accepted or rejected and have a binding power due to an uncoerced discourse. RMAPI instead of seeking agreement here is seeking to use its formal and informal power of governance to induce groups to go along. They may not in fact agree with its priorities or with the way they have chosen to implement the priorities. For example, many groups if asked might not agree with the entrepreneurial emphasis of RMAPIs program.

McMickel's pronouncement also belies the claim of Director Brock that RMAPI does not carry out any aims or exert much power. It clearly aimed to employ authority and power to induce compliance with social service and other groups, those within the RMAPI group but also in the larger community. Yet there would be no discussion in the community at large over the desirability of this process. The complaints of critics that collective impact can act like a monopoly or a cartel seem justified.

Is It Collaboration?

For proponents of the collective impact system change requires however, a substantial degree of coordination and common purpose. As Kanis and Kramer note, collective impact "requires all participants to have a shared vision for change, one that includes a common understanding of the problem and a joint approach to solving it through agreed-upon actions."[5] However, it is too easy within the bounds of collective impacts model of organization for coercive or inducted agreement to take place. The common understanding of a problem is, if properly understood, not strategic but communicative; it cannot be the result of strategic action or any inducements.

At best, RMAPI has taken a long time to establish the alignment it claims to pursue. As the report that Patti Singer unearthed noted, alignment has been difficult to achieve. Significant groups did not want to go along with its main ideas. Brock also noted that older directors did not want to go along with the program but attributed it to the fact they were stuck in their ways. But there is no public evidence to accept his claim. I

[5] John Kanis and Mark Kramer. "Collective Impact." *Stanford Social Innovation Review.* (Winter, 2011) https://ssir.org/articles/entry/collective_impact

think based on public evidence that the collective impact model is bulky unwieldy and incapable in Rochester of achieving a real consensus.

Even if a common understanding could be reached, the question of the legitimate options allowed by the collective impact model is itself restrictive. When collective impact defines problems as system problems, it leaves out normative issues. How is this non normative approach compatible with the claim made by the structural racism group that it measures its progress using an equity measure? Do all members in Rochester for example agree on the individualized approach to remediation proposed in the readings and the programs RMAPI has pursued?

Even sympathetic critics, however, have wondered about collective impacts overly restrictive approach to organization. Landsman and Roimi note concerning another Collective Impact problem, "After a year or so, however, it was clear that RTI was going beyond FSG's five conditions, especially as they relate to coalition building and organizing the communities that would be most affected by the work."[6] They suggest a number of emendations that are more in line with Wolff's criticisms. They argue that the community and the leaders have to contribute to a shared vision and that community voices have to drive shared plans to address inequality.

Connected Communities and Purpose-Built Communities

Early on RMAPI identified revitalization of communities as one of its priorities. In its 2016 report GUIDING PRINCIPLES: Mobilizing our Community to Achieve Self-Sufficiency, community building is one its major principles. Most people impacted by poverty they claim want to stay in their communities. That condition, however, relies on having neighborhoods that meet their needs. These needs include quality affordable housing, access to nutritious foods, neighborhood safety, quality education, youth development, crisis service alternatives to arrest, community health campuses, local business development and job opportunities, transportation infrastructure and neighborhood community centers that connect individuals to appropriate education, training,

[6] Greg Landsman and Erez Roimi, "Collective Impact and Systems Change: Missing Links," *Nonprofit Quarterly* February 12, 2018. https://nonprofitquarterly.org/collective-impact-systems-change-missing-links/

and other support services.[7] However, the leadership of the group also saw the principles of community building as compatible with entrepreneurialism and asset building approaches. These policies often work against the formation of communities of trust and solidarity.

This list of desiderata is indicative of the major problem in poor neighborhoods. They lack access to resources, services, and opportunities. Grocery stores and other stores often leave poorer neighborhoods leaving residents only overpriced and poorly stocked convenience stores. Access to fresh nutritious food is lacking. Often access to financial services is lacking and in addition, many of the poor have poor credit or no credit. Many good jobs are in the suburbs, and without adequate transport, they are inaccessible. Because home ownership requires credit, most rely on renting and often on landlords who are absent and do not care about neighborhoods. Affordable rent is becoming a serious problem. Schools in poor areas are often substandard. This is only to list a few of the serious problems with poor neighborhoods.

The report gives an impressive list of goals to revitalize communities, to promote "self-reliance," create opportunities and empower members of the communities they live in. However, the actual programs enacted follow a similar pattern. These goals are not realized through community action but by solutions formulated by venture capitalists and think tanks. I have already noted that asset building rarely have a non-economic solidarity creating approach: they are rooted in economic approach in which political goals are subordinated to privatization and marketization. They want to privatize schools and other services, and to gentrify poor areas, providing opportunities for them to make profitable investments. Real estate interests play a major role here too. These are not necessarily compatible with the emphasis on local self-sufficiency that RMAPI hopes to emphasize.

One of the initiatives begun by RMAPI is a project to revitalize the Beechwood and EMMA neighborhoods of the City of Rochester called connected communities "utilizing the proven principles of the Purpose-Built Communities framework" These principles include "the need for mixed-income housing, cradle-to-career education, community health and wellness, and long-term economic development, and ultimately reduce poverty." The principles stated on the Connected Communities

[7] RMAPI. *Guiding Principles: Mobilizing our Community to Achieve Self-Sufficiency*: 7, A new version is in a video. https://endingpovertynow.org/guiding-principles/

web site are identical with those of Purpose Driven Communities.[8] As with the collective impact model, I think the evidence for these "proven principles" is limited and at best ambiguous. Groups like RMAPI seem eager consumers of hype pitched as scientific results. I want to look beyond the fancy marketing and rhetoric and take a closer look at what the Purpose-Built Community framework is and what is the main source of its claims to success.

Purpose Built Communities is a foundation concerned with Urban Redevelopment originally started by well-known financial mogul Warren Buffet, hedge fund manager Julian Robertson and real estate magnate Tom Cousins. Its aim is to replicate the so-called success of the East Lake project started by Cousins. To call the East Lake project a success, however, requires deliberate ignorance of its actual operation and effects on the poor.

The East Lake project which is the underpinning of the claims involved a transformation of the East Lake neighborhood in Atlanta by Cousins 20 years ago. In the 1990's it was one of the worst neighborhoods in the area with high crime, poverty, and a rundown public housing project. The East Lake Meadows housing project started like many federal housing projects in 1971 with high hopes but due to poor construction lack of repair and lack of federal aid to residents, rather quickly became rundown.[9] As support for public housing dried up and stigma was attached to living in such places, the project became barely habitable and troubled by widespread substance abuse problems. Cousins came into the area, bought the golf course in the neighborhood, and put a lot of his own money into the project.

Under Cousins' direction, the housing project was replaced by mixed income housing. Not all residents of the older housing were allowed back. There were strict requirements on the new housing. Felons for example were excluded. As a result, 75 percent of the residents of the project left the area. Local public schools were replaced by Charter Schools, but here too students were cherry picked. The best ones attended the charter schools while the rest ended up in depleted public schools. Cousins also

[8] *Connected Communities Breaking the cycle of poverty and revitalizing the EMMA and Beechwood neighborhoods in Rochester, NY.* https://www.connectedcommunitiesroc.org/

[9] This is documented in Sarah Burns and David McMahon *East Lake Meadows: A Public Housing Story* 2020. https://www.pbs.org/kenburns/east-lake-meadows/.

used pressure to get members of his new exclusive iteration of the golf club to give donations to the foundation he set up.

Cousins' initiatives had some success, crime went down considerably, and educational results seemingly improved, but at what cost. His plan did not revitalize the neighborhood as much as induce a forced gentrification and resettlement program which improved the neighborhood through gentrification. What happened to those who used to live there?

A study led by Georgia State University Sociologist Deidre Oakley concluded that despite some marginal improvements, possibly caused by a soft rental market there, was no real change in the situation of those displaced by the East Lake project.[10] She notes that, at least statistically, the communities in which those homes are located are only marginally better than the old Affordable Housing Act (AHA) projects: they still have high rates of violent crime, they are overwhelmingly poor, and are racially segregated. Instead of doing away with pockets of poverty, Georgia State University (GSU's) study indicates that the elimination of the housing projects simply caused most of those pockets to reform elsewhere. Pockets of poverty were simply displaced. Oakley notes, "If you look at it within what the goals of what poverty deconcentrating were for these public housing transformation efforts, those goals really aren't being met. If you look at the goals of self-sufficiency, these residents are still poor. There's little upward mobility going on" Thus, the evidence of success that purpose-built proponents cite is somewhat shaky. More recently, Oakley is cited in another article detailing the decrease in affordable housing in the Atlanta area. She notes this will put more pressure on the displaced poor.[11]

The recent film *East Lake Meadows* on the history of the housing project in the area also provides a dissenting perspective.[12] The film depicts a different set of issues. Despite the poor living conditions, residents of the project and the area developed social bonds that were important to them.

[10] Deidre Oakley, Erin Ruel, Katherine Hankins, Mechelle Puckett, "Forced Mobility: The Relocation of Public Housing Residents in Atlanta," *Environment and Planning* 46: 2932—2949 2016. Cited in Gwynedd Stuart, "Life after the projects GSU study suggests Atlanta Housing Authority demolition only shifted pockets of poverty," *Creative Loafing* Thursday August 25, 2011 http://www.creativeloafing.com/news/article/13062319/life-after-the-projects

[11] Oakley is interviewed about the Atlanta project in Alexis Stephens, "Has the Shift to Mixed-Income Housing Created a Tale of Two Atlanta's?" *Next City* February 19, 2015. https://nextcity.org/daily/entry/atlanta-affordable-housing-mixed-income-housing

[12] Burns, *East Lake Meadows*

In opposition to the common view, they had a genuine sense of community. Such bonds were broken when residents were displaced. The film suggests that we revisit ideas of public housing from a fresh perspective. They contend that in the past, an alternative version of public housing which might have drawn on community solidarity to reconstruct the community with better conditions was not pursued. Instead, we now have a neo-liberal voucher system which is not always in the interests of the poor.

Purpose Built community initiatives have not always been welcome with the alacrity shown in Rochester. A 2012 initiative proposed in Chattanooga brought widespread criticism from residents who objected to forced resettlement when housing projects would be torn down.[13] There was little consultation with the community and little sense of how they viewed their own problems, according to these critics.

It is I think difficult to hold up the model of purpose-built communities in which 75 percent of the poor were displaced and in which public schools are undermined, with the stated goal of the Rochester project to keep people in their neighborhoods when purpose built communities push them out. But this is typical of the naivety with which such projects which come with the promise of foundation money are adopted. Too often RMAPI has relied on programs developed by think tanks and social entrepreneurs instead of community development.

The 2020 Report

Several years later, the Connected community group of Rochester in 2020 released a comprehensive plan for the revival of the community.[14] It is another impressive document full of aspirations for community development. It concerns not just economic but community development. It addresses many of the concerns originally raised by connected communities: housing, transportation, health, education, and community trust building needs. It has a thorough assessment of the problems and needs facing poor communities and especially the EMMA Beechwood area.

[13] James Harrison, "Westside residents speak out against redevelopment proposal" *NoogaToday* February 9, 2012. http://nooga.com/153614/westside-residents-speak-out-against-redevelopment-proposal/

[14] *Comprehensive Plan for the EMMA and Beechwood areas* January 2020. https://static1.squarespace.com/static/56acde712b8dde1d2361c5e2/t/5e1f5663966d9f0902c6521c/1579112251307/01-2020+Comprehensive+Neighborhood+Plan%2C+EMMA+and+Beechwood

However, as earlier statements on community development indicated, with their stress on entrepreneurship, it remains tied in important ways to neo-liberal ideas. First, it proposes the replacement of housing with mixed income housing. While the study says it is committed to keeping people in place, it is clear that other such projects have displaced the poor. How will this be achieved? They claim to be committed to helping people get mortgages and low-cost housing, to improve the existing housing stock and to make housing affordable. However, thus far progress with these goals is limited. Rochester Habitat states it has worked on one house.

Education is also a central focus of connected community. They endorse the idea of a community school which is open late hours and has activities for students. And they endorse collaboration with the University of Rochester which has been working with a high school to increase test scores and graduation rates. The role of charter schools in this process, something found in other community improvement proposals remains unclarified.

The proposal has many small-scale ideas for promoting community. These include a community garden a community hub which includes offices for community groups a party room and health care. They want to possibly build a skating rink, promote community fairs, and add Christmas lights. They hope to make residents feel they are connected and have a stake in the community.

However, questions remain with issues like funding and the community economic plan. Connected Community lists the total costs at 20 million dollars. About 14 million of that is going to be obtained through philanthropy. I do not think much of that money has been obtained yet and I do not know if that number is realistic, but the more important issue is what expectations will philanthropists impose on the community plan. Many venture philanthropists as noted earlier are privatizers with a history of turning public goods into market ones which are ripe for investment. Even well-established foundations have their own agendas. These issues have to be approached with caution. Foundations grants might run counter to the aims of these groups.

Second economic growth is approached in part through the creation of opportunity zones. Such zones are a well-known neo-liberal idea in which designated areas provide incentives such as tax breaks. The particular version passed by Congress in 2017 includes: (1) A temporary tax deferral for capital gains reinvested in an Opportunity Fund; (2) A step-up in basis for capital gains reinvested in an Opportunity Fund; (3) A permanent exclusion from taxable income of capital gains from the sale or exchange of an investment in a qualified opportunity zone fund if the investment is held for at least 10 years. These are supposed to encourage investment.

Since similar ideas have been around for some time, there is some basis for evaluating these. The results are at best mixed, but even good results have been subject to questions. Stuart Butler a conservative economist who was involved in the earlier iteration of these ideas "enterprise zones" is skeptical of the current version. "It's attracting the wrong kind of investment — large-scale investment which may lead to far greater gentrification and removal of people rather than the original intent of the enterprise zone idea,"[15] Political Scientist Timothy Weaver calls opportunity zones a "zombie idea"[16] that wanders the world of urban policy despite its "moribund performance." Weaver notes that studies of the performance of the enterprise zones in England and America found that they had little or no impact on jobs economic growth and poverty. On the contrary, to the extent that they deplete revenue from municipalities, it can have a negative impact. They can also promote gentrification high end development and higher rents. It is really a variant of trickle-down economics. At best, like the local COMIDA grants they simply transfer wealth from one area to another. They do not really attract new investment but give higher profits to those often-outside financiers who invest. I think there is a fundamental tension between the non-economic solidarity building needs of communities and the neo-liberal ideas found in renewal and gentrification and economic ideas like opportunity zones which are in the end commodifying solidarity dissolving projects. Such ideas attempt to square the circle.

[15] Ayesha Rascoe, "White House Touts Help For Poor Areas — But Questions Endure Over Who'll Benefit," *NPR* July 8, 2019. https://www.npr.org/2019/07/08/736546264/white-house-touts-help-for-poor-areas-but-questions-endure-over-wholl-benefit

[16] Timothy Weaver, "Enterprise Zones: The Zombie Idea That Just Won't Die," *Urban Affairs Forum* July 18, 2017. https://urbanaffairsreview.com/2017/07/18/theyre-back-ben-carson-revives-the-enterprise-zone-the-zombie-idea-that-just-wont-die/; Timothy Weaver, *Blazing the Neoliberal Trail: Urban Political Development in the United States and the United Kingdom*, (Philadelphia: University of Pennsylvania Press, 2016).

RMAPI Pilot Programs: Triumph of the Entrepreneurial Self

The pilot programs that the RMAPI report discusses are consistent with those found in the original reading list not simply in substance but in philosophy. They employ an individualized approach to poverty which assumes the problems lie in the behavior of poor individuals lacking cognitive and emotional skills, which it is their obligation to correct. They also sought to partner with other local agencies that aligned with their "entrepreneurial recommendations." Their aim here is to induce more entrepreneurial behavior in individuals. To be sure, RMAPI is at pains to assert that they do not follow a deficit approach, much like the originators of the asset approach deny it. But they still employ what might be called an insufficiency approach. The poor lack the ability to be entrepreneurs without guidance. This may be a kinder gentler version of neo-liberalism, but the aim of pilot programs is to facilitate the entepreneurial self. Whether this ideal is good or proper, or the extent to which is tied to neo-liberal assumptions about social welfare are not questions RMAPI asked. Can a program that truly wants to reduce poverty rely so extensively on community development based on neo-liberal principles like entrepreneurialism. The latter with its emphasis on commodification and financialization of the self, works against the self-sufficiency RMAPI claims to support. When poverty is converted to a management problem, questions of equity are not sufficiently addressed. There is no questioning of the larger inequalities in our political economic arrangements.

In the last years of Director Brock's tenure, the pilot programs that had been stalled for several years finally got underway. Articles on the achievements of RMAPI Pilot programs appeared in local papers at the beginning of 2020.[17] They show however, not just the neo-liberal character of RMAPI reforms but the limited scope and reach of these programs. The first article by Carrie Putnam reports a study by University of Notre Dame which shows progress using the Adult Mentoring Program, Bridges to Success. A mentor is assigned to each participant, he/she guides them through the social service system, and shows them how to access and take

[17] Carrie Putnam, "Study: Rochester's anti-poverty pilot programs see signs of success," *Rochester Democrat and Chronicle* February 13, 2020. https://www.democratandchronicle.com/story/news/2020/02/13/study-rochesters-anti-poverty-project-sees-signs-of-success/4739306002/

advantage of services. However, while the results seem impressive a closer look at the results reported do not yield anything close to a making a dent in the poverty rate. The total number of participants in the program over two years was 160 but the Notre Dame study included less than 100. (had others dropped out?) This is a small program. The report claims a 118 percent income increase and 110 percent in employment. 80 percent of the families have moved from a crisis to a more stable position, "in at least one area of social support" The "at least one" in the statement is a weasel word. It's an attempt to put a positive spin on a less than stellar conclusion. One area does not a significant change make. Similarly, the over 100 percent increase in income looks less impressive when we see that the income went from a monthly average of $119 to something over $900. That is not even enough to get off food stamps. While on percentage terms it is large, in absolute terms it is not impressive. Bridges to Success aims to create economic mobility pathways, but this hardly seems a path out of poverty but only creates individuals who are slightly less poor. The case loads of this mentoring program are small, about 25 per worker and the next cohort is only scheduled to be 75. The program would have to be expanded exponentially are hire many more social workers to make a dent in poverty.

The focus of mentoring projects is individualistic. It is closely aligned with the notion that poor people are insufficient in individual characteristics and that reducing poverty means changing the behavior of the poor not the structures of social power. As one mentor notes help might involve helping people get a car or a bus pass or getting a job or better housing.[18] These are certainly not bad things, but they do not go far enough to alleviate poverty in the community as a whole. Consistent with the individual approach Jeremy Underwood president and CEO of Rochester non-profit ABC and now co leader of the RMAPI steering committee stresses a focus on commitment. He says, "Really the most important work we do in the fight against poverty is with individuals." But these individuals he says have to be motivated. They must have the desire to change and to want to commit to a program. Thus, these programs are successful because it

[18] Alan Morrell, "Bridges to Success mentor helps others come from poverty to a better life," *Rochester Democrat and Chronicle* February 13, 2020. https://www.democratandchronicle.com/story/news/2020/02/13/hillary-bartoszek-among-mentors-helping-break-cycle-poverty/4738844002/

requires pull from the individual not a push from social services. Presumably, the bootstraps are provided.

A mentoring program that reached a significant portion of the population would be prohibitive as well as manipulative. As Greenbaum puts it:

> more than ten million families are suffering from too much scarcity and debt. The idea that every impoverished family could have a coach to help them develop a mentorship plan to escape from poverty is ludicrous on its face in terms of both the potential costs of staffing such a program and the iron limits of the labor market. Not to mention the extreme level of state intrusion entailed in the suggestion.[19]

In the last sentence of this quotation, Greenbaum identifies another problem RMAPI fails to address. Their aims are too often paternalistic.

The second part of the Catholic Charities initiative was begun however from different premises. It is more like the asset building discussed earlier which assumes there are community resources that those in poverty ridden areas can draw on. It draws on a model called FII or Family Independence Initiative.[20] The latter is a program that aims to keep families from falling back into poverty. They note that poverty is not always a permanent condition. While up to 75 percent of families get out of poverty after four years, 50 percent fall back into poverty. They want to provide a technology platform to strengthen social networks, access resources, and allow those in poverty to support one another in achieving mobility. Thus, it is not entirely a deficit approach. They argue that poor people have resourcefulness, what they lack are resources. By harnessing the power of the community, they hope to bypass top-down models. It still however rests on the assumptions of individual commitment to the program.

However, as Feldman's study of asset building approaches illustrated, participants are required to take on the understanding of themselves as agents of self-financialization, "entrepreneurs of themselves." Something of the same is found in the Family Independence Initiative. The program is both intrusive and demands the loyalty of participants. The notion of a

[19] Susan Greenbaum, *Blaming the poor: The Long Shadow of the Moynihan approach on Cruel Images on Poverty,* (Rutgers: Rutgers University Press, 2015):154.

[20] see The *Family Independence Initiative* https://www.fii.org/

community-based approach that focuses on participants is belied by their use of a marketing model and extensive data analyses. Their website claims that they use data analytics and predictive marketing, the same technology used by companies like Amazon to make suggestions about what shoes to buy, or a company like Netflix that collects your preferences and suggests movies for you to see. When an individual searches for something on Google or visit a products web site or a store, and that product shows up in a Facebook ad, that too is predictive marketing. The same data analysis is supposed to be applied to low-income communities to help families to win control over their lives. The process involves providing over 200 data points to the process and a strong commitment to "initiative." The latter is supposed to show one's willingness and worthiness to participate.

While such predictive analytics are trendy and promote new religion of big data, critics have expressed some significant reservations about such analysis. First, critics argue that such models assume that preferences are fixed. Thus, past patterns are predictive of future ones. This does not turn out to be true. Changing social, economic or political conditions could easily change preferences, and even human variability could change preferences.[21] A strong economic upturn or downturn could change our consumption patterns. Even more problematic, such data analytics are highly intrusive and contentious. How many times have you heard of someone being irritated by having ads for something they browsed online show up in their browsing? These may just as easily promote a negative reaction rather than a positive one. The very act of collecting and using data may affect the result. Second, such models are often wrong. There are some notable failures in the use of big date predictive models. Often it turns out not to include all the variables or relevant conditions. Third, such analytics when applied in the social sciences have often reproduced biases, profiling and repressive norms. For example, the use of data analytics by police departments to identify area of potential crime and to identify possible criminals has led critics to claim that not only do they fail to predict crime with any accuracy they target minorities. A study by the RAND corporation seems to back up this critique. Looking at the Chicago data analytic policing model they found "that CPD did not use the algorithm to

[21] Eric Siegel, *Predictive Analytics: The Power to Predict Who Will Click, Buy, Lie, or Die*, (Wiley: Hoboken New Jersey, 2016). "Pros and Cons of Predictive Analysis," https://scsonline.georgetown.edu/programs/masters-technology-management/resources/pros-and-cons-predictive-analysis

administer social services so much as to create a short list of people it would target to arrest next."[22]

More broadly, the use of data analytics is intrusive because it can be used for surveillance and the results of data mining can be sold for profit to other companies who want either to control behavior or to sell goods. The individual here is reduced literally to a commodity a set of data to be exchanged for other goods. It violates the need for personal integrity. This is ethically problematic on its own terms but even more so when data mining becomes a condition for receiving services in the guise of showing commitment and initiative. In my view, it is demeaning and disrespectful. One should not have to agree to be a subject of manipulation to get into a social welfare program.

FII was a small pilot program that reached about 150 people. It followed a peer mentoring approach in which employs co-workers, friends, neighbors, and other heads of households to create support networks and reach financial goals. Under this program, it is claimed there was a 32 percent increase in family income and a 29 percent increase in employment.

The larger problem is whether participants had to convert their self-understanding to see themselves as instruments of self-financialization and be subject to intrusive monitoring, While FII claims argues that its peer mentoring approach is a true community-based one, it stays within the neo-liberal model of creating the entrepreneurial subject. Its primary concern is with the economic success at the expense of other issues in civil society. Its notion of participant input is limited to helping others be better workers and have more appropriate middle-class economic virtues. In contrast a true grassroots approach would also include political and social issues and citizen empowerment that is, the creation of an independent capacity to evaluate policy and institutions both economic and politics. Only with the latter can citizens become engaged and reflective participants. The demand for proof of loyalty by agreeing to data mining is more along the line of the neo-liberal paternalist outlook in which the poor person is subordinate than a relationship of equals.

[22] Manuela Ekowo and Iris Palmer, "The Promise and Peril of Predictive Analytics in Higher Education," *New America* October, 2016. http://www.lonestar.edu/multimedia/The%20Promise%20and%20Peril%20of%20Predictive%20Analytics%20in%20Higher%20Education.pdf

Conforming to Norms

RMAPI and some of the groups that administer programs express some traditional biases about poverty. Foremost is one that poverty is most often a problem with single mother families that do not have fathers. RMAPI's web page prominently features statistics on poverty in single families While it is no doubt a fact that many such families are poor, the interpretation of this fact reflects a conformist outlook. Instead of dealing with the changing nature of families, it looks to stabilize traditional forms. For example, in a radio interview on the local NPR station with Leonard Brock and Catholic Charities discussing RMAPI programs, a catholic social worker stresses the need for marriage counseling or family stability, instead of something addressing gender biases about the freedom and autonomy of female head of households. The tendency to blame poverty on matriarchal African American family goes back to Moynihan. Reagan notably blamed welfare queens for abusing the system.

It is a mistake however, to blame poverty on single mothers. The traditional family is not the norm anymore, Thus, it is not the fact that poor women reject marriage that is a cause of poverty. On the contrary, they fear marrying in strained economic circumstances as a recipe for divorce. The solution lies more in support for single mothers so that poverty is not prevalent. Obviously, single mothers are often paid low wages, don't have access to childcare or paid leave, and few educational opportunities, but perhaps it is these structural barriers more than the need for a traditional family that keep poor women subordinate.[23] Pro marriage policies are not the solution. Moreover, these approaches do not consider the new social vulnerabilities associated with changed gender roles. LGBTQ individuals for example, have a higher rate of poverty than heterosexual men and women, and transgendered individuals fare the worst. I do not think RMAPI took sufficient account of the LGBTQ community in any of its programs until recently.[24]

[23] Ellen Friedrichs, "4 Ways the US Keeps Single Moms in Poverty—And What We Can Do About It," *Everyday Feminism* October 28, 2015. https://everydayfeminism.com/2015/10/keeping-single-moms-poverty/

[24] Muri Assancao, "Poverty rate for LGBT people in U.S. 'much higher' than straight, cisgender individuals: study," *New York Daily News* October 23, 2019. https://www.nydailynews.com/news/national/ny-poverty-rate-lgbtq-williams-institute-study-transgender-20191023-nss3jztnkjewtlzbq6amct4xeu-story.html

Social Work agencies and advocates have often adopted aims that are consistent with neo-liberals. Another group that carried out RMAPI programs is Action for a Better Community. This is a Community Action Agency that was created as a part of the war on poverty in the 1960s. It has a track record of community service, and administers Head Start and other programs, In the 1960s they created a community health center still in operation today. In the late 90s however, it adopted elements of the Clinton work for welfare agenda. Today it states its mission as follows: "Action for a Better Community is a Community Action Agency that promotes and provides opportunities for low-income individuals and families to become self-sufficient."

Its newest director Jerome Underwood, head of the aforementioned ABC was recently appointed a co-director of RMAPI replacing Rev. Martin McMickle. While Underwood no doubt has good ideas, he still takes an individualizing approach to poverty that reflects the changes in ABC in the 90s. In a 2020 video posted on the RMAPI website, he stresses the need for individual change less than institutions like the quote I cited above.

There are similar assumptions found in other major Rochester organizations, The Rochester Urban league, whose ex-leader William Johnson was the first African American Mayor of the City of Rochester, also stresses the notions that are compatible with business models. They seek "economic self-reliance, parity and power, and civil rights" and equal opportunity.[25] Recently they too have adopted the model of collective impact to describe their competing Interrupt racism program.[26]

Another important program touted by RMAPI is a jobs initiative working with several already established programs such as Rochester Works. They collaborate with the city of Rochester and a local businessman to create training programs. In a Feb 2019 radio interview, Brock states that over a period of two and a half years, about 218 people were trained and about 150 have jobs in local warehouses and manufacturing. This program too seems small in scope, and Brock stated that he had not approached many companies because he was not sure he had enough workers. Once again, RMAPI has had trouble convincing people to participate in their programs. Perhaps they don't believe they will help them; but a program that cannot convince people of the worth of their initiatives is not going

[25] Urban League Website's Mission Statement https://www.urbanleagueroc.org/mission-vision

[26] https://www.urbanleagueroc.org/interruptracism.

to be very successful. But when asked about the small number of participants, he claims he does not count the numbers and any improvement is a victory. Each job, he says, is a job for a family and gas a big impact. An organization formed to address poverty, however, needs better results.

In the aforementioned radio interview Brock however, dips into some deficit thinking that indicates why he thinks there are problems. Many of the people enrolled in the program are not only lacking technical skills but also employment related social skills. They do not show up on time or lack other similar skills. To get into the program you must show initiative and show you are "deserving."

At the end of his tenure, Leonard Brock presented a summa of RMAPI successes some of which I have discussed.[27] These give a good idea of the self-understanding of RMAPI leadership of their accomplishments. The first two are the mentoring programs and the job training programs reviewed in a previous section. These are pilot programs and at least one of them, the mentoring program seems implausible on a large scale. The third success is in an advocacy role which I discuss later. The last two derive from the collective impact model. One is the rationalization of services so that access is more easily available, and information is integrated in a way that allows service providers to give better service. The last is the alignment of principles: "Funders have aligned priorities with RMAPI's and integrated its guiding principles to the funding applications to ensure dollars invested in poverty alleviation are in line with a community strategy." Rochester's Borg problem remains in this proposal.

A good deal of the RMAPI program focuses on managerial and administrative issues, not political ones. The programs it does adopt often reflect the priorities of neo-liberal reformers, who seek to change individuals into more market conforming subjects and do not address the larger economic and political changes leading to stagnant wages and increasing poverty. I do not see the uniquely local focus in Bridges to Success or the Financial Independence initiative or workfare programs. The aim of self-sufficiency is ambiguous. It remains tied to the idea that welfare creates dependency and a deficiency theory of poverty. It is based in a notion of human agency that sees economic behavior as the central component of being human. In contrast, an emphasis on autonomy sees agency as rooted in social and political freedom within a context of common projects. Political agency requires a notion of autonomy that goes beyond economic self-sufficiency.

[27] Smriti Jacob, "Brock sets his exit from RMAPI." *Rochester Beacon* December 12, 2019.

Bibliography

Assancao, Muri. "Poverty rate for LGBT people in U.S. 'much higher' than straight, cisgender individuals: study." *New York Daily News* October 23, 2019. https://www.nydailynews.com/news/national/ny-poverty-rate-lgbtq-williams-institute-study-transgender-20191023-nss3jztnkjewtlzbq6amct4xeu-story.html

Burns, Sarah, and David McMahon. *East Lake Meadows: A Public Housing Story* 2020. https://www.pbs.org/kenburns/east-lake-meadows/\

Comprehensive Plan for the EMMA and Beechwood areas. January 2020. https://static1.squarespace.com/static/56acde712b8ddc1d2361c5e2/t/5e1f5663966d9f0902c6521c/1579112251307/01-2020+Comprehensive+Neighborhood+Plan%2C+EMMA+and+Beechwood

Connected Communities Breaking the cycle of poverty and revitalizing the EMMA and Beechwood neighborhoods in Rochester, NY. https://www.connectedcommunitiesroc.org/

Ekowo. Maunela and Iris Palmer "The Promise and Peril of Predictive Analytics in Higher Education." *New America* October, 2016. http://www.lonestar.edu/multimedia/The%20Promise%20and%20Peril%20of%20Predictive%20Analytics%20in%20Higher%20Education.pdf

Friedrichs, Ellen. "4 Ways the US Keeps Single Moms in Poverty—And What We Can Do About It." *Everyday Feminism* October 28, 2015. https://everydayfeminism.com/2015/10/keeping-single-moms-poverty/

Greenbaum, Susan. *Blaming the poor: The Long Shadow of the Moynihan approach on Cruel Images on Poverty.* Rutgers: Rutgers University Press, 2015.

Harrison, James. "Westside residents speak out against redevelopment proposal" *NoogaToday* February 9, 2012. http://nooga.com/153614/westside-residents-speak-out-against-redevelopment-proposal/

IBM. "Rochester, USA Smarter Cities Challenge report 2015." www.cityofrochester.gov

Jacob, Smriti. "Is RMAPI misunderstood?" *Rochester Beacon* October 25, 2018.

Jacob, Smriti. "Brock sets his exit from RMAPI." *Rochester Beacon* December 12, 2019.

Kanis, John and Mark Kramer. "Collective Impact." *Stanford Social Innovation Review.* (Winter, 2011) https://ssir.org/articles/entry/collective_impact

Landsman, Greg and Erez Roimi. "Collective Impact and Systems Change: Missing Links." *Nonprofit Quarterly* February 12, 2018. https://nonprofitquarterly.org/collective-impact-systems-change-missing-links/

Morrell, Alan. "Bridges to Success mentor helps others come from poverty to a better life." *Rochester Democrat and Chronicle* February 13, 2020. https://www.democratandchronicle.com/story/news/2020/02/13/hillary-bartoszek-among-mentors-helping-break-cycle-poverty/4738844002/

Oakley, Deidre, Erin Ruel, Katherine Hankins, Mechelle Puckett. "Forced Mobility: The Relocation of Public Housing Residents in Atlanta." *Environment and Planning* 46: 2932—2949 2016.

"Pros and Cons of Predictive Analysis," https://scsonline.georgetown.edu/programs/masters-technology-management/resources/pros-and-cons-predictive-analysis

Purpose-Built Communities Web Site. https://purposebuiltcommunities.org/

Putnam, Carrie. "Study: Rochester's anti-poverty pilot programs see signs of success." *Rochester Democrat and Chronicle* February 13, 2020. https://www.democratandchronicle.com/story/news/2020/02/13/study-rochesters-anti-poverty-project-sees-signs-of-success/4739306002/

Rascoe, Ayesha. "White House Touts Help For Poor Areas — But Questions Endure Over Who'll Benefit." *NPR* July 8, 2019. https://www.npr.org/2019/07/08/736546264/white-house-touts-help-for-poor-areas-but-questions-endure-over-wholl-benefit

RMAPI. Guiding Principles: Mobilizing our Community to Achieve Self-Sufficiency.

Siegel, Eric. *Predictive Analytics: The Power to Predict Who Will Click, Buy, Lie, or Die*. Wiley: Hoboken New Jersey, 2016.

Standing, Guy, *The Precariat-The New Dangerous Class*. London: Bloomsbury, 2011.

Stephens, Alexis. "Has the Shift to Mixed-Income Housing Created a Tale of Two Atlanta's?" *Next City* February 19, 2015. https://nextcity.org/daily/entry/atlanta-affordable-housing-mixed-income-housing

Stuart, Gwynedd. "Life after the projects GSU study suggests Atlanta Housing Authority demolition only shifted pockets of poverty." *Creative Loafing* Thursday August 25, 2011 http://www.creativeloafing.com/news/article/13062319/life-after-the-projects

The *Family Independence Initiative* https://www.fii.org/

Urban League Website. Mission Statement. https://www.urbanleagueroc.org/mission-vision

Urban League. Interrupt Racism. https://www.urbanleagueroc.org/interruptracism.

Weaver, Timothy. "Enterprise Zones: The Zombie Idea That Just Won't Die," *Urban Affairs Forum* July 18, 2017. https://urbanaffairsreview.com/2017/07/18/theyre-back-ben-carson-revives-the-enterprise-zone-the-zombie-idea-that-just-wont-die/

Weaver, Timothy. *Blazing the Neoliberal Trail: Urban Political Development in the United States and the United Kingdom*. Philadelphia: University of Pennsylvania Press, 2016.

CHAPTER 8

Rethinking the Map

Sympathetic and unsympathetic critics alike have pointed to a need to revise the framework of collective impact. Many of these cite the need to develop equity principles within the collective impact program. In response, questions of equity have begun to play a role in collective impact. While this change does address a lacuna in collective impact theories, the question of exactly how equity principles are compatible with the managerial and marketizing orientation of Collective Impact remain. Wolfe, for one, doubts that collective impact can be compatible with a justice perspective.

Collective Impact 3.0

Mark Cabaz and Liz Weaver have proposed a new iteration of the paradigm they call Collective Impact 3.0.[1] They remain committed to the collective impact model because they claim it has "good bones." They propose to transform collective impact from a management model to a

[1] Cabaj, Mark and Liz Weaver, "Collective Impact 3.0 an evolving framework for community Change," *Tamarack Institute* (2016). https://cdn2.hubspot.net/hubfs/316071/Events/Multi-Day%20Events/Community%20Change%20Institute%20-%20CCI/2016%20CCI%20Toronto/CCI_Publications/Collective%20Impact%203.0%20Liz%20Weaver%20Mark%20Cabaj%20Paper.pdf

B. Caterino, *The Failure of the Neo-Liberal Approach to Poverty*, https://doi.org/10.1007/978-3-031-10606-4_8

movement one. They want to incorporate other models of collective change that can provide a more inclusive vision of equity. The management model they claim, entails that "the leaders of institutions responsible for a domain—such as health, education, or criminal justice—come together to find ways to get better outcomes than they might achieve independently. While they may consult with the broader community on the nature of the problem and how it might be addressed, they perceive themselves to be primarily responsible for developing and implementing new responses to an issue "[2] While they think that the earlier approach can bring results, for example in the Strive education initiative in Cincinnati that raised test scores, there are other types of problems that require a different approach "In a movement-building approach, by contrast, the emphasis is on reforming (even transforming) systems where improvements alone will not make a difference."[3] Here movement building means expanding the scope of participation beyond traditional leaders and institutions in order to include other stakeholders. The greater inclusion of community members can open groups to possibilities for change. They aim to create a visionary process that changes hearts and minds. Managerial approaches want to improve systems. Movement approaches want to change society and systems.

They suggest some changes in the five principles of collective impact to reflect their conception. Among them, a shifting emphasis from "continuous communication" to "community engagement," shifting from a common agenda to shared aspiration, and transitioning from shared measurement to strategic learning. These emendations are all meant to shift the emphasis to a community-based approach.

Collective impact in its first formulations overemphasized the organization of cross sectors of CEOs to the detriment of the community. The emphasis on greater inclusion gives everyone a stake in the project and increases commitment when times are hard. In addition, community participation is necessary to gain insight into the problems experienced in the everyday life of members of an affected community. Thus, community members need to be involved in all elements of the process.

While they accept to a large extent the need to create some type of common agenda, they recommend moving in the direction of a "big tent" approach in which many individuals work on related problems. Agendas

[2] Cabaj and Weaver, "Collective Impact 3.0": 3-4.

[3] Cabaj and Weaver, "Collective Impact 3.0.": 4.

that are framed too narrowly tend to encounter the problems of unintended consequences of social engineering that can sometimes be perverse.

The data heavy approach of Collective Impact is also seen as limited. Giving the example of General Motors who used a data heavy approach to management in the 1990s, they contrast Toyota whose learning heavy approach proved more successful. Thus, they recommend that measurement be combined with a more robust social learning approach. They are somewhat skeptical that such measurement techniques are more suited to static systems in opposition to the dynamic character of social systems.

Another version of the revised paradigm is less concerned with social movement but power. Coryanne Payton Scally and her associates at the Urban Institute try to fuse a stress on the multisite cross sector approach to systems change with their concern with power, In their definition, collective impact is "a new, connected set of activities that were planned and implemented to achieve a goal, that span more than one site, and that involve a mix of institutions from the public, nonprofit, philanthropic, and/or private sectors The definition of a site varies, but common examples are a neighborhood, a school, a city, or a region."[4] Their definition of a system however is vague. A system is defined as a set of entities that is either affected by or influences a common problem. There is little in the way of analysis of systematicity, or of the pathologies of that can ensue.

System change here includes three distinct dimensions in which fundamental conditions at the source of problems are addressed: explicit changes to policies and practices; semi explicit changes in relationships; and dynamics of power and implicit changes to mental models.[5] These however are more example of social change.

The urban institute report also stresses the causes of problems like poverty and especially racism. These cannot be understood simply analytically but conclude that such system problems like race are "expressions of power that have long historical roots" However, the processes of change seem ill defined. One suggestion is that those in power must be willing to voluntarily surrender some of their power through a process something like consciousness raising. I think however, the list of any social group with power surrendering it without significant protest and social conflict is

[4] Corianne Payton Scally, Lydia Lo, Kathryn L.S. Pettit, Camille H. Anoll, and Kassie Scott, "Driving Systems Forward: Leveraging Multisite Cross-Sector Initiatives to change systems, Advance Racial Equity and Shift Power," *Urban Institute* August 3, 2020.

[5] Scally, "Driving Systems Forward," Executive Summary

quite small. Making collective impact act more like a social movement would involve it engaging in such social conflict.

Each of these brings up questions of communicative rationality and communicative power. The latter is not contained in the ability of individuals or a group to achieve a goal but refers to the creation of binding relations a social world. Relationships of power and domination for example do not just limit the ability of some to pursue their own aims, it also involves the asymmetrical relations with others and their own understanding; they can, for example, affect the very identity of those subject to domination. Moreover, changing attitudes is more a matter of insight and self-reflection on the relation between one's own attitudes and social relations of power and domination; it requires insight not a simple change of attitude. What is needed is a diagnosis of the social and political pathologies of power and domination.

These suggestions are interesting, but they do not address the problem of how to link the systems change perspective with one that emphasizes social change nor whether in the long run Collective Impact can incorporate both. Questions of power and domination simply do not fit into its approach. It does not provide any account of the origins of problems it seeks to change. Are the sources of poverty and race, mostly cultural problems are they economic and political problems or some combination? Without a clear conception of these, much of the discussion of power remains abstract.

Social movement theory in contrast is a collective action model that stems from the participants' perspective. It considers mobilization of citizens central.[6] Not just knowledge but effective political organization based on creation of ties of solidarity and commitment among members are important. However, I do not think that the social movement perspective can be subordinated or fused with the aims of collective impact. A more fruitful approach would be to subordinate collective impact and system approaches to a community development approach. The former might provide suggestions, but they need to be guided by normative and practically oriented perspectives. Such a transition would require a shift in perspective. It would require leaving the largely third person perspective of the observing expert, to the second person perspective of the

[6] Alan Touraine. *The Self-Production of Society,* (Chicago: The University of Chicago Press, 1977); Charles Tilly, *Social Movements, 1768—2012,* (London: Routledge 2012).

participants themselves. In such a case, it would be better to scrap collective impact and focus on more traditional community organizing.

In response to criticisms of its project, RMAPI also makes some concessions to these new approaches. They do not go as far as Collective Impact 3.0, and they do not truly reject the managerial model. For example, RMAPI did try to incorporate the voices of the community in its governing structure, but it is not clear to what extent they suceeded. There is only one "community member" on the steering committee and he is a former head of ABC. It has also made gender and racial equality and addressing structural racism part of its agenda an especially important issue for members of the Rochester area with its record of deep-seated racial inequality. More recently, it has lobbied for changes that would affect equity.

The New Focus?

The last year for which there is a written report, 2018, shows, four years into its work, a stalled program. Even though there has been little progress, they present an optimistic vision of their activities as the agent of systems change. They state, "In 2018, Rochester-Monroe Anti-Poverty Initiative coalition members made significant strides in putting resources toward the kind of systemic change necessary to achieve the poverty reduction that has eluded the area for so long. Through this coalition's focus on workforce development and the accessibility and affordability of basic needs, we are creating dramatic improvements to the wider systems that address and often perpetuate poverty."[7] These dramatic improvements did not yield much in the way of results. It seems to be based more on aspiration then achievement. Much of what they tout is bureaucratic data collection. In 2018 the fourth year after their inception, they finally set out to collect data to map social services. Their new strategic plan resets the bar backward. It indicates that the first five years of their program is involved with making process changes rather than system changes. The latter will not come until 2021 or later. They list as major achievements the aforementioned pilot programs which were delayed in their start up, and which were small in nature. and participatory budgeting. The timeline they develop however, once again stresses that change takes time and outlines in more detail the 15-year plan with little actual change achieved

[7] RMAPI, *2018 Year in Review.* rmapiannualreport.pdf (endingpovertynow.org)

until the latter 5 years. In reality, there is then little forward movement, mainly organizational imperatives. There is not much in these organizational developments to provide much hope of an immediate remedy to poverty.

Yet hope is needed. The poor in Rochester are discouraged and lack hope for a better future. The bureaucratic reorganization of Rochester's social services even if they are successful hardly provides a compelling version of social hope or visions of a more just community that would motivate them to act collectively to fight poverty. It was more a bureaucracy then a movement.

It seems a new direction was needed. For several years, RMAPI had been giving indications of a change in focus. It was going to shift from a set of pilot programs to a focus on larger social issues. According to the RMAPI 2019 Policy Agenda, the initiative has developed a set of priorities the aim at addressing the root cause of poverty. "These policy priorities" it states, "were developed by RMAPI's Policy Working Group after several months of meeting with local experts' community and government leaders, and representatives from non-profit agencies to determine which actions would be the most effective and the most needed to effect poverty."[8] Similarly, the 2020 agenda employs the exact language with only one change, perhaps as an afterthought: "and people directly impacted by poverty."[9] In the end, though it does not appear there was any public debate about these issues. In 2019, RMAPI lists Bail Reform, Eviction Protection, Tax Credits for Families in Poverty and Transportation as important issues. The 2020 agenda included increasing Tax Credits for Working Families, Funding to improve Child Care, again Funding increases for Public Transportation, Parole Reform, the non-suspension of license for unpaid violations, and improved housing access. Mayor Warren saw this as evidence of a reinvigorated anti-poverty initiative largely on the basis of a new Democratic county executive. Adam Bello who she hoped would be more cooperative.[10]

There is no description of the actions RMAPI has taken and no year-end reports for the years 2019-2021 that state in more detail what has been done. There is only a web video. The new activities are lobbying

[8] RMAPI, *2019 Policy Agenda.* https://endingpovertynow.org/article/rmapi-2019-policy-agenda/

[9] RMAPI, *Policy Agenda 2020. http://endingpovertynow.org/wp-content/uploads/2020/01/RMAPI-Policy-Agenda-2020.pdf*

[10] Brian Sharp, "New Anti-poverty agenda rolled out highlights tax help for eligible filers," *Rochester Democrat and Chronicle* January 31, 2020.

activities. These political activities certainly can be seen as better than pilot programs since they impact the environment in which poor people live. I wonder however, what specifically is the role of Collective Impact here. Do we need an institutional structure with its unwieldy framework and funding issues in order to lobby for changes like a higher minimum wage? These are ideas on the radar of many social reform groups and progressive organizations and even some mainstream groups. They do not require a whole governance structure to pursue. Policy lobbying activities however, fall short of the large-scale activity needed to address poverty in Rochester.

While the long lag between startup and results remains a serious problem, information on the time that other collective impact programs took to get organized shows different results. One Collective Impact program that was addressing homelessness problems in the Palm Beach area took only a few months to find information, and set up and begin programs.[11] A project in Tennessee took on reforming Health care services, took about a year and a half.[12] On the other hand, a program in St. Louis took over 3 years just to get to the stage of appointing a backbone organization.[13] Still Rochester's plan seems on the long side. Despite the skepticism that some have expressed about collective impact, the RMAPI report touts it as capable of radical system change. Yet as I have noted, the notion of systems changes employed remains in many respects unclarified. At best, system change is supposed to change the service delivery system using the model of a market in administrative services. The link between an efficient delivery of services and a just society are less clear. The causes of systematic poverty and inequality cannot be found in inefficient services.

Popular Democracy and RMAPI: Contradictory Impulses

In line with collective impact 3.0, RMAPI has interpreted its efforts as consistent with participatory democratic notions. In its 2018 report, RMAPI emphasized how it incorporates community input. To be sure,

[11] The Homeless Plan: Palm Beach County's Plan to End the Cycle of Homelessness. http://thehomelessplan.org/

[12] *A Strong Start*. https://www.strongacc.org/process-timeline/

[13] *Vision for Children at Risk Collective Impact chronology*, https://visionforchildren.org/strategic-action/collective-impact-chronology/

this emphasis goes back further, but the emphasis simply does not meet the reality. The decision-making structure and principles of governance is not based on democratic deliberation. It does not challenge the backbone structure that underlies RMAPI. Without such a change, the claim for a decentered control seems unfounded.

RMAPI did, to be sure, experiment with participatory budgeting in which they asked community members to vote on which projects it wanted RMAPI to pursue with $200,000 of grant money. For some enthusiasts, this was a genuine move toward participatory democracy.[14] However, the amount of less than $200,000 is not large.

The example of participatory budgeting is a step in the right direction but is far too limited. It consists simply of giving citizen participants a chance to choose among several alternatives presented by leadership. A model of participatory governance would be considerably more robust. It would have to include a non-coercive model of deliberative dialogue in which citizen members were significantly involved in all parts of the policy process, from formation of ideas to agenda setting. Citizen participation requires an equal right to give reasons to contest others and put forward alternatives, It had to focus on developing the deliberative competence and expertise of all participants. Frank Fischer provides a characterization of the basics of participatory governance:

> Participatory governance, as a subset of governance theory, emphasizes democratic practices. Grounded in the theory of participatory democracy more generally, it offers a theory and practices of public engagement through deliberative processes. Advanced largely as a response to a —democratic deficit in contemporary political systems, it extends the citizens' role beyond that of voter or watchdog to include direct deliberative involvement with pressing policy issues. It seeks to develop practices that are founded on a more equal distribution of political power, a fairer distribution of resources"[15]

The latter would mean genuine control over the entire agenda of RMAPI.

[14] Velvet Spicer, "Anti-poverty agency seeks community's ideas," *Rochester Business Journal* April 21, 2018.

[15] Frank Fischer, "Participatory Governance," *Jerusalem Papers in Regulation & Governance* Working Paper No. 24 (August 2010): 2.

Early on in its formation, RMAPI announced its intention to make sure community members had a seat at the table. Members of the community were to be included in each of the original work groups. This would seem to give the impression of participation, as the members were to provide input that informed the work of the committees.[16] However this participation turned out to be limited, The elite oriented structure of collective impact proved to be inimical to real participatory policy making. [17]

One reporter interviewed a community member, Isabelle Bartter, who was decidedly unsatisfied with the commitment to community participation and input. She hoped that RMAPI was going to be a true community organization, a grassroots movement run by and for the community. Instead, she found the suggestions of her working groups put to the side and not implemented. "We thought we were going to propose these ideas and that's gonna be that. I got the sense and I think a lot of other people got the sense that these things are gonna happen within the next couple of years," The groups came up with 33 recommendations which they hoped to implement. However, she felt that the whole effort was a waste of time. It was a good deal of discussion with no follow through. "there was zero political will and money behind making the ideas we came up with a reality"[18]

Subsequently the community member asked a question on the aforementioned radio interview. The RMAPI representatives state that they are interested in community input, and in fact, are interested in the proposals of the ex-member who has left the group; it is clear in the interview they talk right by her. They appear to consider these ideas in the same way a superior might do without any real commitment. The ex-member argued that it is not a true grass roots organization. While her working group may have made suggestions, that was the end of their input. To be a true community organization, members would have to be involved in most aspects of the process. The key here is the idea that "they" that is, RMAPI leaders and corporate and institutional members are the decision makers; the

[16] Patti Singer, "Poor to get seat in groups addressing poverty," *Rochester Democrat and Chronicle* April 7. 2015.

[17] John F. Forester, *The Deliberative Practitioner: Encouraging Participatory Planning Processes,* (Cambridge MA: MIT Press, 1999); Frank Fischer, *Democracy and Expertise: Reorienting Policy Inquiry,* (New York: Oxford 2009). *Reframing Public Policy: Discursive Politics and Deliberative Practices.* (New York: Oxford, 2002).

[18] Veronica Volk, "Anti-poverty Initiative working group participants feel slighted," *WXXI AM News* Feb 5, 2019.

community members really did not have the power to set the agenda or make authoritative decisions. Just having a community input group does not make a democratic community organization.

The lack of attention to participants perspectives is sustained by internal documents from one of the original 8 working groups: housing. They made a number of suggestions that seemed crucial to addressing the housing issues. Their recommendations focused on anti-gentrification efforts, by directly helping "indigent working poor" through rent caps and subsidies in area where working poor live. This includes eliminating "benefit cliffs," situations in which a slight increase in income lead to loss of benefits, making the poor worse off. They are punished for earning more. It also included city loans, and significantly the expansion of anti-discrimination laws to include discrimination on the basis of income.[19]

Even if in a small way, these proposals propose a decommodification of housing, and move in the direction of recognizing housing as a human right. For example, it proposes to eliminate or at least reduce means testing as a criterion for aid. However, this implicit emphasis is lost as the proposal changes emphasis in the hands of the staffer who wrote the document. The emphasis on secure housing is interpolated into a neo-liberal framework not the human right to housing. He reinterprets these ideas to conform to the neo-liberal terms of RMAPI's project. He views these proposals as useful because they support an asset building approach. They will encourage the poor to save and make them better capitalists.

Of course, the problem here is not that housing security is important for making the poor asset builders, it is important because housing security is a basic need in our society independent of any financial status or potential economic benefit: it is a social right. To be evicted or threatened with homelessness, is not just an economic crisis it is an existential one that effects basic security/In the end however, the point became moot. As one of the conveners noted, housing was not a high priority for RMAPI and was not included in the three major areas of focus. It only appears piecemeal, in other proposals.

The citizens who made these recommendations are not cultural dupes. They had a clear understanding of their situation and some of the barriers they faced. They were not lacking in emotional self-control or lack reasoning skills. Their ideas reflected notions of social rights that RMAPI is unable to incorporate into their program.

[19] Personal correspondence with Isabelle Bartter

Thus, the citizen participants are doubly slighted. First of all, the suggestions were not taken up in any meaningful way and housing issues were not deemed a priority by RMAPI leadership. It wasn't the concerns of the citizens that set the priorities, but a more elite group. Second, even its own suggestions were interpolated to fit with pre-existing assumptions of the leadership that involved neo-liberal assumptions about asset building and enterprise.

However, the solutions proposed for the housing crisis among many of the least well off in Rochester, including the poor and the near poor, would have provided immediate relief for those in poverty and near poverty, and rent subsidies could have made an immediate dent in the poverty rate, showing the results the initiative needed to make in its early days. Citizen participants understood this better than RMAPI leadership.

In an editorial in the *Democrat and Chronicle* which addressed the general lack of community participation in groups addressing racial issues like structural racism, local activists. Howard Eagle, Minister Clifford Florence Sr., and Cilanda Florence-Yarde included RMAPI among those groups who they felt were unresponsive to calls for more community inclusion.[20] Instead, they felt the same community leaders were involved in these projects again and again with few results. Eagle also reported that he submitted developed proposals on structural racism and anti-racism education, and never received a reply. [21]At least there should have been an effort to engage with interested community members. Despite claims to consult the community, there seems to be a disconnect between RMAPI and some of its engaged community activists. There is little evidence of an effort to be a true community organization.

Despite the claims of the 3.0 iteration, critics have been concerned about the way feedback and solutions from the community especially communities of color tend to be downplayed. More generally, it raises some concerns about the openness of the RMAPI process. As with many groups the collective impact framework tends to pre-structure what is important and what is peripheral. This is not a framework open to full participation. Here the members of the community at best are consulted about the plans formulated by the group. They do not get to participate

[20] Howard Eagle, Reverend Clifford Florence Sr. and Cilanda Florence-Yarde, "Essay: Watchful Eye, Community Input needed on RASE Commission," *Rochester Democrat and Chronicle* September 22, 2020.

[21] Personal Correspondence Howard Eagle

in the formulation of policies as equal partners with RMAPI leaders. In addition, the need for a common front tends to marginalize those whose perspectives are not in agreement with the plan.

A New Leader

In December 2020, Aqua Porter was appointed the new director of RMAPI replacing Leonard Brock. She had been interim director since May. Porter was formerly a Vice President at Xerox, in charge of business transformation. She had no previous non-profit experience. Though her emphasis may be different, Porter still combines the contradictory elements of commitments to racial equity with neo-liberal ideas.

Co-Chairs of RMAPI Jerome Underwood and Dann Braverman cited her business experience as a key factor in her hiring noting she is what the coalition needs now. "We already have a group of community leaders who are working together and beginning to see real change. Her experience in leading complex teams, her change-management skills and her passion for equity will solidify the gains we made." They emphasize the need for a "culture of results and accountability" that will keep RMAPI on the course of creating equal opportunity for all.[22]

Porter did not propose any immediate changes in the RMAPI agenda, especially given COVID, which presented new conditions. She did say however, that she wished to bring more businesspeople into the process. In the short term, she wanted RMAPI to focus on immediate needs of the poor during Covid, which in its early stage intensified poverty. She too employed the notion of self-sufficiency to describe the goals of RMAPI.[23] The emphasis on business experience, the introduction of business management practices, and on reaching out to more businessmen do not seem to indicate emphasis on the community engagement principles of the 3.0 version but a deepened commitment to a management model.

Some of Porter's statements illustrate her concern for equity and for racial justice. She wants to emphasize that the poor don't choose to be poor or that they are less capable. The experiences of poor people are important, she says, and they ought to be "included" in the discussion. However, she seems to have come to the job without a full knowledge of the poverty problem. "Even as a citizen of Rochester for so long the depth

[22] Smirti Jacob, "Porter picked as new RMAPI leader," *Rochester Beacon* Dec 1, 2020.

[23] James Brown, "Porter made Permanent RMAPI leader," *CITY* December 1, 2020.

and breadth of poverty was unknown to me." It seems odd that only when she took the job did she begin to see the true impact of poverty on all aspects of life.[24]

Structural Racism Revisited

RMAPI leadership has continually stressed the need to address structural racism. In 2017 for example, Reverenced Martin McMickel stressed the central role of addressing racism in the poverty initiative.[25] In 2020, Jerome Underwood and Daan Braverman noted that asymmetries in health care during COVID once again illustrated the need to address structural racism.[26] Yet there has not been a lot of progress in this area. Other than a mention of a few issues, the 2018 report barely mentions it. At the very end of the report, it does note that it has "worked with St. Joseph's Neighborhood Center to expand implementation of its Structural Racism Initiative." This is a two-year Program that according to RMAPI helps businesses and agencies to understand structural racism. But other than consciousness-raising, there is no indication of action.

One initiative undertaken recently is the 21-day Racial Equity Challenge. This program has been run in communities throughout the country, based on the idea that it takes only 21 days to break a habit. Local groups like the United Way and Rochester Institute of Technology (RIT) endorsed this. It is a self-directed learning program. At RIT, participants get an email each weekday for 21 days with 10 minutes of content on racial equality. In most versions of the challenge, reading or other media are included as daily suggestions or assignments. Much of the effort of the equity challenges seems to be directed at leaders in businesses or large organizations.

This program seems to be much like the Urban Leagues suggestions, that individuals voluntarily give up power and dominance. While the promotion of racial equity is obviously a good thing, I think there are reasons to be skeptical of such individualized practices. Is it really proper to call the lack of racial equity a habit, like smoking or chewing your nails? Racism is more of an ingrained social attitude that can have deep psychological roots. It requires serious insight and reflection.

[24] Patti Singer, "Meet the new executive director of Rochester Monroe County Anti-Poverty Initiative," *Minority Reporter* December 1, 2020.

[25] Patti Singer, "Community needs to address racist policies to turn the tide on poverty say leaders," *Rochester Democrat and Chronicle* June 13, 2017.

[26] Jerome H. Underwood and Daan Braverman, "Current events serve as an unfortunate reminder that racism is thriving," *Rochester Democrat and Chronicle* June 8, 2020.

The other problem with this program is that it seems to assume that changing racial attitudes and structural racism is a painless matter of proper cognitive attribution. I suggested that social changes of any significance involve conflict. Those in power rarely give up power willingly. Much of the discourse on structural racism in the public has certainly provoked reaction, both on the national level and in the local Rochester area.

As I write this, there is in fact significant backlash to perspectives that might discuss structural racism. Despite the fact that it is not taught in any grade schools critical race theory has become a bogeyman for the cultural right. Local suburban school board meetings have found parents speaking out against supposed views that make students feel guilty for racial injustice!!

The other initiative during this period concerned a pledge to commit to a \$15/hr. minimum wage. (As of 2022, the state minimum wage will be \$15 for New York City and downstate counties, but only \$13.20 upstate. All New York State fast food workers, however, must be paid \$15.) The pledge has been signed by a number of local employers. Employers are recognized as Level Up Champions and get to display a Level-Up Badge that signifies to employees and potential employees their commitment and allows consumer to choose business that "align with their values."

Thus, while the move toward lobbying efforts and away from individualized programs seems like a much better strategy, RMAPI still has chosen one of the most voluntaristic means of pursuing it: individual pledges. To be fair it has lobbied for an even higher living wage in its most recent 2022 policy agenda. The state is urged to speed up the transition to the \$15 wage upstate and the \$15 dollar pledge is to be supplemented by a continuing commitment to a living wage that would go beyond the minimum wage.

Still collective impact still seems to be a point of emphasis. In the same document from September 2021 discussing results, they speak of the vast coalition of partners all working toward the same goal. In another section of document describing the Level UP Champion initiative: "Through the nationally respected collective impact framework, we are collaborating in ways never experienced here before" However instead of speaking of system change, RMAPI wants to "create culture-shifting improvements that reduce poverty in Rochester long term."[27]

[27] RMAPI, "Level Up Champions move thousands of Rochester residents to \$15/hour in 2021," September 2, 2021.

The shift in language from system change to cultural change is subtle but important. It may indicate a shift from projects based on neo-liberal assumptions about the individual. Yet elements of collective impact still remain. Despite its claim to listen to the poor, the programs initiated here are still top-down. The cultural change that RMAPI seeks is a change in the leadership culture of Rochester, and not the empowerment of the poor. Both the $15 initiative and the 21-day challenge are directed at the business professional class, and are not initiatives from the community. It's still a form of governance which is not open to any public accountability.

Wither System Integration?

While RMAPI still regards collective impact as important, one element of its program is no longer under its auspices. Since the start, the problems of system change and system integration have been important RMAPI priorities. RMAPI participated in the IBM smart cities study and had one of its subcommittees dedicated to systems integration. It appears however, that systems integration is no longer part of its program. Its oversight has been taken over by the United Way.

In their 2021 report, "The Monroe County System Integration Project: A United Way Innovation Case Study", the issue is explained. "Over the last two years {since 2019--bc} United Way of Rochester, in Rochester New York, has emerged as a leader in establishing the Monroe County Systems Integration Project (SIP)." Originally, as noted, this was a part of RMAPI, but a duplication of interests led to a reconsideration of its role. At the same time as RMAPI's initiative, Rochester's Healthcare Community and Community Based Organization (CBOs) were having discussions about improving services for the poor. Some of this work, the United Way document states, involved a Medicaid redesign begun in 2014(!). Thus, it seems that since both RMAPI were addressing the same population with overlapping services this overlap was creating its own inefficiencies. There needed to be one place where these services could be addressed. The United Way provided a "neutral staffing space and eventual oversight for SIP which was essential as diverse sectors with competing interests worked to build trust and consensus."[28] The director of SIP also noted that since

[28] United Way of Rochester, *Monroe County Systems Integration Project: A United Way Innovation Case Study,* 2021: 1 https://unitedwayrocflx.org/media/yo0dzgv5/uwrochester_casestudy-monroe-county-systems-integration-project-final-5-11-2021.pdf?lang=en-US

the United Way didn't have any skin in the game it could more directly serve the community good.

Unpacking this bureaucratic language there was obviously a turf war between the Medicaid redesign team and RMAPI leading to an undisclosed conflict severe enough to cause a change. I wasn't able to find out more about this conflict, but I do have some questions. I think it shows more weaknesses in Collective Impact projects. Clearly, in this case it wasn't able to create a consensus or enforce any governance over the system integration issue. There were people from local health care systems on the RMAPI board, so I think it is fair to assume that the issue was discussed. Since the original initiative on Medicaid redesign was carried out in 2014, it's hard to understand why this conflict hasn't come to light earlier. In RMAPIs 2016 update as part of their implementation and design initiatives they include Medicaid redesign as one of the programs they want to align with.

> At the macro-level, this priority aims to account for and align the significant number of poverty-reduction efforts and complimentary initiatives being implemented across the community, including but not limited to Connected Communities, ROC the Future, Medicaid redesign and the Finger Lakes Performing Provider System, efforts from the Mayor's Innovation Team, the Finger Lakes Regional Economic Development Council's Pathways to Prosperity initiative, etc.[29]

Clearly in the case of Medicaid redesign, this alignment failed. This seems to be in conflict with RMAPI statements claiming they were achieving consensus and alignment. But the break seems to be more radical than that. If seems as if the whole project of systems integration has been removed from RMAPI. Alignment is central to collective impact, yet I found no significant discussion or criticism in any article or report on the problems of alignment and collective impact.

Losing control over systems integration whether one likes the project or not, is certainly a blow to the authority of RMAPI and its ability to bring the community together and align interests. Seemingly, it was not successful in creating the "trust" necessary to such integration projects.

[29] RMAPI, *2016 update*. my copy. This is no longer available at the web site.

Equal Opportunity or Expanded Social Rights?

Martin Luther King: Social Democrat

Every year on the celebration of Martin Luther King's birthday, we are subject to the platitudes from establishment liberalism and conservatives touting his legacy. Conservatives especially love to cite King's declaration that we ought to judge others by the content of their character not the color of their skin, as proof that King shared their commitment to a meritocratic color-blind society in which the problems of race have largely been solved. Liberals were satisfied to see his work as advocating little more than equal opportunity with a modicum of affirmative action.

King would have rejected both of these alternatives; He was skeptical about the capacity of liberal democracy to solve the problems of structural racism and poverty. He certainly wouldn't have endorsed the savage inequalities of the neo-liberal era with its notions of responsibilities or creation of an entrepreneurial self. Nor would he have accepted the notions of economic self-sufficiency that simply made the poor better competitors in the rat race of a destructive economy.

The view King articulated was social democratic. He believed that social justice and equity required more than a formal conception of equal opportunity but required a substantive version of equity.[30] He also thought that structural racism had not just cultural but economic roots, so it too required a social democratic solution. Most important it required addressing the structures of social and political power. Returning to some of these ideas provides a useful reminder of the type of social equity needed to address poverty and structural racism.

King drew on a number of traditions to develop his vision of social democracy, The religious traditions of the social gospel and some of its messianic and redemptive overtones as well as Christian socialism based in an ethic of brotherhood. He also drew on the African American movements of the depression era and W. B Dubois and Phillip Randolph who advocated for economic and political rights. His notions drew as well on the notion of social citizenship of Marshall. While not a Marxian socialist,

[30] King's relation to theories of social rights and citizenship are documented in Sylvie Laurent, *King and the Other America: The Poor People's Campaign and the Quest for Economic Equality,* (Berkeley: University of California Press, 2018).

he did draw on Marx's critique of society. Like Marxism, Social Democracy entailed a critique of the market economy especially in its harshest forms.

King's social democratic proposals are primarily associated with his last period and the Poor People's Campaign (PPC), a multi-racial effort to bring together the poor of all races to demand social rights like decent wages, jobs, better housing, and education. However, ideas go back further. Central to this effort and to his social democratic outlook was an economic bill of rights. This proposal required extensive redistributive policies and a call for a guaranteed annual income. In the language of the time, he favored people over property. The economic bill of rights contained the following propositions

1. A meaningful job at a living wage for every employable citizen.
2. A secure and adequate income for all who cannot find jobs or for whom employment is inappropriate.
3. Access to land as a means to income and livelihood.
4. Access to capital as a means of full participation in the economic life of America.
5. Recognition by law of the right of people affected by government programs to play a truly significant role in determining how they are designed and carried out.[31]

These propositions outline a notion of social citizenship in the sense that Marshall understood it: the notion that all members of a polity ought to enjoy and to share at least a basic level of social-economic and cultural well-being.

While the PPC was burdened with the death of King in 1968 and was a victim of the Nixon administration, its failure to put these ideas into policy was more the result of the backlash to civil rights and to anti-war protests that would usher in the Nixon era, than the content of the ideas. Today when there is renewed interest in economic rights and guaranteed annual income, his proposals are newly relevant. The larger issue however was the challenges to social power that these proposals represented. King understood that the struggle for economic rights also included moral and political imperatives. It was the struggle for human dignity and equal respect.

[31] SCLC. https://www.crmvet.org/docs/68ebr.htm

Certainly, there are elements of these ideas in the more recent turn by RMAPI. They have finally come to support a minimum wage, no matter how late in the game, and sometimes adopt the imperative for satisfying basic needs. The adoption by the City of Rochester of a rather limited guaranteed annual income is welcome, but they still take place in the context of a theory of equity that stresses individual initiative and not collective responsibility. It generally accepts economic arraignments and even the provision of welfare services without challenging its basic in social and economic power.

Social Economic and Cultural Rights concern the conditions required to carry out democratic rights as citizens as well as the necessary conditions for well-being that democratic citizenship requires. Thus, in addition to political rights like the extension of franchise they include the right to a decent standard of living, housing, food security health care and mental health care, basic education, social security and welfare, and environmental safety. Because we are subject to vulnerabilities, we depend on cooperation with others in order to protect and develop our abilities. Many of these bring the argument back to the social contract discussed in earlier chapters. The relation between workers and employers and between members of society recognizes basic conditions and obligations. Social justice provides a vision of social equity based on equal respect of others that involve human solidarity and mutual recognition of others. We can be harmed not only by material conditions, but also by forms of disrespect based in exploitation and cultural domination.[32]

The American version of the welfare state has always tended more to the liberal more than the social democratic end of the scale, but under neo-liberalism all notions of social rights and social justice are under siege. This alone limits the effectiveness of anti-poverty programs and restricts its scope. It makes anti-poverty initiatives less capable of responding to new social conditions and needs. I think RMAPI needs a more robust notion of social equity guiding its outlook, in order to address these needs.

[32] In 1795, Thomas Paine proposed a system of old age pensions and disability benefits. While Paine's version was based on an agrarian society, in which an estate tax would be levied on all cultivated land, he held that all those who owned such land owed the community a ground rent.

Bibliography

A Strong Start. https://www.strongacc.org/process-timeline/

Bartter, Isabelle. Personal Correspondence.

Brown, James. "Porter made Permanent RMAPI leader." *CITY* December 1, 2020.

Cabaj, Mark and Liz Weaver. "Collective Impact 3.0 an evolving framework for community Change. https://www.tamarackcommunity.ca/library/webinar-collective-impact-3.0-dynamic-disruptive-times-mark-cabaj-liz-weaver#:~:text=In%202016%2C%20Mark%20Cabaj%20and,as%20a%20movement%20building%20strategy.

Eagle, Howard, Reverend Clifford Florence Sr. and Cilanda Florence-Yarde. "Essay: Watchful Eye, Community Input needed on RASE Commission." *Rochester Democrat and Chronicle* September 22, 2020.

Eagle, Howard. Personal Correspondence,

Fischer, Frank. "Participatory Governance." *Jerusalem Papers in Regulation & Governance* Working Paper. No. 24 August 2010

Fischer, Frank. *Democracy and Expertise: Reorienting Policy Inquiry*. New York: Oxford, 2009.

Fischer, Frank. *Reframing Public Policy: Discursive Politics and Deliberative Practices*. New York: Oxford, 2002.

Forester, John F. *The Deliberative Practitioner: Encouraging Participatory Planning Processes*. Cambridge MA: MIT Press 1999.

Jacob, Smriti. "Porter picked as new RMAPI leader." *Rochester Beacon* Dec 1, 2020.

Laurent, Sylvie. *King and the Other America: The Poor People's Campaign and the Quest for Economic Equality*. Berkeley: University of California Press, 2018.

RMAPI. 2019 *Policy Agenda*. https://endingpovertynow.org/article/rmapi-2019-policy-agenda/

RMAPI. 2016 *update*.

RMAPI. 2018 *Year in Review*. rmapiannualreport.pdf (endingpovertynow.org)

RMAPI. *Policy Agenda* 2020. http://endingpovertynow.org/wp-content/uploads/2020/01/RMAPI-Policy-Agenda-2020.pdf

RMAPI. "Level Up Champions move thousands of Rochester residents to $15/hour in 2021." September 2, 2021.

Scally, Corianne Payton, Lydia Lo, Kathryn L.S. Pettit, Camille H. Anoll, and Kassie Scott. "Driving Systems Forward: Leveraging Multisite Cross-Sector Initiatives to change systems, Advance Racial Equity and Shift Power." *Urban Institute* August 3, 2020.

SCLC. https://www.crmvet.org/docs/68ebr.htm

Sharp, Brian. "New Anti-poverty agenda rolled out highlights tax help for eligible filers." *Rochester Democrat and Chronicle* January 31, 2020.

Singer, Patti. "Poor to get seat in groups addressing poverty." *Rochester Democrat and Chronicle* April 7, 2015.

Singer, Patti. "Community needs to address racist policies to turn the tide on poverty say leaders." *Rochester Democrat and Chronicle* June 13, 2017.
Singer, Patti. "Meet the new executive director of Rochester Monroe County Anti-Poverty Initiative." *Minority Reporter* December 1, 2020.
Spicer, Velvet. "Anti-poverty agency seeks community's ideas." *Rochester Business Journal* April 21, 2018.
The Homeless Plan: Palm Beach County's Plan to End the Cycle of Homelessness. http://thehomelessplan.org/
Tilly, Charles. *Social Movements, 1768—2012*. London: Routledge 2012.
Touraine, Alan. *The Self-Production of Society*. Chicago: The University of Chicago Press, 1977).
Underwood, Jerome H., and Daan Braverman. "Current events serve as an unfortunate reminder that racism is thriving," *Rochester Democrat and Chronicle* June 8, 2020.
United Way of Rochester. *Monroe County Systems Integration Project: A United Way Innovation Case Study*. 2021: 1 https://unitedwayrocflx.org/media/yo0dzgv5/uwrochester_casestudy-monroe-county-systems-integration-project-final-5-11-2021.pdf?lang=en-US
Vision for Children at Risk: Collective Impact chronology, https://visionforchildren.org/strategic-action/collective-impact-chronology/
Volk, Veronica. "Anti-poverty Initiative working group participants feel slighted." *WXXI AM News* Feb 5, 2019.

Index[1]

[1] Note: Page numbers followed by 'n' refer to notes.

B. Caterino, *The Failure of the Neo-Liberal Approach to Poverty*, https://doi.org/10.1007/978-3-031-10606-4

The manufacturer's authorised representative in the EU is Springer Nature Customer Service Centre GmbH, Europaplatz 3, 69115 Heidelberg, Germany. If you have any concerns regarding our products, please contact ProductSafety@springernature.com

Printed and bound by CPI Group (UK) Ltd, Croydon, CR0 4YY
30/09/2026
02225490-0006